# THE RULES
# THAT MAKE US

# THE RULES THAT MAKE US

How Culture Shapes the Way We Act,
Think, Believe and Buy

## OLIVER SWEET

Copyright © Oliver Sweet 2026

The right of Oliver Sweet to be identified as the Author of the Work has been asserted by him in accordance with the Copyright, Designs and Patents Act 1988.

First published in Hardback in 2026 by Wildfire
An imprint of Headline Publishing Group Limited

1

Apart from any use permitted under UK copyright law, this publication may only be reproduced, stored, or transmitted, in any form, or by any means, with prior permission in writing of the publishers or, in the case of reprographic production, in accordance with the terms of licences issued by the Copyright Licensing Agency.

Cataloguing in Publication Data is available from the British Library.

Hardback ISBN 978 1 0354 1746 9
Trade Paperback ISBN 978 1 0354 1747 6

Designed and typeset by EM&EN
Printed and bound in Great Britain by Clays Ltd, Elcograf S.p.A.

Headline's policy is to use papers that are natural, renewable and recyclable products and made from wood grown in well-managed forests and other controlled sources. The logging and manufacturing processes are expected to conform to the environmental regulations of the country of origin.

Headline Publishing Group Limited
An Hachette UK Company
Carmelite House
50 Victoria Embankment
London EC4Y 0DZ

The authorised representative in the EEA is Hachette Ireland,
8 Castlecourt Centre, Dublin 15, D15 XTP3, Ireland (email: info@hbgi.ie)

www.headline.co.uk
www.hachette.co.uk

**For Martha and Tilly –**

**my greatest teachers**

**Culture** is the shared way of life of a group of people. It shapes our *identity*, how we connect to a *community* and our *belief systems*.

Driven by anthropological understanding.

**Cognition** is the way our brain learns, understands and makes decisions. Fear, desire and motivation all affect how our brain works.

Driven by psychological understanding.

There's a balance between culture and cognition when it comes to understanding why we do what we do. A lot has been written about the role of cognition, so instead, this book will look at the hidden rules of culture, and how we can use them in life, business and society.

## Contents

Introduction 1

### Part One: Analysing Culture

1. Finding the Rules That Make Us 13
2. How Culture Affects Life, Business and Society 40
3. Culture Makes an ASS Out of U and ME 65
4. Culture Starts at Home 97

### Part Two: Changing Culture

5. Finding the Rules That Change Us 119
6. How Tribalism Makes Us and Breaks Us 153
7. Social Silences Create Social Consequences 176

### Part Three: The Future of Culture

8. How Technology Creates New Rules in Life 205
9. The Future Is Here, It's Just Not Evenly Distributed 228
10. Life Lessons from a Business Anthropologist 254

Acknowledgements 275

References 277

Index 286

# Introduction

Whenever I tell people I'm writing a book about culture, there are two responses.

The first is a series of questions about culture: *Why are Brazilians so good at football? Is religion a good thing? Why are levels of equality so high in Scandinavian countries? Why is K-pop so popular? Which nationality blurs their background the most on video calls? What's the effect of the 'manosphere'? Why are young people so obsessed with social media? Why don't British people talk about sex? Why do they drink so much tea in India? Why is it rude to smile at a stranger in Denmark?*

The second response is a series of curious and amusing stories.

> I went to a French school in the 1980s and we were allowed to smoke in the playground from the age of sixteen. I was speaking to a Swedish friend who said they had a sauna at school for everyone to use after PE.

> When I started my job in Seoul, my boss insisted we go out drinking every Friday night, and that I drink shots with him. But when I wore red nail polish to work, I was discreetly told it was 'too much'.

> I took a flight from Delhi to Nairobi with a stopover in Riyadh. At the airport in Riyadh, the men were ushered in front of me (a white, Western woman) without a word being said. When I landed in Nairobi, I was ushered to the front of the queue in front of all the men.

I was in Cairo during Ramadan visiting a friend who was atheist. Every evening a cannon boomed from the Citadel, signalling it was time to eat. When it went off my friend paused to take a gulp of water. 'It's just what you do,' he said with a shrug.

Questions about culture are endlessly interesting as they help us formulate ideas about why the French are French, why the Americans are American, and how to make a 'proper' cup of tea in England. The constant questions show a human yearning to understand the dividing lines between us, and where they've come from.

Everyone's got a cultural story to tell – they are fun, fascinating, sometimes enraging, occasionally inappropriate and often joyous. Culture belongs to everyone because it's part of everyone, which is why everyone wants to talk about it. Our culture has shaped who we are and given us stories to live by, and it opens our mind when we travel abroad.

This book answers big cultural questions about small and fascinating behaviours. It's a book that looks at how social media affects our lives, why stereotypes make us laugh and cry, and what wearing a mask in public means. It is a book that tells stories and starts conversations, some that will make you smile, others that will frustrate you, but all with a purpose of seeing culture.

### Culture creates the hidden rules that make us

We like to think we are a product of our own free will, that our decisions, unique personality and desires come from our brain rather than from someone else's. But as we'll see throughout this book, culture creates the rules that make us who we are. We are a product of the world we grow up in, and we reinforce how the world works by conforming to the rules.

Culture simultaneously lives within us and is a force placed upon us. I don't like defining culture because as soon as it's defined, it's often wrong – but many of the elements that make up culture show this double-edged influence.

### Culture is shared
Culture binds people through shared behaviours and symbolic acts – shaking hands, bowing, fasting, feasting. We engage in these acts because they are the 'right way' to act, and they are the right way to act because we always do them.

### Culture is everything we don't think about – until we do
It's the invisible script guiding what we believe, how we behave and who we think belongs (and who doesn't). It's in the stories we tell, the gestures we share and the norms we follow without question – you don't need to think about it because everyone else also knows it. Until they don't.

### Culture is felt
Being in a group with a shared purpose creates a wonderful feeling inside us. Conversely, when we find ourselves in a culture different from our own, we can feel confused or disoriented.

### Culture has meaning
Words, colours and symbols can mean different things to different cultures. 'Thank you' can mean friendship or obligation. Red can scream passion or war. Culture gives meaning to the mundane.

### Culture grounds us
It roots identity in place and memory. You can leave Scotland for forty years and still be Scottish. People carry places inside them, even if they've never actually lived there. Culture ties us to a home, both real and imagined.

**Culture gives us instinct**
Culture tells us how to behave before our brain kicks in. It's individual and collective, emotional and habitual. To understand ourselves, and other people, we have to understand culture.

**Culture can divide us**
That 'click' of belonging or division isn't logic, it's culture at work. The side-eye can create silence, exclusion and alienation when associated with a divisive culture.

**Culture is absorbed**
You weren't born with it. You absorbed it – through stories, mimicry and experience, often without knowing.

My grandmother tells a story about Ron, a larger-than-life politician who befriended my grandfather years ago. One evening he came round to dinner and met my then three-year-old Uncle Tony, who was playing on the floor. He had turned a bench upside down and was rowing back and forth in his imaginary boat.

Ron looked at Tony and said, 'That looks like a lot of fun – can I get in with you and row?'

'No,' said Tony, 'you're too fat to get in.'

'Where did you get that idea from?' asked Ron, taken aback by this forthright toddler. Then, with an air of suspicion, he added, 'Did your father say that about me?'

'No,' said three-year-old Tony, 'I've got eyes, haven't I?'

Ron was speechless, my grandmother was mortified and Uncle Tony carried on rowing.

Uncle Tony may have been right, but he had broken all the rules above. His toddler innocence clearly didn't understand the shared code, he created a (bad) feeling in everyone around him, his instinct was to be truthful instead of kind, his offhand remark created a clear division, and he hadn't learned this wasn't what you say to a guest.

Uncle Tony's story is a great example of how, in time, we internalise the external rules that surround us. We follow the rules of the culture we're part of, which we learn as we grow up, or when we move to a different culture. This book is about that process of absorption. We are not born to binge drink on a Friday night, we learn it. We are not born to be hierarchical and stay in the office until our boss leaves, we learn it. We are not born to shake hands, sing songs, wear make-up, write poetry, play video games, run marathons, roller-skate or take drugs – these are all things we absorb when we are part of a culture. Many of these things may feel like they originate inside us as personal problems (drug-taking) or achievements (creative writing), but more often than not they originate outside the brain in the culture that we live in.

### The rising tides of culture

Anthropology is the study of culture, and it is an essential tool for understanding why we do what we do. Anthropology decodes the meaning behind how people learn, share and interact, to create a way of thinking.

Culture is responsible for a lot of recent changes in the world – *vibe shifts* have created seismic changes in governments, and new cultural trends make people millions of dollars. Keeping up with culture is a busy business, and planning ahead can feel like trying to catch fog with a butterfly net.

I've spent nearly two decades helping brands, governments and NGOs unpick some of the knotty cultural problems they face by applying the academic principles of anthropology in an accessible way. Working at Ipsos MORI, rated the most innovative research agency in the world,[1] I've run hundreds of anthropological projects for clients working in consumer goods, financial services, government departments, healthcare, tech, PR, transport – all of whom want deep cultural thinking presented in a structured manner. Many of these projects had a specific, business-oriented goal in mind: to understand how culture was affecting the way people act, think, believe and buy.

The guiding principles outlined in this book come from anthropology, and the anthropologist's toolkit centres around good conversations and watching what people do. The data in this book is mostly stories I've gathered over years of anthropological fieldwork, talking to people around the world, and observing what they're doing.

These stories provide a way to focus on analysing culture, changing culture and the future of culture. An example of this can be summarised in a single story from a trip I took to Shanghai in 2016. I have a vivid memory of the way my taxi driver constantly used his phone as he drove. Shanghai traffic is multi-laned chaos even through the city centre, and his dedication to using WeChat was petrifying. He had one hand on the wheel, while the other swiped his phone with instinctive hand gestures.

He jumped between different chats and I realised that instead of reading through typed messages, he was listening to a string of voice notes. In the same way that I read through chats in my WhatsApp groups, he was doing the same, but in audio. This was his form of entertainment as he drove, his personalised chat radio station.

Despite my having zero understanding of Mandarin, it was fascinating to watch. He jumped into a particular group, listened to the back-and-forth between several people, dropped his own message in as a response to what he'd heard, and then went on to the next group. In my desire to create order in madness, I assumed one was a family chat, one a friends' chat and another a work chat, just from the way he seemed to respond. But honestly, I really didn't know.

What fascinated me was that I was watching someone use exactly the same piece of technology that I do in a different way, so I started to come up with my own hypothesis. Was this purely about convenience when driving? Maybe he was illiterate? Was this a technologically inclusive solution for a country struggling with literacy rates, particularly among those in the service economy? I felt confident that I'd come up with a clever answer and I started making assertions about how naive Western tech developers are when it comes to creating inclusive design.

Later in the day I met my Chinese colleague, Luna, a cultural analyst born in Shanghai who had previously lived in the UK. She laughed at my analysis. Voice chats weren't about convenience – did I think that everyone else on those group chats were driving at the same time as him? Probably not. Voice chats weren't about illiteracy – did I think all his friends and family are illiterate too? In a country with 96% literacy rates?

She then showed me her phone, where voice notes were normal. 'Voice chats are a nice way to interact,' she said. 'They give you extra context in an otherwise depersonalised digital world.' *Why isn't everyone using voice chats?* the look on her face told me.

Back in the UK, my work WhatsApp group of fifteen colleagues were weighing in on whether a particular article was offensive. It was pretty standard work chat, but I couldn't type fast enough to get my point across as the conversation moved on too quickly. So, I held down the record button and sent an eleven-second voice note into the chat. It certainly felt new, even emboldening. *If the taxi man can do it, why can't I?* Nobody replied to my point. Had people simply ignored me? I dropped in another voice note, and that got ignored too. My third one didn't get ignored; instead, the group turned on me for being a weirdo.

At our next team meeting in the office, I suggested being more Chinese for a week and using voice notes in our WhatsApp group. 'It's really convenient,' I suggested. 'It's good because you don't need to type it out, and you can add more context to everything you're saying. Why wouldn't we?' I was convincing enough that they agreed to trial it, but the group went deathly silent for a whole week until they all decided to take the piss out of me again for being a weirdo.

The different manner in which Chinese and British people adopt the same piece of technology is down to culture. It's an obvious statement perhaps, but it's something that's often overlooked by clients I've worked with over the years, particularly in the tech world. However individual people think they are, WhatsApp communication conforms to a set of social norms about how to act, which is where my experiment became unstuck.

My taxi ride in Shanghai taught me a lot about cultural insight, and how you can read an enormous amount into small behaviours. Analysing culture is fascinating because it exists everywhere, even in taxis. It underscored the importance of not making crass assumptions, and how important it is to engage with the people you are analysing. It also showed me that changing culture isn't just about giving people a convincing reason; changing behaviour requires everyone else to do it with you. Nobody else wanted to be called a weirdo in my UK WhatsApp group.

It also gave me a glimpse of the future because when it comes to technological adoption, China is a good five-plus years ahead of the West. And a couple of years after my failed WhatsApp experiment, the next person I got a voice note from was my cousin, who is fifteen years younger than me.

## Culture vs cognition; anthropology vs psychology

Both psychology and anthropology ask the same core question: Why do we do what we do? But they look for answers in very different places.

Psychology turns inward. It maps the architecture of our minds – our thoughts, feelings and behaviours – and offers us tools to cope, heal and grow. It explains how people tick, how we break and how we mend. But psychology often assumes the individual exists in isolation, floating in a vacuum of personal choice and internal motivation.

Anthropology, by contrast, turns outward. It studies the unseen frameworks that shape our lives – identity, community and belief systems. While psychology explores how fish swim, anthropology dives deeper to show us the shape of the reef and the currents of culture guiding their path. It's less about what's in our heads and more about what's in the water we all swim in, usually without noticing.

This difference is not academic; it has implications in life, business and society. In a world increasingly governed by behavioural economics and psychological nudges, psychology has taught us that every action is about personal choice. The result is a culture of hyper-individualism, where the burden to change rests squarely on the individual. Anthropology reminds us that behaviour is rarely just personal. It's social. It's structural. It's cultural.

Psychology helps us treat symptoms. Anthropology helps us diagnose the system. We need both. As a psychology graduate, I have seen it help people increase in confidence, reduce anxiety and overcome trauma. But psychology's success has also blinded us to its limits. It's time to balance the equation by seeing culture not as background noise but as a powerful force that shapes the rules that make us.

\*

In this book, we'll explore the way that culture is rooted both within us and in the people that surround us. We'll explore everyday culture questions, like whether stereotypes are true, how we set up our homes as a place for cultural apprenticeships, and many, many more. We'll also discuss how to change culture and how culture changes us through the continued rise of political tribalism and technological echo chambers, and what the future of culture looks like.

This book lays out how to see the rules of culture in life, business and society. Many of these rules hide in plain sight, and knowing how to see them allows you to see both your behaviour and other people's in a new light.

# PART ONE

# ANALYSING CULTURE

Culture and cognition walk into a bar, and the barman hands them a cocktail menu.

Cognition studies the menu in detail, wondering what each drink will taste like, which one they're in the mood for and whether the barman will make it well. Cognition leans over and points at the menu: 'I've made a choice.'

Culture looks up. 'I'll have what they're having.'

# 1

## Finding the Rules That Make Us

People care about culture because it is everything and everywhere. It's a word that is bandied around in business – 'culture eats strategy for breakfast'[1] – and has also become part of today's political narrative, with politicians engaging in 'culture wars', supporting or rejecting 'woke culture' while running the risk of 'cancel culture'. 'Culture vultures' go to the theatre and art galleries, and travellers have become mini anthropologists, reporting on cultural differences between countries: 'Thai culture is so welcoming.' People are often described as 'cultured' when they learn the rituals of other nationalities but can quickly be accused of 'cultural appropriation' if they go too far or try to make money out of it. Looking at these various uses of the word, 'culture' is a powerful concept.

But when we look at the use cases above, it becomes clear that culture is something that happens between us. Culture is an interaction, an idea passed around, a story shared between generations, an attitude developed in a community, or a body of knowledge that grows among a group of people. Culture sits between people, it connects people; it is something that's outside our bodies, but we are fundamentally part of it. Culture binds us together and keeps us apart; it's something that controls our behaviour, yet we are in control of it. Culture sits around us, yet it lives in all of us.

Dr Adam Gamwell, a business anthropologist who applies the principles of anthropology to everyday life, says we should think of culture as 'more of a vibe than a concept'.[2] It's the way people share their values and beliefs through everyday behaviours, like eating together, shaking hands or the level of formality among friends. It's communicated through the small and sometimes imperceptible behaviours that make up both the individual and the interaction.

Vibes are recognised by other people and are always shifting. Youth culture evolves in the shadows of parental surveillance, creating new codes of communication through slang, style and secret meet-ups. Corporate culture teaches new employees how to behave through mimicry, like the awkward silences when a junior employee throws out a new idea in a hierarchical company, or the way some workers eat lunch at their desks for fear of being seen as slacking. Cultures vary enormously: some are kind or forgiving, others are focused on accountability; some believe in decisive action, others promote reflection before change; and some are highly competitive, while others promote collaboration. Many of these traits are often seen as individual characteristics, when in fact individuals are simply acting in accordance with the culture they live in.

But herein lies an unspoken paradox of today's world: it's culture that connects us, but in terms of understanding *why we do what we do*, the world is obsessed with psychology. The number of people in therapy steadily increases year on year, we're constantly analysing our own and others' mental states, and psychological frameworks are entirely accepted in business and politics. Popular psychology books fly off the shelves as people are looking for self-improvement, and 'therapy speak' – like 'boundary setting' and 'self-care' – is common in everyday chat. Psychology has become as much part of how we heal our mind as medicine has for the body.

The obsession with psychology has transformed it from a discipline that helps the individual, to a way of analysing society at large. In political campaigning, the use of psychology has fundamentally changed many Western democracies, as seen in the Brexit vote in the UK and Trump's presidential victory in the US. In 2016, Cambridge Analytica was able to segment the electorate for the Brexit and Trump campaigns through using psychological personality types, and then used that analysis to feed each personality type a different campaign message. This was the first time political parties were able to offer so many different promises to the electorate in a single campaign. This has further exacerbated political polarisation in the US through creating a political culture of competition and animosity.

Psychology has infiltrated business to a huge extent, whether it's understanding consumer motivation for buying products, setting performance-based targets for individual employees, or the constant goal-setting to keep people motivated and focused. In business, psychology is used to make sure customer needs are catered for and employees are driven to perform, which in turn creates the type of culture we live and work in. Our belief that human cognition can improve how people interact with one another is valiant, but there are other, more collaborative ways to change behaviour and outcomes.

### Psychology for me, anthropology for the world

As a business anthropologist, I spend a lot of time hanging out in people's homes around the world. I also shop, play and eat with them, watch them have their nails and hair done, take their kids to sport practice, and I always meet their friends and family. I become an investigator into people's lives, trying to find out why they really do the things they do. I spend time with people because that's often the best way to answer some of life's trickier questions. In essence, I get a more accurate read of people by watching what they do rather than asking them what they think.

But I haven't always signed up to this worldview. Like many, I was once obsessed with the answers psychology had to offer. I would talk about the *real* reasons people did things, and would hypothesise that a friend or family member was being particularly egotistical or repressed or in denial. I read Carl Jung's *Man and His Symbols*, which allowed me to extend my psychology chat into an analysis of dreams. I would talk about my own dreams, offering up some deeper meaning behind why I was sitting on a horse as all my teeth fell out, and make sweeping statements about someone's personality based on a dream they told me about. I'm not sure how much fun I was to hang around with, but I thought I knew a lot about people.

My interest in psychology did allow me to talk about emotions and feelings, and helped me make sense of life as an only child and connect with my parents when I was at boarding school. And most importantly, it allowed me to talk about emotions when my dad died without having to address the pain directly. It gave me permission to talk about my feelings as a young, inexpressive boy in a culture where boys aren't supposed to cry. I owe a lot to the ideas and concepts that psychology taught me.

Psychology explains why we do what we do through looking at how the brain sees and interprets the world, showing that our decisions come either from response to slow, rational processing or from fast, subconscious processing that is harder to pinpoint. Most psychological approaches recognise that the majority of our behaviours are not driven by rational decision-making, and instead come from a place that's quite instinctive. Evolutionarily, our brain has evolved from a more primitive state to one that also includes rational thought – which differentiates us from most other animals – but our instinctive processing is still very dominant. Mapping the development of the brain over thousands of years shows humankind's journey to becoming civilised animals, a process that has helped us keep our instincts in check. Psychologists explain *why we do what we do* as a balance between primitive fears and desires on the one hand, and knowledge and motivation about what's best for us on the other.

What's more, we find evidence for this in everyday life. We eat fatty foods when we should be on a diet, we have another beer when we know we've got an early start, and we pay for a gym membership that we know we'll barely use. Sometimes those instincts drive us to levels of destruction, and we punch a stranger in the face if they insult us, have sex with someone that we shouldn't, or steal because we want what someone else has. Our fears and desires make us fallible, even stupid, and they are responsible for more of our behaviours than many of us would like to admit.

The discipline of psychology has been great at helping us understand our subconscious and instinctive mind. Therapy, in its numerous approaches, helps us recognise why we think or act in a particular (often problematic) way to help us see the patterns of our life (and hopefully not repeat them). That might be through having a deeper understanding of ourselves, or through changing the way we respond to different stimuli in the world. On a larger, societal level, the recent rise of behavioural science (aka 'nudging'[3]) has shown how psychological insight can be used in government and business to tap into people's instinctive responses on a group level, offering a framework for influencing people's fears and desires for more favourable outcomes.[4] According to psychology, our brains have developed rules on how to survive.

As an undergraduate, the psychology I learned focused heavily on experiments that either test how we think or how we behave in groups. The cognitive and behavioural psychology that was popular at university taught me about the biases in the human brain but gave me little insight into the human condition. Many people go to university and fall in love with their degree; I went to university and fell out of love with psychology. What I loved about reading the likes of Freud, Jung and Winnicott was that their form of psychology looked for the reasons why people are different, rather than the contemporary psychology which demonstrates how quirks of the brain show we are all the same. I parked those ideas for a while and went in search of something that helped describe the world as it really was, outside of a lab experiment.

By contrast, anthropology assumes that no person lives in a vacuum, and it answers the question of *why we do what we do* by looking at the context of everyday life, assessing people's upbringing, their social setup, and the cultural milieu that surrounds them. Where psychology starts from the position of the brain, anthropology starts from the position of culture, recognising that we are products of where and how we live. As a result, psychology is much more inward-looking, studying the individual, while anthropology studies how the individual behaves by looking at the group.

Again, the evidence surrounding us is palpable. If you grow up in New York, you'll have a very different experience of life compared to someone living in Tibet, and when describing *why we do what we do* in these two places, there will be a completely different set of influences driven by religion, family structure, wealth, job opportunities, language, trade and political freedoms, to state just a few. On a smaller but no less important level, a Londoner growing up on a council estate in Hackney will have a wholly different perspective to someone growing up five miles away in a manor house in Highgate. Again, family structure, wealth, job opportunities, accent, purchasing power and safety are going to influence *why we do what we do* in very different ways. According to anthropology, our culture has developed rules on how we flourish (and fail!).

While psychology and anthropology are not exactly aligned, they both come up with very compelling arguments. We can see the psychological argument about how we are instinctive beings trying to tame our animalistic desires. We can also see the lesson from anthropology on how we are the product of our upbringing, our parents, and how the world around us teaches us right from wrong. Both arguments are impossible to ignore.

I see the disciplines of anthropology and psychology as a parallel to what happens within us, as people. Sometimes we need to be culturally astute to navigate a situation, and at other times we need to be cognitively aware of what people are thinking. If we face a difficult choice in a familiar environment - like how to discipline someone in the workplace - our cognition goes into overdrive to create the right response. If we face a straightforward choice in an unfamiliar environment - like ordering from a menu in a roadside café in Thailand - our cultural instinct looks for cues to form the right answer. This mix of culture and cognition makes up the broader spectrum of how we navigate life.

## The historic interaction between culture and cognition

Whenever we are faced with a situation or a decision, we may well find ourselves with an internal struggle. Do we want to let our instincts govern our response, or do we follow the culturally appropriate way of doing things? You may really want pizza for breakfast, but you've got a breakfast meeting with your boss, and you end up choosing eggs Benedict instead. When breakfast comes, you might want to ask about your long overdue pay rise, but instead you make small talk about their kids and then discuss the resourcing difficulties the team are having. When getting up to leave, you might desperately need the toilet but your boss asks you to walk back to the office with them instead. Or maybe . . . just maybe, you turn up to breakfast, order a Domino's pizza to arrive at the café, demand a pay rise from your boss and sit out the rest of the morning on the toilet reading the news on your phone. This push and pull between our culture and cognition is the real description of *why we do what we do*.

Kids are a great example of following cognition over culture. A baby's instinct to feed, sleep and cry keeps them nourished, safe and warm. Newborns have what's called a 'Moro reflex', which causes their hands to involuntarily flail out to grab someone when they think they are falling. This reflex is hardwired into humans from day zero in response to a fearful situation. As children grow up, one of the main jobs of a parent is to help them manage their instincts, to tell them they can't have cake for breakfast and that they shouldn't get naked in the playground. However, while parents are unified in trying to temper their children's instincts in favour of more measured behaviour, what they are implicitly doing is teaching them about the culture they live in, because the rules that kids are taught vary from New York to Tibet, and from Hackney to Highgate.

One consequence of pandemic lockdowns was that we were no longer compelled to be quite so culturally rule-abiding. When we weren't allowed to leave the house, some of the cultural rules that had been hardwired into us were no longer mandatory. Anyone working from home could wear pyjama bottoms all day. As our cultural trappings became less necessary, people stopped brushing their teeth so regularly, wearing perfume, or buying expensive wine. Lockdowns meant that we bent the rules and started to make up some new ones because we were living in a different environment. As lockdown eased, some had forgotten what the polite rules in public were – like dressing formally for the office, or wearing smart yet uncomfortable shoes – because our cultural standards had changed.

## Psychology: codifying cognition

Psychology really took off when people started to recognise that there was a lot more going on in their brains than they realised. The more people looked into the brain, the more complex cognition looked. The more people looked into behaviour, the more inconsistent we appeared to be. And the more unhappy we became, the more we realised it couldn't be solved by simply not thinking about it. The success of psychology came through codifying cognition and giving people a common language around how and why people think in different ways.

Daniel Kahneman often suggested that we think far less than we think that we think. This phrase encapsulates how psychology developed as a discipline, recognising that our brain is full of so many thoughts that sit below the conscious surface. In 2002, Kahneman was the first psychologist to win the Nobel Prize for Economics, 'for having integrated insights from psychological research into economic science',[5] after which he proudly announced he hadn't taken a single course in economics. His book *Thinking, Fast and Slow* describes how the brain has two systems – System 1, a fast-thinking, instinctive side, and System 2, a more deliberative, rational side. Kahneman does a fantastic job of showing that we like to think System 2 is in charge, but in reality, System 1 is controlling more than we realise.

Jonathan Haidt, the social psychologist, noted the difference between our deliberate vs instinctive thinking by describing our brain as an elephant rider and an elephant: the elephant rider has influence over the direction of travel but ultimately only has a small amount of control over how the elephant actually behaves. Haidt uses this analogy to explain the battle people face between the instinctual, animalistic part of the brain (the elephant) and the mechanisms with which they can tame that beast (the elephant rider).

In *Blink*, Malcolm Gladwell shows that people are incredibly good at assessing a situation in the blink of an eye – that people's instincts are often better than the slower, more cognitively laborious part of their brain. He argues that intuitive judgement is developed over time, from multiple different factors like experience, upbringing, training and knowledge. His analysis demonstrates that your past will help you solve any problem that you face in the present without having to think about it too hard. The more expert you are in a subject, the more you should follow your instincts, and thinking about it too much (like an economist assumes people think about things) can lead us to factor in misleading information.

The behavioural scientist's contribution to understanding cognition has been huge and groundbreaking. Most of us now accept the psychological hypothesis that humans are innately biased. Many of us think we know how biased we are, and some of us accept that we are biased in ways we don't always recognise. And a small number of us may even acknowledge that we are biased in ways that we don't like, and certainly don't like to admit. *We think far less than we think that we think* because we believe our rational, conscious brain does most of the work, but it doesn't. This lack of insight into how we really behave suggests that the elephant rider doesn't have control of the elephant and, in many cases, doesn't actually know what the elephant is like or capable of.

Discovering these hidden rules of cognition has made psychology an exciting discipline in the last twenty-five years, but some big blind spots remain. These rules have been discovered through behavioural experiments, in which scientists have documented over 180 cognitive biases that influence people's actions, often in ways that are completely unknown to them.

One of these experiments – known as the Stanford Prison Experiment – was conducted by Philip Zimbardo in 1971 when twenty-four male students were randomly assigned the role of either prisoner or a prison guard.[6] Even though participants were aware it was an experiment, they started to play out their imagined identities, and the experiment spiralled out of control within days. 'Guards', empowered by their assigned roles, began exhibiting authoritarian and even sadistic behaviours, imposing humiliating punishments on the prisoners. Conversely, 'prisoners', stripped of their autonomy, grew passive, distressed and increasingly submissive.

While the experiment could never be repeated based on moral grounds, its core lesson endures: under the right conditions, ordinary people can commit extraordinary acts of cruelty – or fall into helplessness. The experiment's implications extend far beyond prisons, offering insights into how power, authority and identity shape behaviour in workplaces, schools and even families. The stark divide between the roles demonstrated how quickly individuals could internalise an identity and act it out according to social hierarchies, even when they knew those hierarchies were part of an experiment.

Another famous experiment – the Implicit Association Test (IAT) – was developed by researchers at Harvard University in the late 1990s and revealed striking insights into the unconscious biases many people related to race.[7] Unlike traditional surveys or interviews, which rely on self-reported data and may be influenced by social desirability, the IAT measures reaction times to pairings of concepts and attributes, such as 'Black' and 'good' or 'white' and 'bad.' By clicking on a series of images, the test measures the speed at which respondents associate certain terms with different races.

The results – data gathered from over 50 million tests, predominantly completed by people in the US – are startling: 65% of people associated 'good' with 'European American', and only 17% associated 'good' with 'African American'. Regardless of people's explicit beliefs or intentions, they repeatedly demonstrated a preference for white over Black individuals. This suggests that implicit biases – subtle, automatic associations influenced by societal norms, media portrayals and historical inequalities – are pervasive against Black people, even among those who consciously reject racism. The data challenges the widespread notion that racism is limited to overt acts of discrimination, and instead suggests that prejudice and discrimination are baked into our belief systems without us consciously being aware of it. This has real-world implications for hiring, healthcare and policing, to name but a few pertinent issues that are present in the US today.

These psychological insights have changed the way we see risk, judgement and decision-making. By creating experiments that mirror conditions in the real world, psychology has shown us there's a hidden side to our brain, a fast-thinking System 1 that allows our inner elephant to run wild. These beliefs aren't something we are born with; they have grown over time and developed from the sum total of our experiences, and need to be checked when thinking about how we solve some of societies' more thorny challenges.

## Anthropology: codifying culture

While our cognition has been effectively codified, mapping our culture in an accessible manner is about as sophisticated as spotting animal shapes in passing clouds. Gillian Tett, anthropologist and editor at the *Financial Times*, suggested that 'asking someone to describe culture is like asking a fish to describe water.'[8] In common parlance, 'culture' is a 'fat word', a term that is used loosely to mean many different things to different people. In the same way that psychology has codified cognition, anthropology has defined a set of rules for how we behave in groups – but culture is more complex than first meets the eye, and anthropologists get great joy in finding the hidden rules in culture. There is a code for how culture operates that can be cracked.

We know culture influences us in a million different ways – from the books, TV and news we consume, to the food we eat, and to the different countries we travel to (or don't). All of these things make up modern culture, both reinforcing it and morphing it into something new. We shake hands as an age-old gesture to introduce ourselves, and then we add a twist according to our subculture, be that a secret Masonic symbol or a fist bump among friends. Our gestures, actions and interactions come from a set of rules that help us define what is socially acceptable, but they are changeable, complex and country specific. These are the rules that make us, whether we see them easily or not.

Anthropology guides us to look at the social side of life, the interactions between people and the way people learn to behave in similar ways. Culture also looks at systems of meaning, whether that's how words are used or why symbols take on associations, by taking a historical-cultural narrative. Anthropology looks at evidence in the real world, rather than evidence created in an experiment. It doesn't rely on a reaction-time machine to tell us whether we're racist or not; it gets us to look at our interactions to see if there's a system that perpetuates racist beliefs. Anthropologists help us see the systemic web of racism – rather than claiming it's one bad egg – showing that it's up to all of us to fix it.

Anthropologists use historical and present-day data to form a narrative of how people behave in groups, whether that's socio-political movements, cultural failings in the workplace or how different minorities have been treated around the world. Put this way, an anthropologist's response to the injustices acted out during the Stanford Prison Experiment would be, 'No shit!?'

The idea that people play out identities they are given is a core tenet of anthropology, with numerous historical examples to draw from, such as how previously kind and liberal Germans joined the Nazi party and participated in the active discrimination against and killing of Jewish people; how Hutus and Tutsis were triggered into killing their own neighbours after a power battle in Rwanda's government; or how the dissolution of Yugoslavia created a new set of national identities that quickly turned to violence. There are also plenty of examples of people switching between identities without much trouble, just as participants did in the prison experiment: for instance, when we see workplace bullies described as loving parents at home, or a terrorist that's known for extreme acts of kindness in their community before committing a heinous crime. When anthropologists study identity, they assume that people are playing out a role in the group, even if that role has been given to them by others. Being part of a group has a powerful effect on how the individual behaves, which they then adopt into their identity.

Again, an anthropologist's view of the Harvard implicit bias test might also be, 'No shit, America is racist!?' While the results of the test are shocking, describing 65% of Americans as implicitly racist doesn't feel like a new statement to an anthropologist –

it is sadly in keeping with everything we know about American culture to date. It is supported by numerous statistics in the US like the average white family having ten times more wealth than the average Black family,[9] and that Black people are incarcerated at more than five times the rate of white people.[10] This is mirrored in media and advertising, where 62% of gang members in films are Black[11] while only 9% of doctors are. The skewed portrayal of race in the media is widespread, be that through cinema, news, advertising or fiction, which are all core drivers in the creation of cultural symbolism. All these different factors link together to create a belief system that is prejudiced towards Black people, whether we like it or not.

When Malcolm Gladwell first took the implicit bias test, he came out as being moderately in favour of 'European American' equating to 'good' – which utterly shocked him given he is half Black, and made him question how culture had infiltrated his belief system in a way that made him biased against people like himself. The cultural association of Black people being labelled with negative attributes is so prevalent in American culture that it becomes built into the assumptions and rules that guide our thinking – whether you are Black or not.

The important thing to note here is not that psychological experiments don't tell us anything – they really do. Having taken the IAT myself, I also came out as moderately in favour of 'European American' equating to 'good', which gave me a big personal shock, given who I think I am. The psychological tests offer individuals a moment to address their own biases, but as a social commentary, it's not that surprising.

The headline should be that these tests confirm what we already know from the study of anthropology. By using the principles of anthropology to look at what connects us, we can analyse how culture influences our behaviour as individuals, which the psychological experiments corroborate. Psychology has done an incredible job of documenting the rules of cognition – it's time anthropologists started documenting the rules of culture.

## The Cultural Trinity – finding the rules of culture

In my work as a business anthropologist, I started to see patterns across all the projects I worked on.

This pattern is what I call the Cultural Trinity, a framework that analyses culture through looking at the rules of life. It offers a structured way to decode what people do, believe and feel, in the context of real life rather than controlled experiments. The Cultural Trinity breaks culture down into three interlocking parts:

- ▲ **Identity** – How people see themselves and express that identity in the world.
- ● **Community** – Who people belong to, interact with and feel validated by.
- ■ **Belief systems** – What people believe about the world, and how they decide what's right, wrong, valuable or not.

Its simplicity is its beauty, but underneath it lies a depth of understanding that's true to anthropological thinking. Each element on its own is interesting, but combined, they give us the depth of understanding that culture warrants.

By demonstrating how this framework is part of everyday life, we start to codify culture in the same way that psychology has helped us codify cognition. These are all concepts that people see and talk about on a daily basis, and they all contain stresses, joys and patterns that anyone can understand. Furthermore, it allows everyone (not just academics) to have

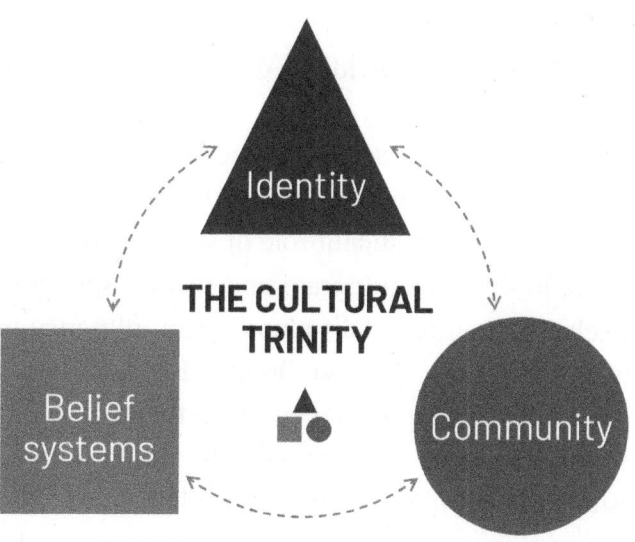

a nuanced conversation about culture, to be specific and concrete, while also grounding it in concepts that we all know and understand.

What's more, it makes it easier to see that there are rules attached to how you express your identity, who's allowed or not allowed in the community, and how belief systems give us a purpose to describe who we are. These rules may be hidden, but they are present in our behaviour and are part of what makes us who we are. This book and the conversation about the Cultural Trinity should allow us to ground culture in our everyday lives in the following ways.

### ▲ Identity – how we play out different roles in life

The concept of identity, as part of the Cultural Trinity framework, revolves around how individuals perceive themselves and are perceived by others. In everyday life, identity informs the way people dress, speak and behave. For example, a person might express themselves in line with their cultural or racial heritage, showing it through clothing, food or use of language.

This sense of identity also influences career aspirations, hobbies and personal goals, as individuals often align their actions with how they are seen by society.

Identity is not static; it evolves based on experiences, societal expectations and interactions with others. Social media, for instance, plays a significant role in shaping modern identity by enabling individuals to curate and project specific versions of themselves. An individual's identity can influence how they approach situations – someone identifying as a feminist may prioritise advocating for gender equity in their workplace. These expressions of identity interact with the other components of the Cultural Trinity, like community affiliations and prominent belief systems. In many cases, the way our identity aligns with community and beliefs actually means we switch our identity around depending on the situation.

- **Community – the peer-to-peer relationships we have in life**

Community examines the networks and relationships that bind individuals together. Communities are characterised by peer-to-peer interactions and provide support, shared norms and a sense of belonging. For example, an individual who belongs to a tight-knit neighbourhood may feel a sense of duty to participate in local events or uphold shared values such as mutual respect or environmental sustainability. A member of a sports team may drink excessive amounts of alcohol or join their peers in late-night activities, even if it's against their better judgement. These shared experiences reinforce the bonds between members, creating a cycle of communal influence.

In workplaces, community manifests through team dynamics, organisational culture and shared objectives. People are often motivated by the expectations and recognition of their communities, whether it is a professional group, religious congregation or online fandom. This sense of collective identity can lead to cooperation, conflict resolution and innovation. Interactions within communities also contribute to shaping personal identities and strengthening shared belief systems, underscoring the interconnectedness of the three components.

### ■ Belief systems – what guides us in life

Belief systems, the third component of the framework, encapsulate the values, traditions and ideologies that guide people's actions and perceptions. These systems can range from religious and spiritual frameworks to secular moral codes and political ideologies. In daily life, belief systems influence decisions both big and small – such as dietary choices based on ethical or religious values, or acts of charity motivated by a sense of justice or compassion. A trained scout may value preparedness more than their friends do, as a soldier values loyalty and discipline. These guiding principles often serve as the moral compass for individuals and communities alike.

Belief systems also shape societal norms and rituals, which people follow consciously or unconsciously. For instance, cultural celebrations such as weddings or festivals are often steeped in belief systems that reinforce a shared sense of identity and community. Likewise we typically learn our ideas of mourning and burial rites from these belief systems. These rituals, in turn, create opportunities for individuals to reconnect with their values and social networks.

The power of a model like this is to a) create definitions of identity, communities and belief systems that relate to the specific topic at hand, and b) make sure that each section of the model fits together on any given topic. There are many ways to further codify identity, community and belief systems, but the most common ones I use are the following.

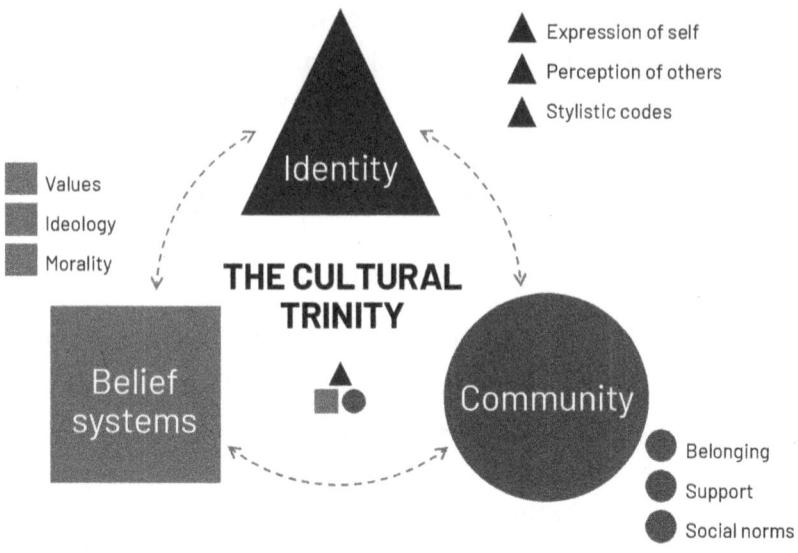

- ▲ **Identity** – Who an individual is – is often broken down into:

    *Expression of self*, because we project (and protect) an image of ourselves that we try to uphold,

    *Perception of others*, because what other people think of you influences the role you play out in life,

    *Stylistic codes*, because identity is often communicated non-verbally.

- ● **Community** – The nature of our peer-to-peer interactions – often gives people:

    *Belonging*, because people need a place that feels like home,

    *Support*, because a community is there to improve your life during the good times and look after you in the sad times,

    *Social norms*, because people need a place where their behaviour is considered normal.

ANALYSING CULTURE

- **Belief systems** – The guiding principles of how we live life – are often constructed through:

    *Values*, which give people a set of guiding principles on how to act in situations, and interact with others,

    *Ideology*, which is a system of beliefs about how society should be organised,

    *Morality*, which helps people determine right from wrong in terms of personal conduct.

## The Cultural Trinity in action

At twenty-four, I stumbled across the best boss in the world. I was a lost psychology graduate who happened upon an apprenticeship with a fantastic business anthropologist, Johanna Shapira. Shapira had spent years running an anthropology department at Ogilvy, one of the largest and most respected advertising agencies in the world, dropping nuggets of cultural gold into advertising strategies for the biggest brands in the world. She balanced whip-smart commentary that made the room pause for contemplation with a huge heart for the people in her corner, and I recognised that being on Team Shapira was going to be a great ride.

In one of my first projects, I was tasked with finding ways to get teenage boys in Tower Hamlets to use youth centres, which were well funded but largely empty. Tower Hamlets is one of the most deprived and diverse boroughs in the entire country, with the highest levels of child poverty in London. It has severe levels of overcrowding, with children often sharing bedrooms or sleeping in the living room, which often means older kids head out to the streets to avoid the family glare and find some independence. Once on the street, they show off their new-found swagger and are seen by others as intimidating and antisocial. Teenage kids hanging out on street corners had been brought to the attention of the local authority, which was where I got involved.

This was exactly the kind of job my young, idealistic self wanted – a chance to create meaningful change in the part of London where I lived. I contacted some local schools who also thought my cause was worthy, so they identified some young people I could speak to. Given it was my first project, I was happy with my chats – these teens told me their siblings were annoying and they couldn't invite their friends round, so they hung out on the streets most evenings. *Would you prefer to go to a youth centre?* Yeah, they were happy to go to a youth centre, but they weren't sure what was there. *What would make you go there?* The teenage boys I interviewed were classic boys: they'd go to the centres if there were video games, table tennis and pool tables – simple. *Give them what they need, and they will come*, I thought.

But when I came back with these findings, Shapira gave a wry smile and said, 'I don't think that's the answer.' She sent me back to Tower Hamlets, and this time I spent several evenings with the teenagers, hanging out on the streets, on park benches, and just going where they went. Many of the evenings were actually quite dull – they didn't have enough money to go to a café or pub, and they didn't want to be at home with their parents, so they were on the street with very little to do. But despite the mundanity, there was always an air of possibility that 'something' might happen. On several occasions I suggested that they could go to the youth centre if they were bored, but they would shrug and say, 'Maybe later.' What were the groups of boys really looking for each evening? Groups of girls.

What I actually found from hanging out on the streets was that getting the boys to the centre had nothing to do with improving the facilities. The local authority had already stacked the centres with video games, table tennis and pool tables. Teenage boys didn't go to the youth centres because the teenage girls didn't go there. The video games, table tennis and pool – all the things the boys said they wanted – were the things that put the girls off. The girls were the ones who had nothing to do at the youth centre, so they went to find fun on the street, and the boys followed. We looked at what connects people and were able to see that by making sure the youth centres catered to the boys *and* the girls, uptake of the services increased.

In retrospect, this was the first report I wrote that highlighted the importance of identity, community and belief systems – the Cultural Trinity. The report talked about the identity of teenage boys, how they were perceived as antisocial and intimidating, and how that perception informed their actions and the clothes they chose to wear. Being out on the streets at night became a badge of honour, and was considered a rite of passage for kids that age in the area.

I also talked about the role of community, in that the youth centres were not a place that either teenage girls or boys felt like they belonged. I could see the boys were 'adulting', playing out older versions of themselves, but bumping into a group of girls caused them to melt and become small children in big clothes. The youth centres had been designed to support kids at an age when they were big enough to not be at home but too young for adult nightlife. But in reality, the social norms of the youth centres weren't right for the girls, because they weren't designed for them, or for the boys, because the girls weren't there.

The report also laddered up to a belief system that suggested teenagers in Tower Hamlets were often treated as young adults by their parents, who were predominantly white working class or first-generation South Asian immigrants, because they had also been given a lot of responsibility when they were growing up.

Letting their kids go and play with other kids, whether at home or on the street, was a very normal thing to do. To mainstream society and the people who complained to the local authority about rowdy teenagers, they were still kids that needed supervision and oversight – but to their families, they were old enough to demonstrate independence.

This experience revealed how much more was going on beneath the surface, and how the dynamics I was observing could be neatly encapsulated through the three elements of the Cultural Trinity.

- ▲ **Identity** – Teenage boys who are seen as antisocial are simply trying to navigate a new, fluid identity shaped by peer pressure and 'street' fashion, while discovering emergent ideas of masculinity.

- ● **Community** – The unsanctioned street becomes the site for peer validation and belonging, contrasted with youth centres, which are perceived as sterile, irrelevant spaces where the teens can't play out new adult roles (flirting).

- ■ **Belief systems** – Tension between institutional views of adolescence (represented by the oversight of the youth club) and familial-cultural beliefs (that youth is a moment of self-discovery) creates unspoken codes of teen nightlife.

Anthropology helps us see what happens between people, and focuses on what unites us as a group rather than defines us as an individual. It prioritises insight from culture over insight from cognition, and through this first report, I began to see why cultural factors are more influential than personal motivation in driving people's behaviours. Anthropology factors in the wider cultural context of people's lives, meaning you need to go out on the street and see how people are living their lives, rather than simply asking them.

Compared to psychology, anthropology taught me about life's complexity. As the anthropologist Eric Wolf declared in 1964, 'Anthropology is both the most scientific of the humanities and the most humanistic of the sciences.'[12] This can be hard for businesses and governments to get to grips with, as they prefer the straightforward and immediate solutions that psychology seems to offer. While these can work for targeted individuals, sadly they are often short-term fixes for the whole group or simply don't work at all. Taking the time to understand people and the complexities of the societies in which they operate offers governments and companies lasting solutions and long-term behavioural change for the whole community.

Anthropology helps us understand an individual's action through the lens of the Cultural Trinity. All of these factors are hugely influential in why people do what they do, but they are not easily explained in a Q&A scenario. People are notoriously bad at describing their identity, community and belief systems, even when they are very open to discussing various aspects of their lives. People just aren't good at remembering or describing their behaviours in an accurate manner. Anthropology gave me a language with which to understand the real motivation behind decisions, and allowed me to build up a level of cultural intelligence that differed from the cognitive understanding that psychology offered.

## SO WHAT?
### Why knowing the rules that make us matters

One of the differences between *academic* and *business* anthropologists is that anyone advising businesses needs to answer a simple but important question: So Fucking What? Now that you've done your clever analysis, what do I actually do?

'SFW' was a catchphrase a (different) boss used repeatedly to focus our thinking on what our clients should do with our cultural analysis. This is a phrase that continues to ring in my ears, and it is how I will finish each chapter.

Knowing the rules that make us helps us in life as people are often playing with their identity. Being aware of how our image and interactions affect our identity helps us see our role in culture, such as the influence of how we dress and behave if we want to be part of certain communities. If we start to think about how our identity influences the culture we want to be a part of, then we become a more active participant in the world we want to create.

Businesses are a community in their own right as a group of employees that cooperate around a shared goal, creating a workplace culture that sets standards for behaviour. Many businesses are also creating culture through communicating with their customers or clients, and the specific way in which they communicate creates an image of how people should think about them. Knowing that a business needs to be a place of belonging and support that sets standards for how to behave can sharpen the minds of leaders who want to foster a particular workplace culture.

Our society is a complex interplay between various cultures and subcultures – all of which are guided by their own Cultural Trinities – that are dictated by government and civil society. The task of anyone trying to create a peaceful and cooperative society is to find a set of beliefs that everyone can get behind to act as a uniting force, whatever culture they come from. This is the role of national culture which might revolve around the idea of *liberty* in America, *paternalism* in France or *tolerance* in the UK.

So herein lies the Cultural Trinity as a model to analyse the rules that make us. The next chapter will look at how these elements interact with one another, which leads on to a series of chapters about how culture has made us and changed us in all walks of life.

# 2

# How Culture Affects Life, Business and Society

I was never very good at dancing, but then again, neither were my parents. I remember the three of us at a French village fete, celebrating the end of the harvest. There were lines of trestle tables and benches in a large hall where people sat, ate and chatted together, and the atmosphere was buzzing from everyone coming together. After dinner, a local band played songs of various styles – rock and roll, jazz and some more classical pieces – and everyone got up and danced to the music they liked.

The local farmer, who looked and acted more like he was from the Marais in Paris than the fields of rural France, invited my mum to dance. He led her in a ballroom waltz, elegantly traversing and gliding around the room. At the end of the song, my mum sat down looking flushed in the cheeks, feeling rather pleased that a Frenchman had shown her how to dance. For the next song, the equally glamorous sister of the farmer asked my dad to dance, also to a waltz, expecting him to lead. My dad floundered with his two left feet, wiggled his hips in a classic 'this is how we dance in England' manner, and then tried to twirl her around the room in the same way her brother had done with my mum on the last dance. It didn't end well as the French lady burst into fits of giggles and then yelped as my dad accidently trod on her toe, and they both agreed to sit back down with only a minute having passed.

In rural France, kids learn to dance at school, which creates a nation of people who know the basics in how to move their bodies. In the UK, teenagers learn to drunkenly wiggle their hips in a dark nightclub. When the two cultures meet, it's like a remake of *Beauty and the (Drunken) Beast*. Dancing is a great analogy for culture: it's learned; if you know it, you know it; and it's a bonding force that drives people to practise and perfect.

## For the love of travel

In 1997 I was seventeen and found myself in India's Rajasthani desert, staying with an NGO for a month as part of a school trip connected to an international development programme. I was there with three other classmates to document a Bedouin tribe that the Rajasthani state refused to recognise. Non-recognition by the state meant they had no access to healthcare, education, formal work or even community water sources, which further exacerbated their nomadic tendencies and exclusion from society. Our job was to go out into the desert to photograph the tribe (back in the day when I needed a dark room to produce the pictures) so that the NGO could make a case to the state government that these people were real, had needs and deserved recognition. Without knowing it, this was my first anthropological project.

As a seventeen-year-old Londoner, I encountered so many people, customs, habits, manners and rituals that were alien to me. Out in the desert, we lived with the locals, dressed like the locals, ate with the locals and sang songs with the locals (I can still remember the words to 'Pardesi Pardesi', the number-one hit at the time). We copied their morning routine, which meant getting up with the sun, doing a small amount of yoga and breathing exercises, and brushing our teeth with a neem twig picked from a tree in the courtyard. Using a neem twig to brush my teeth took a bit of getting used to, and involved peeling off the bark, chewing the moist core until it became frayed and then using the frayed ends to get between the teeth. I was deeply sceptical of this behaviour as a source of good oral hygiene, but I knew there was no way I could replenish my Colgate, so I went with the flow.

One part of the daily routine that none of us could get on board with was the toileting practices. We'd been told before our trip about using our hands to clean ourselves after going to the toilet, along with a few tips and tricks to make it easier (hot tip: pour water on your bottom before pooing to prevent it sticking), but it was a step too far for this city boy. As a result, my classmates and I brought toilet paper with us on the trip, along with some paper bags which we used to collect the soiled toilet paper because the septic tank couldn't handle it. Each evening, we took the full paper bags out into the desert to burn them to avoid a public health issue. The process became an end-of-evening ceremony in which we would wander off into the darkness, stare at the endless stars, have a cigarette and light a little fire before heading back to camp.

At some point in the second week, our stomachs had submitted to a light but troublesome bug, and when it came to our evening ritual, we struggled to light the fire because the toilet paper was a bit moist. We kept adding dry twigs from the desert floor as kindling to get the fire going, but our pile was too wet and refused to burn. All four of us stood around the failing fire, scratching our heads, looking gormless. At that point, what seemed like out of nowhere in the twilight of the evening, an elderly Bedouin man who we had met a couple of days earlier appeared. We greeted each other, and as a kind offering, he got down on his haunches to help us with our struggling fire. He clearly thought that to get the fire going, it needed more oxygen, and before any of us knew what was happening, he had his hands in the fire, tossing it around so that it would draw better.

The four clueless city dwellers jumped into action, gesturing that he move back, shouting *nahin, nahin* (Hindi for 'no', a language he didn't even speak). Chuckling, he clearly thought our soft city approach of not touching a fire with your hands was laughable, so he tossed it some more and blew hard into the failing embers at the base. In doing so, the outer paper bag blew off and revealed the contents of the fire, at which point he stopped and looked deeply puzzled.

This story still troubles me to this day and is a classic example of how familiar behaviours can be entirely unsuitable for foreign contexts. From getting up at sunrise to do yoga to using a neem toothbrush, being in India felt very strange. Our refusal to engage with Indian toileting practices was a reaction to this discomfort. To the poor Bedouin man who tried to help us, we evidently had a deeply strange evening ritual that he wished he'd never known about.

While we could never fully explain our bizarre toileting practice to the elderly Bedouin man, we were able to convey to him with our facial expressions that we all felt his disgust. We immediately got soap and water out of our backpacks for him to use. He left in good spirits, and when we met him again a few days later, he showed us a coming-of-age ritual in which his nephew killed a goat for a celebration the following day. Our previous interactions had added a level of familiarity between us, despite the massive language barrier.

The story also troubles me because of the obvious historical connotations of a white, inexperienced kid going to India with a camera to 'save a tribe'. Through years of colonial rule, the British exacerbated the caste system that I was there to document, and the idea that I was there to whitewash the sins of the past does not fill me with pride. While my work had value, I was there as part of an ongoing problem of international inequality and white privilege.

This is the very problem that anthropology is grappling with as a discipline which was founded from white colonial privilege, treating tribes in far-off lands as 'strange' and 'other'. But as I reflect on my role documenting the Bedouin in Rajasthan all those years ago, and the ethical considerations that have developed since, I can only try to avoid those power imbalances in the work that I do now and how I push anthropology to develop.

### Culture is a 'web of meaning'

During my career I have sat on a lot of sofas and drunk a lot of tea. No matter the topic that I am researching – parenting, shopping, beauty, finance – being an anthropologist means I start by understanding the person in front of me.

In the UK, tea is a facilitator of conversation that transcends age, gender, race and, most importantly, class. Tea sits at the cornerstone of British culture as a ritual that allows everyone to start a conversation. The weird thing is that many people in the UK – me included – don't really like drinking tea. It's more like an activity that helps pass the time than a beverage I enjoy, but as soon as someone comes into my house, I offer them a cup of tea.

The anthropologist sees tea as an act of reciprocity that formally starts an exchange of information, allowing people to get to know one another. Tea helps the British overcome their deep sense of awkwardness and allows the host to avoid eye contact while the guest secretly judges their home. The cup should be large enough to buy about ten to fifteen minutes of small talk before proceeding on to the real reason the person has come to visit (to fix the boiler, share news or ask a favour). I always say yes to tea just to get the small talk going (though, to be honest, I prefer coffee). Our lives are imbued with so many rituals – and they often start with tea.

The anthropologist Clifford Geertz said that the role of the anthropologist is to look at culture as a 'web of meaning', suggesting that 'man is an animal suspended in webs of significance that he himself has spun'.[1] The primary job of an anthropologist is, through conversations and observations, to discover that meaning. The clothes we wear, the trinkets in our home, the food we eat, the flowers we buy, the ads we see, all the quirky behaviours that people display around us – everything reveals something about us.

The way that we serve tea has significance because both the maker and receiver know that they are entering into small talk. It's a shared ritual. If you start replacing builder's tea (a generic term for a strong cup of tea) with lapsang souchong (a smoky tea from China), you are into a completely different web of significance, even though the liquid hasn't changed *that* much.

You often need to be part of the web of meaning to know when it's gone wrong. To the uninitiated non-Brit, the warm, murky cup of tea might not seem like a difficult drink to make, but do not be fooled – there is a right and a wrong way to make a cup of tea depending on which class you are from (everything in the UK is about class). Tea is imbued with history and connotation and is used as a way of assessing whether you are middle class (who use a *cup* and make a pot of tea) or working class (who use a *mug* and make the tea in the mug). Again, there is very little difference in the end result, but the process reveals your different belief system.

Geertz says, 'Culture is both meaning and the process of making meaning.' Culture is static in that there are common reference points (tea drinking) while also being dynamic and changing over time. For example, the UK tea market is now about 94% tea bags and 6% loose leaf tea,[2] which on a day-to-day level, means that most people have converted to making tea in a mug. Does this mean everyone has become working class? No, but it does indicate that perhaps how we take our tea is less of a class distinction than in previous generations. Many middle-class people now ask for builder's tea because there is an implicit understanding that the tea on offer will be made in a mug, the working-class way. Nobody thinks about class origins when asking for tea (apart from an anthropologist), but the meaning gets embedded ever so subtly into our behaviour and language. Hence tea has a meaning that is static but also ever changing.

## Mapping tea around the world

In China, a woman I was visiting offered to show me her 'tea ceremony'. This was quite different to my many British tea exchanges. My first mistake was that I started to talk as she was performing the ceremony, something my Chinese colleague immediately stopped me doing. You must be calm and respectful when someone performs a tea ceremony in China; it is not a signal for small talk. You are supposed to focus on and respect the elaborate ritual of pouring water and tea between various pots and cups, because it symbolises a sharing of knowledge, happiness and respect. The process is about removing distractions like noise or stress so that you can connect in a meaningful manner. It is still a reciprocal act with which someone welcomes you into their home (similar to the UK) but performed with a wholly different meaning.

In India, chai is consumed at every possible opportunity – first thing in the morning, waiting for buses and trains, when shopping, working or socialising, as well as before and after food. A variety of ingredients and flavours are used: cardamon, cinnamon, cloves, ginger, black pepper, nutmeg and more. Tea in India has a long and complicated history as it is thoroughly entwined with British colonialism and the East India Company plantations. In response to the Great Depression in the 1930s, the export market for India's tea decreased enormously, just at a time when production was becoming ever more efficient, so marketers tried to create a domestic market for tea. Tea took on a cultural significance that became linked to India's economic growth. Powdered tea leaves became readily available even in the smallest villages, which meant each region could add their own ingredients and spices, linking chai recipes to individual villages. Tea's rise to everyday consumption over a twenty-year period is unparalleled compared to any other food or drink in the world. Now, at every truck stop and train station you see people from every caste and class drinking tea from the same *chaiwallah* (tea-seller), and chai allows strangers to talk to one another. Chai is Indian, and India is chai – it connects unknown people and signifies India's growth to a stronger and more unified nation.

By viewing something as everyday as tea through the lens of identity, we see that tea performs a social ritual which is about welcoming people into one's home, shop or workplace. If we took that act at surface level, we might assume that tea plays out the same role around the world. However, by laddering in community and belief systems we see there are different levels of expectations, uncovering the distinct 'webs of meaning' that shape how this simple act plays out in different countries:

**In the United Kingdom . . .**

- ▲ **Identity** – Tea signals a desire to welcome others, masking awkwardness while performing the role of a polite host.
- ● **Community** – Tea serves as a social lubricant that cuts across class and culture, facilitating small talk and softening interactions.

- ■ **Belief systems** – Deeply coded with British class dynamics, tea-making rituals subtly signal social standing. On the surface, this is a demonstration of equality, but the underlying meanings – pot vs mug, tea type – speak volumes about class heritage and shifting norms.

In China . . .

- ▲ **Identity** – Serving tea is a welcoming act, showcasing that a host is respectful and deeply intentional.
- ● **Community** – The tea ceremony structures connection through shared silence and attentiveness. It creates a community of mutual respect within a quiet, disciplined space.
- ■ **Belief systems** – Tea is embedded in a philosophical web of meaning that values harmony, mindfulness and tradition.

In India . . .

- ▲ **Identity** – Serving chai is both welcoming and inclusive; it is an informal yet deeply rooted cultural practice.
- ● **Community** – Chai transcends caste and class, enabling spontaneous conversations among strangers in public spaces – from train stations to roadside stalls – showcasing a web of belonging to the new India.
- ■ **Belief systems** – Chai's history is layered with colonial legacy, economic innovation and regional pride. It reflects a belief in self-sufficiency, symbolising India's evolving national identity.

In anthropology, 'culture' starts with the everyday, not the momentous. The way in which we drink tea tells us a lot about the culture that we live in, and the culture that we live in tells us a lot about how we structure our lives. In the UK, our world is structured around class, in China around respect and in India around unification. In all of these cases tea provides moments of connection in a potentially fragmented world, and it creates inclusive cultures where people can take a moment to trust one another. Metaphorically, tea culture embodies the purpose of anthropology, a medium through which we can unite rather than divide (which makes me think I should like it more).

## Applying anthropology to business

American anthropologist Horace Miner said that anthropology can 'make the strange seem familiar, and the familiar seem strange.'[3] Anthropology encourages us to juxtapose what we find unusual next to what we find familiar in order to figure out what other people think is normal, and why they might think that you are strange.

This idea can be applied to thorny public policy areas such as healthy eating, or to life when trying to understand why your neighbours' kids leave their bikes lying in the street. However, this concept works best in getting businesses to understand the lives of the people they need to engage with. Companies like Airbnb were able to take the utterly novel concept of staying in a stranger's house and normalise it by showing that someone else's home is actually more familiar than a hotel. Dove also did this through questioning the entire system of beauty advertising. Using 'real' women with a range of body types and untouched photos, they disrupted what had become *familiar* visual norms in the beauty industry. If there's a problem that relates to how people see the world, using an anthropological lens will often help you find new ways of looking at the same issue.

Twenty-five years after my trip to Rajasthan, and with over 200 anthropological projects under my belt, I found myself working for Sensodyne, a specialist toothpaste that helps people overcome sensitivity and gum disease. From a scientific perspective, it's a great toothpaste, highly effective at improving oral health, and the people who use it normally swear by it (it has some very loyal users). While they were the number-one brand for gum issues in the UK and the US, their growth was naturally limited by the fact that gum health in these countries is actually quite good – in order to grow, they needed to help people in countries where oral hygiene was more of an everyday issue.

I started working with Sensodyne in 2018 to find opportunities in India and China. From my time staying in the NGO in India I knew that the morning routine was a crucially important moment in the day, highly ritualised, and a process of transformation that was very specific to Indian culture. When we went to people's homes in Delhi and Mumbai, we found the morning routine was just as ritualistic as it was in the desert, and brushing your teeth happens before breakfast, washing or getting dressed. Symbolically, it is actually considered to be a spiritual reawakening of the soul, which is thought to disconnect from the body when in a deep state of rest during sleep. Brushing your teeth isn't a cleaning process, more a purification ritual, with Hindu mythology suggesting that Brahmins (the priest caste) were born from the mouth of Brahma (the purest of all gods), and the mouth represents a place of purity. Suddenly, the morning routine I had seen in my teens was reimagined as a transformation whereby the soul reconnects to the body every morning.

Sensodyne's allopathic claims of including sodium bicarbonate to improve gum health was factually true, but it had little ritualistic connection to the reawakening of the soul. This cultural insight repositioned the behaviour of brushing teeth from a clinical act to prevent tooth decay (Sensodyne's viewpoint) to a ritual focused on using Ayurvedic principles to help reawaken and purify the soul after sleep (the consumer's viewpoint). This shift to an Ayurvedic mindset recognised that mind, body and soul are all interlinked, and this intergenerational theory of health is immune to fads given its longevity as a system of knowledge. Sensodyne shouldn't position itself as a new saviour against tooth decay; it should use ingredients like neem to implicitly position it as an old sage. This was a huge leap of consciousness for a Western consumer healthcare brand to add Ayurvedic variants to the range, but they soon realised that doing so was a way of showing efficacy in a culturally relevant way. And the financial results were as effective as the oral health improvement, with sales rising to over £13.2 million in the first three years of the repositioning.

Sensodyne used the same anthropological approach when looking at how to gain access to the Chinese market, where the cultural narrative was about the past being entwined with the present (due to the incredibly fast development of the country). This meant it was important to combine Sensodyne's efficacious model with principles from traditional Chinese medicine (TCM), which is as much a philosophy for life as it is a cure for illness. A core tenet of TCM is about balancing internal heat – if your body gets too hot from stress or poor diet, you can end up with inflammation, irritability and spots; being too cold comes from too many raw foods or emotional withdrawal, and you can end up with fatigue, diarrhoea or low libido. Managing internal heat is a juggling act between behaviour and food, and TCM has a list of herbs and plants that assist with the balance.

In January 2019, Sensodyne Herbal infused with centella was launched. Clearly positioned as a Western brand with its clinical look and feel, it used centella as TCM shorthand to show Chinese consumers that it would cool internal heat and prevent bleeding gums. Later that year, they released another variant infused with rhodiola, a plant extract signalling it would detoxify the blood and slow acute reactions. This TCM double act showed consumers there was a variant to cool internal heat with centella, and a warming, energising variant with rhodiola: Sensodyne was there for all their TCM oral health needs. Playing both sides of the cultural track made Sensodyne relevant in a market where Western brands were struggling for recognition, and over the same three-year period, Sensodyne increased sales to the tune of £15 million.

By using the Cultural Trinity in our analysis we were able to show Sensodyne how to convince Indian and Chinese consumers that their product was efficacious, not because it was clinically the best but because the company understood local belief systems. Ayurveda and TCM aren't just curative extracts; they represent a deeper meaning of oral health in India and China that Sensodyne could become part of.

**In India . . .**

- ▲ **Identity** – Brushing teeth is not just a hygiene habit but a personal ritual that connects the soul and body each morning, and toothpaste is part of spiritual renewal and daily purification.

- ● **Community** – Morning routines are a household ritual that come with a sense of collective discipline, where Ayurvedic variants have spiritual currency.

- ■ **Belief systems** – Oral care is tied to Ayurvedic health, which sees the mouth as a sacred space and brushing as an act of spiritual cleansing. Health products are trusted when they align with this symbolic worldview.

**In China . . .**

- ▲ **Identity** – Oral health reflects both personal status and cultural continuity, and individuals want TCM ingredients to 'cool' and 'detoxify' their mouth and body.
- ● **Community** – Rapid social change has led to a blend of past and present practices, so people trust products that are a combination of Western science and traditional wisdom.
- ■ **Belief systems** – TCM frames oral health as part of a broader balance of internal energies. Sensodyne became credible by adopting TCM ingredients as cultural shorthand for efficacy.

The greatest skill anthropology can teach us is to *watch* and *listen* effectively, which requires us to take part in the experience of life. Even though the brand managers couldn't understand local beliefs on an instinctive level because it wasn't their culture, they still managed to change the toothpaste formulation based on walking a mile in someone else's shoes.

### Culture can even sell pet food

One of the most entertaining studies I did was looking at how people feed their pets across Latin America, and it takes a certain kind of researcher to get excited by this kind of thing. Before we got to Brazil, our client at pet food company Pedigree told us that the problem was that pet owners in Brazil fed their pets human food, predominantly scraps from the table, rather than pet food. Human food can be very bad for pets, and if we could find the right psychological hooks to convince pet owners to buy dry kibble, then they would have healthier, shinier, better-smelling pets – an easy win, we thought.

When we got to meet people in Brazil, all the pet owners told us that they love their pets. Sure, who doesn't? I imagine most pet owners would agree. But when we met families that owned pets in Brazil, we realised we'd vastly underestimated their love. The dogs we met in Brazil were the pride and joy of the family, often inconveniencing their owners in the night by sleeping in the middle of their bed like a child. One family told us, somewhat bitterly, that Roger the cat (real name) got to eat fresh minced beef every day, whereas the family were only allowed meat every other day.

Pet owners in Brazil weren't feeding their pets *leftovers*; they were making a full meal for them twice a day. That meant chopping and frying onions (not recommended as they can be toxic to dogs), adding in mince, mixing in a bit of gravy, while also boiling up some rice in another pan. If it wasn't mince, it might be shredded chicken, or maybe a different cut of beef. Because their pets ate the same food as they did, the same rules applied about what constituted good food, namely that it must be fresh and cooked from scratch. Conversely, they also had strong views on what constituted bad food for their beloved companions.

There's some logic in this: if you really loved your pet, would you give them dry pellets every day? Well, we gave the families we met a free bag of kibble as an experiment and none of them had used it two weeks later, because they genuinely didn't consider kibble to be food.

Instead of pushing dry kibble, we went with a premium product that has small chunks of meat hermetically sealed in a pouch. It's more expensive than kibble, and it's the closest thing to fresh meat, which was enough to make it equate to 'real food' in a Brazilian mindset. We placed this product in the fresh produce aisle of the supermarket, where shoppers are thinking about what both they and their pets will eat. In this instance, dog owners bought a small pouch of Pedigree meat rather than expensive mince from the butcher, but still cooked the sauce and rice, serving what they considered a meal worthy of their animal. Win-win!

This supermarket experiment sent purchases of wet pouches through the roof, increasing sales in Brazil to the tune of $10 million. A similar insight in Mexico showcased the importance of the home-cooked meals, which led Pedigree to launch a dog cookbook teaching pet owners how to cook various recipes, often substituting expensive fresh meat with a wet pouch. Rather than trying to force our idea of what pets should eat on to other cultures, we were able to help pet food producers understand the society they were trying to break into. Once we accepted that Brazilians and Mexicans were never going to feed their dearly beloved pets a diet of dry kibble, we were able to suggest a product that was much closer to the existing idea of pet food in these countries. The wet pouches saved pet owners time and money, and led to a multimillion-dollar increase in sales.

Through collaborating with pet owners in Brazil, we were able to find ways to change behaviour that weren't based on the psychology of persuasion. There were no scare tactics about onions and diarrhoea, nor were there glossy adverts showing how shiny their dogs would be if they ate Pedigree. What Pedigree came to understand is that pet owners in Brazil have a very different belief system: the role of the pet in the family is different, the concept of fresh food is different, and nutrition and health are different. By adopting a new belief system into their thinking, they were able to find new answers right in front of their very eyes. The Cultural Trinity shows us that an apparently irrational behaviour is actually a deeply embedded cultural practice.

- ▲ **Identity** – Pets are treated as full family members, often like children, and feeding them is an act of love and care that reflects one's identity as a responsible, nurturing owner.
- ● **Community** – Home-cooked meals for pets mirror communal norms around fresh food and shared mealtime values. Owners extend their household food rituals to include pets, reinforcing social bonds through cooking.
- ■ **Belief systems** – 'Real food' means fresh, home-prepared meals. Dry kibble doesn't qualify as food because it lacks the emotional and sensory cues of proper nourishment. Feeding practices are guided by a belief in food as a marker of love and worth, not just nutrition.

Tricia Wang is a tech anthropologist who has stressed the importance of creating 'thick data', which places importance on observations, feelings and reactions as a source of understanding. Essentially, what Wang is advocating is adding a layer of empathy and context on top of some very big datasets to avoid colossal misunderstandings.

If Pedigree hadn't sent us to meet people in Brazil and instead relied on the masses of data they had at their disposal, the problem would have looked a bit more like this: i) pets in Brazil eat human food, ii) pet owners will give their pets leftovers, so iii) educating pet owners about how cheap and healthy kibble is will perform best. This would be what Tricia Wang describes as 'thin data' – insight based on randomly selected data points leading to assumptions and leaps of faith.[4] Thin data can often lead to one-size-fits-all results, such as finding a specific group that are most likely to buy kibble, which gives a false idea about how acceptable that is to a majority of pet owners.

Thick data can be applied to much broader audiences, through understanding what's important to them and how their belief systems are structured.

## Finding rules for a healthier society

Over a six-year period, I supported various public health programmes in the UK looking at how the government could help people become healthier through a better diet, quitting smoking, reducing alcohol and exercising more. UK public health initiatives are often labelled as a move towards a 'nanny state', not because the Brits don't like state intervention in their lives but because of their deep-seated cultural beliefs about privacy: what happens in the home stays in the home.

This cultural importance of privacy is the reason many public health messages have fallen flat. In 2009 (before my involvement) the UK government launched a flagship campaign, Change4Life, and based a lot of its communications around helping children lose weight.[5] It started with a worthy cause – getting people to recognise that a) an overweight child will go on to have poorer health in later life, and b) there are simple ways to do this, such as cooking healthy food at home. It was a big campaign that used a number of celebrities for wide-ranging appeal.

In the first few years, the campaign struggled because it was essentially trying to fight a culture where *parents know what's best for their child*. A campaign that told families that their child was overweight was seen to damage a child's sense of pride – it was bullying via a poster. Telling a parent their overweight child would have reduced life chances was implicitly telling them their child was doomed to failure. This was an unkind message, and parents were not open to collaboration.

Having created a confrontational feeling with parents, the healthy home cooking campaign with ideas for 'recipe switching' felt patronising. Parents doubled down on their own (unhealthier) home cooking because the home was their private business and their child loved these meals (food is a common means of communicating love between parents and kids).

As a result, a movement arose among parents seeking to instil 'body confidence' in overweight children, the belief being that if a child felt good in their body, they could achieve anything they wanted. While self-confidence is of course worth nurturing in children, sometimes this message of 'body confidence' meant a child would eat whatever they desired – and children are notoriously bad at choosing the 'healthy' options! Parents perceived their children's loss of confidence at school among their peers to be far more damaging than the effect of being 'big boned' or overweight, which meant that the spiral continued. This counter-intuitive response to public health campaigns was the result of applying psychological principles to attempt to change people's behaviours, while simultaneously ignoring the more important cultural beliefs that truly drove the behaviours.

When I delivered this message to Public Health England (PHE) in 2014, the room fell silent. Up until that point, the campaign had been built on delivering scientific and nutritional advice in an accessible manner to create positive health outcomes. PHE were using behavioural science techniques to guide people to make the 'right' choices, under the philosophical guise of libertarian paternalism. But the right choice for a professional nutritionist who believes diet is more important than anything else is different from the right choice for a busy family living on an estate who want their children to feel confident at play time and loved at dinner time. More often than not people's cultural beliefs define what the 'right' choices are, not science.

The campaign created a problem for parents: their child's current emotional wellbeing was being pitted against their future health prospects. This is a classic example of behavioural science putting the onus of responsibility upon the individual to change, even if that change requires going against the prevailing winds of culture. Instead, parenting culture in the UK prioritised creating a sense of autonomy and self-belief in children, and parents felt patronised and bullied into doing the 'right thing' all the time. That belief system was more important when people made choices about what to buy and eat. Applying the Cultural Trinity to explore the PHE campaign shows that the resistance wasn't irrational; it was rooted in how families felt about identity, family life and privacy.

- ▲ **Identity** – Parents see themselves as loving caregivers who know what's best for their children. Their self-worth is tied to how they provide, protect and nurture confidence, not just health.
- ● **Community** – The home is seen as a private, protected space where outside interference – even from well-meaning public health campaigns – is viewed as intrusive. Social norms support the idea that parenting choices are personal and not open for public scrutiny.
- ■ **Belief systems** – Autonomy, emotional wellbeing and expressions of love (especially through food) are more culturally valued than expert advice or future health predictions. Public messaging that ignores these beliefs risks being seen as patronising or bullying, even when it is factually correct.

But the story doesn't end there. From 2014, I worked with PHE to embed the lived experience of families into policy-making, which led to a shift in strategy from behavioural change to cultural impact. Spending time with families showed that giving children choice over food is one of many life lessons parents are teaching children – they may not be making the healthiest choices, but they are learning about autonomy, compromise and self-restraint (not just calorie control and healthy eating). We also observed that kids were learning life lessons when playing video games in the sitting room as a family, and it became apparent that telling them to run around outside was never going to work (particularly in rough neighbourhoods). We noted the enormous portions that children were eating, particularly in poorer households, which was a way for parents who couldn't afford much else to treat their kids. These were all lessons that PHE had to learn the hard way because they realised that psychological behaviour-change strategies would never trump culture.

We noted something else, too. Family life isn't all sweetness and roses. Hard-working families are exhausted, and however much they love their kids, watching TV together is the easiest solution after a twelve-hour shift. Tired parents don't make good choices, and when kids want sweets, they often get them. Sugary treats often result in difficult behaviour – especially in the eyes of tired parents. After spending time with families across the country, it was clear that both PHE and families had a common enemy: sugar.

In 2015, PHE started a campaign around the problems of sugar instead. Sugar reduction was a message that families were ready to hear because they all knew their kids became hyperactive when they had too many sweets, but they didn't know how to deal with it. Simple, effective messaging about the number of sugar cubes in everyday items of food – from canned soup to a can of Coke – showed parents what they couldn't otherwise see. PHE developed an app that scanned barcodes, allowing parents to see the number of sugar cubes in a product when they were wandering around the supermarket, which meant some sugary foods no longer made it into the home. Sugar became a means for engaging with health because it was a problem all parents could get on board with, not just parents that had overweight children – it gave PHE and parents a common goal, instead of being at odds with each other.

Change4Life became relevant to everyone, and by 2018, 91% of parents said they remembered the campaign, over 5 million parents had downloaded the app and excess sugar intake in children had reduced by 33% over a three-year period.[6] The speed of this impact was phenomenal and shows the importance of not segmenting an audience, and instead, finding common problems that everyone wants to deal with. Deep down, the parents of overweight children knew there was an issue. In moving away from a psychological model to a more anthropological, cultural view of the world, PHE had shifted the debate from a confrontational campaign to a collaborative movement.

The elephant in the room was the marketing budgets and seductive power of the food and drinks industry, which had successfully lobbied against all previous attempts to legislate against cheaply priced high-sugar items placed at child height in the supermarket. The cultural landscape shifted between 2010 and 2018 as sugar became demonised by parents and health practitioners, allowing PHE to push the Soft Drinks Industry Levy (aka the 'Sugar Tax') through parliament, which taxed soft drinks based on the amount of sugar in each drink.[7] Manufacturers could either pass that cost on to consumers (i.e. raise prices and become uncompetitive), slash profits (and face a shareholder backlash) or reformulate their recipes with less sugar (which they all did). As a result of the Sugar Tax, the number of soft drinks sold stayed relatively stable, but the amount of sugar in those drinks decreased by 44%.[8] Through collaborating with parents and creating a joint mission, PHE managed to reposition sugar within the 'cultural web of meaning' to create long-lasting, sustainable change and improve the lives of millions of children.

Initially, the government focused on a set of beliefs that weren't in line with how parents around the country felt – that parents, rather than the government, are responsible for the health of their kids. But with a good dose of empathy and a smart strategy, they found a set of values that they could agree on – being anti-sugar and better behaved – which meant the rest of the puzzle pieces fell into place. This belief system triggered a different identity, one which empowered parents to stand up to children on sugar, which changed family dynamics across the UK.

By reframing public health through culture rather than cognitive mindsets, PHE discovered that lasting change wasn't about telling people what to do, but about aligning with their values, identities and the shared realities of everyday family life.

- ▲ **Identity** – The new campaign showed parents as empowered agents of change. Saying no to sugar became a way to show love through care and protection, not indulgence.
- ● **Community** – Families across social groups bonded around a shared enemy: sugar. The home became a site of collaboration between parents and kids, reinforced by simple tools like the sugar app, which supported joint decision-making in the supermarket and at home.
- ■ **Belief systems** – Rather than abstract health goals, the campaign aligned with everyday frustrations that families already faced, like hyperactive kids, tired parents and overstretched budgets. This created a shared value rooted in practicality, emotional relief and better family dynamics.

## SO WHAT?
## Culture gives us more holistic answers to life, business and society

During my career consulting for governments and businesses I have seen a desire for quick, measurable outcomes. It's human nature to look for certainty in the unknown, and psychological models give us an illusion that we can control outcomes immediately. Targeting a group with a social or political message based on their specific desires and motivations makes good, intuitive sense. Secretly, we'd love the world to be designed around us. This fits with our egos, it makes us feel special, and it feels like an effective way to change the world. Our own cognition tricks us into believing that what works for one person works for everyone.

As we've seen time and again throughout this chapter, the one-size-fits-all psychological approach rarely succeeds in creating lasting, large-scale change. Sensodyne didn't factor Indian belief systems into their scientific formulations; PHE didn't recognise that body confidence was more important to parents than weight.

In life, we often think of culture as something we visit or experience. While theatre and art galleries reflect interesting ideas that can challenge our beliefs, many of our curious cultural traits are hiding in plain sight. We might think that many of the products we have in our bathroom are purely about product choice, but in reality, we can use the Cultural Trinity to dissect the meaning behind many of the products we buy, as they're often a reflection of our identity.

In business, it's important to work within existing belief systems. Creating cultural change often requires changing one or two elements of the Cultural Trinity – trying to change all three elements can feel like living in a foreign country, requiring a lot of acclimatisation. The reason Pedigree, PHE and Sensodyne were so successful is that they didn't try to change what people believed in; they worked *with* their beliefs to create an offering that was acceptable to the people they served.

In society, we see a heady mix of the Cultural Trinity across policy areas and public services. However, the most important element of the Cultural Trinity for policy-makers and governments to focus on is how their messaging works within the communities they're looking to support. By their very nature, governments are often intervening on topics that people are highly concerned about, so telling people they're wrong or they should think something else doesn't work. By understanding the conversations that are already going on in communities around the country, governments can help with solutions that people haven't yet figured out how to solve.

# 3

## Culture Makes an ASS Out of U and ME

My mum and dad once jumped the queue to board a plane in Russia. They were travelling back to London from India and routed via Moscow on an overbooked Aeroflot flight, and they were obediently queueing to board the plane. People were pushing in, and there was a general sense of panic that there wouldn't be enough seats. My dad decided enough was enough and complained to the stony-faced steward that 'this isn't fair' and they had been 'waiting patiently in the queue for long enough' and it was now their 'turn to board'. The surly Muscovite stared at my dad, didn't even grace him with a word, and with a tough guy nod of his head gestured he get back in line. Dad rose to the occasion and decided he would tough guy him back, raised his voice and pointed his finger. Story has it, the steward grew two feet taller and gestured that he get back in line again, and this time my dad obeyed. A Brit trying to enforce a fair queueing system man-to-man in Russia was a cultural challenge he would lose every time.

National stereotypes are funny because they're true but offensive because they are incomplete. They become amusing reference points for everyone to understand but fail to show the depth of national character and the belief system that lie behind them. Stereotypes are good at explaining what people do – an expression of group identity – but they offer no explanation for why that's the case. For me as a Brit, queueing is deeply important because it is a symbol of living in an equitable society, where following the process means everyone will get the reward. Foreigners regularly laugh at this statement, noting that Brits live in a highly stratified class system, and the presence of a hereditary monarch as the head of state is almost the definition of an unequal society... but that conceals a cultural truth. Over many, many years, British culture has developed a set of small but crucially important rituals - like queueing, elaborate handshakes and constantly saying sorry - to establish equity.

Equally, a Russian would find the story above an overly simplistic description of the flight steward's actions - and thankfully, my mum understood that too. After my dad was unceremoniously turned away, my mum burst into tears and told the steward that her four-year-old son (me) would be waiting for her at the airport in London, and she hadn't seen him in two weeks (true story), and could they please let them board the flight to reunite the family? Mum - having lived in Budapest behind the Iron Curtain for several years - recognised that Russians live in a highly collectivist society that prioritises the family unit over individual need, and despite the strongman stereotype, Russians have a set of values that validates emotion as a reason to act. In Russia, mothers hold a lot of power. Dad thought it was only fair that they should get on the plane because they were in the queue, but Mum convinced the steward it was fair to let them on the plane because of a greater, more culturally relevant need (seeing a four-year-old me).

National stereotypes are offensive on a personal level because we don't want to believe we are a product of our culture, a mass-produced clone, living next door to a cultural replica of ourselves. That's our cognition at play, feeding our belief that we are unique individuals with free will. We believe we are in charge of our own destiny, and we believe we are fundamentally different to our neighbour. This is what Freud termed the 'narcissism of small differences', a psychological factor that emphasises small variations to make them feel larger than they are and serves to increase our sense of free will and uniqueness.[1]

When stereotypes move beyond amusing national quirks and start ascribing characteristics to people's race, gender or sexuality, they start to erase someone's core identity. For example, when Black women are repeatedly portrayed as 'angry' or LGBTQ+ individuals are caricatured as flamboyant sidekicks in the media, these depictions flatten complex lived realities into lazy tropes. For many, especially those who've fought to express their true selves – like trans people navigating public spaces or Muslim women asserting their right to wear the hijab – being reduced to a stereotype feels like a cultural betrayal. It invalidates the very identity they've struggled to have recognised. Meanwhile, the comments are often dismissed as 'jokes' or cultural shorthand. But for those on the receiving end, it chips away at their dignity and humanity. The narcissism of small differences hides the effect culture has on our identity and the choices we make. Given our culture hides in plain sight, we generally sweep these influences under the rug. However, whenever we meet people with a different set of values, our respective cultures become more visible, either when visiting another country or being in a culturally diverse place, like a large, multinational

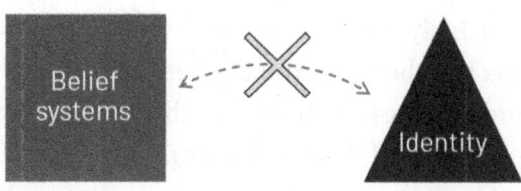

Values – it's harder for other people to see the rules that guide your life, so they are discounted

Perception of others – stereotypes thrive based on who other people think you are

**National Stereotypes**

corporation. Stereotypes lack depth and nuance because they mask the belief system that sits behind them, but they are useful as a shortcut for realising that culture plays a large role in why we do the things that we do.

## Change is dictated by how 'tight' a culture is

Dr Michele Gelfand, professor of psychology at Stanford University, coined the term 'tight and loose cultures' based on how closed or open a culture is to outside influence.[2] Tight cultures have high levels of conformity and people do not accept outside influence easily, whereas loose cultures – in which rules are more principles for life rather than hard and fast ways to behave – allow for a greater degree of personal choice.

Japan is a famously tight culture which has a very strong set of social rules that people must follow or else risk being cast out, and foreigners are rarely given the same social status as indigenous Japanese people. Rules are followed to the letter with little room for deviation, which is part of the reason Japan produces some of the best engineers in the world.

On the other side of the world, Sweden also displays some tight cultural traits. Swedish culture is notoriously difficult for foreigners to truly be part of, and the greatest aspiration of most Swedes is to be the same as everyone else. On the surface, Swedish and Japanese cultures might appear wildly different, but the tight nature of these cultures point to many deep-seated characteristics that make them similar. Both cultures require people to demonstrate a calm, controlled self that doesn't show vulnerability, both have high levels of social isolation as a result of non-intrusive behaviour, and both have a level of stoicism and personal responsibility that inhibits people seeking help. Standing out is actively discouraged in both Sweden and Japan, and group needs are prioritised over individual wellbeing. On one level this creates a wonderfully harmonious society with minimal competition and high levels of cooperation, but on the other, Japan and Sweden have two of the highest suicide rates in the world because they do not accept people who want to be different.

Loose cultures, like the US, allow people to rebel against the cultural rules with fewer recriminations. Americans famously express themselves and behave as they like. American youth are constantly striving to express themselves in new and different ways, so standing out is the only way to fit in. This has helped America become a 'cultural melting pot', where various diaspora can both be themselves and keep their traditions. On the flip side, the looseness in the culture means there is little solidarity with your fellow man in the street, creating a deeply lonely and often competitive society with no security net. America actively encourages people to have different belief systems, allowing people to express various different identities at will.

Gelfand argues that the level to which a culture is tight or loose has a direct impact on people's mindsets and how people

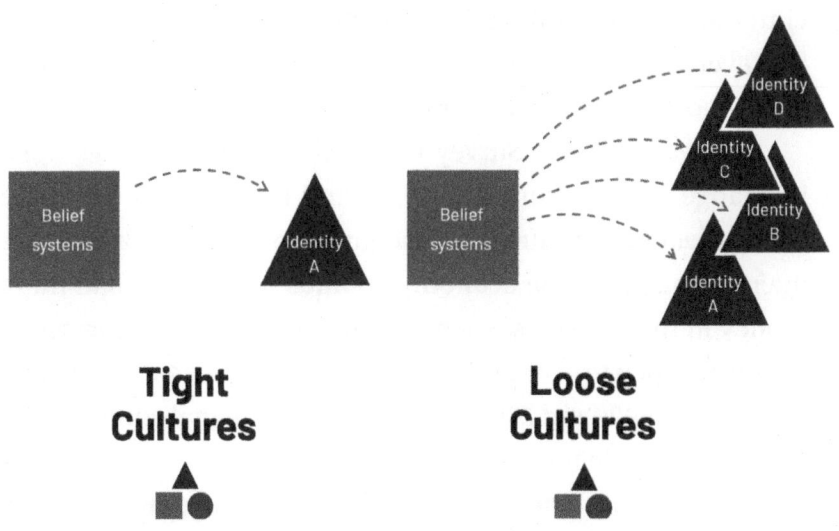

express themselves. The culture that we live in influences how we behave in the presence of others, as well as how we feel about rules, routines, creativity and impulsivity. Of course there are differences between individuals within the same culture, but when measured against everyone in the whole world, our identity – how we express who we are – is not so much a result of our own individual psychology as it is the culture we've grown up in.

## Belief systems dictate the pace of change

One of the reasons the US was able to become a global superpower in the aftermath of the Second World War was its ability to transform itself into a modern, technological nation through adapting to new and emerging circumstances. This economic, social and digital transformation was only possible because of the cultural values that underpin the US. These values meant, on the whole, that people in the US were open to the country changing and saw the opportunity as a positive development. The transition that the US went through was both exciting and entrepreneurial, while also being disruptive and uncertain, and even though this was often couched as an economic shift, it was most certainly a cultural transformation too.

The World Values Survey rates whether a country is 'open to change' or 'resistant to change', and tracking this over time makes clear that cultures are changing.[3] In the 1980s Britain was open to change as the economy boomed and people had more money in their pockets, encouraging increased self-expression. Brits were open to economic deregulation, greater social equality and, in the 1990s and 2000s, ever increasing digital connections.

Following the financial crash in 2007, with the apparent lack of accountability and widening economic inequality, Britain started to swing towards resistance. The UK general election of 2010 ended with a coalition government between the Conservatives and Liberal Democrats, who mandated higher taxes and reduced public spending. An Ipsos survey that year showed that 47% of people felt 'children born today would be worse off than their parents', compared to 29% who thought children would be better off.[4] People were starting to view the past as better than the future, and change was not felt to be positive, which led to a culture that, in 2016, ultimately voted to leave the EU based on the idea that the UK should take back control of its own destiny. When conditions change, so too do people's beliefs.

Over the same forty-year period, China changed more than any other nation on the planet. Since 1980, China has lifted over 800 million people out of absolute poverty,[5] which is more than the entire population of Europe. It has created phenomenal levels of infrastructure that have seen the standard of living move from a bicycle to an electric SUV, literally and metaphorically. Between 1978 and 2005 the Chinese economy grew at a rate of over 10% *each year* based on huge government investment to stimulate manufacturing, technology and finance, meaning that it is now the second-largest economy in the world (it was the tenth largest in 1980).[6] If you live in Shanghai or other tier one cities in China, you can receive your grocery shopping at your door within thirty minutes of clicking 'buy', and the level of digital connection through WeChat, Alibaba and Tencent is unparalleled in the rest of the world.

This development has come at a cost, including the severe political, social and digital restrictions that the government have placed upon the Chinese people, but on a *cultural* level, this development has hugely shaped the Chinese mindset. Chinese people are open to change, to new products, and to new ways of thinking because the future is more exciting than the past.

By comparison to the UK, only 5% of people in China believe that children born today will be worse off than their parents, compared to a whopping 77% who believe their children will be better off than they are.[7] The pace of change in China dictates the level of opportunity they see in the world, which shapes their belief system and how people live.

India, Brazil, Mexico, Nigeria, Indonesia, South Korea and many other nations were previously quite static cultures that have become far more open to change through the introduction of personal wealth and technological transformations, driven through economic growth. Some – such as India and Brazil – have seen populist backlash which is often a signal that people are wary of the pace of change, but the long-term direction of travel is that they are open to change itself.

It is these social and historical narratives that the anthropologist uses to map belief systems. The types of values that people hold within a culture lead to differences in self-expression and how people want to be seen, which in turn leads to the types of identities that are valued over others (e.g. withholding your emotions vs letting them out). When you start to map cultural values around the world, you can see that belief systems drive identity on a mass scale. And some of the countries I've studied in the last fifteen years have thrown up surprising insights through interesting combinations.

### Strange cultures need to be made familiar

In Beijing, one of the most polluted cities in the world, residents open their windows every morning to create a 'flow' of energy through their home. In the leafy suburbs of the US, locals keep their windows and curtains closed because of the fear of people entering their home. When you look at their behaviours on a cognitive level, they don't make sense, but culturally, they are utterly normal.

The role of the anthropologist is to make the strange parts of culture appear more familiar, and one of the main ways to do this is to dig deeper into the cultural values underpinning behaviour. Another way of saying this is: context is everything. Getting into the cultural values helps us understand why the stereotypes are true. But cultural values also help us understand what sits in the everyday behaviours beyond the stereotype. Values help us look into the stereotypes, as well as beyond them.

One of the greatest challenges for a business anthropologist is how we ladder down from big ideas in people's belief system into what that means for people, businesses and society. Often, I study the same problem in two or three different countries. When I'm able to look at WeChat usage in China, I get greater clarity about WhatsApp usage in the UK.

By asking the same question in different countries at the same time, we can see what people are *not* doing, thinking or believing. Comparing two countries often means comparing two different belief systems, such as the collectivism of China with the individualism of America, or the indulgence of Mexico compared to the restraint in India. By comparing the way people live in different countries, you can see how communities act in very different ways, such as the family support that people get in Brazil compared to the state support that people get in Sweden. And when you make comparisons between people you know, you realise that your Mexican and Canadian friends have quite different identities. The following write-ups are a series of observations from various countries that demonstrate how cross-cultural analysis illuminates the national rules that become guardrails for our lives.

## The UK – equity in a class-based society

The British national stereotype is funny because it's true. The rest of the world sees the Brits as stuffy, buttoned-up and self-entitled people that were either born with a silver spoon in their mouth or born to serve the silver spoon people. The unelected king is still the head of state, and a small number of lords and ladies seem to own about 30% of the land.[8] All our cultural icons – be that Boris Johnson in politics, James Bond in fiction or James Dyson in business – were born to wear a tuxedo. The British stereotype feels very stable, very stoic and very nineteenth century. And sadly, a bit too male and stale.

### 'Actions speak louder than words'

And much of this stereotype is true. Brits pay over the odds for Victorian terraced houses that are cold and in constant need of repair, which are then filled with overpriced antique furniture, which is in desperate need of fixing – all in the name of 'character'. It is this same character that means Brits 'mustn't grumble' and should 'grin and bear it'. British character is based on being authentic, and Brits judge others' characters by their actions, partly because they're not very expressive with their words.

This unmoving, 'authentic' character is present at all levels of British society, be that on an estate in Aberdeen, in a penthouse in Manchester or on a farm in Devon. This is how the British class system works: we learn our character traits early in life, and we crystalise them in adulthood to a point where we live out the characters we've learned to be. We learn class-based character traits from the people around us – our parents, schoolmates, colleagues and friends. Authenticity is valued above all else and there's nothing worse than getting above your station or pretending to be something you're not. To change class is not just hard, it is inauthentic.

## 'Children should be seen and not heard'

If culture starts at home, then British children are taught to be subjects rather than participants in family life. The role of children is to learn dutifully, play in their rooms and appear for family duties without 'making a scene'. They are taught from an early age to mask their emotions in public, learning a key British value which is to keep your affairs private.

Anyone who has ever met a small child will know this level of emotional regulation is entirely unrealistic. I have spent a large part of my working life hanging out in British homes studying family structures, and quickly realised the way Brits bring up their children creates huge tensions. Being sent to your room is a common punishment for children who are upset or behaving badly, which is why parents feel uncomfortable taking their kids out to a café, pub or restaurant because they are constantly worried that their children will 'act up' in a place they can't be sequestered (compare this to a place like Italy, where 'acting up' is the equivalent of 'being a cute kid').

I vividly remember spending the day with a working-class family in south London. We were in the park and a four-year-old boy wanted to play with another boy's football. The other kid didn't want to share (it happens), and tears soon followed. On seeing the situation evolve, the dad of the crying boy felt he had to frog-march his own son out of the playground to another part of the park to avoid feeling judged. We discussed this moment afterwards, and I'll never forget his words as we walked off with a crying child in the buggy:

> It's not [my son's] fault, and it's not my fault, it's the ignorant child's fault. Which isn't actually the child's fault, it's those

posh parents' fault. [My son] doesn't understand that situation. I find it embarrassing because it feels like their eyes are on me, and on my kid, so we just had to get out of there.

This, along with many other quotes from the project, describes the loneliness associated with British parenting. This Victorian Era identity of the Brits being buttoned up, class-ridden and emotionless is largely true. British culture is highly individualistic and private. Layer on top a whole heap of moral stoicism, then you start to see the importance of having *character* – a cultural identity to live by, that is also restrictive and static.

### 'It's just not cricket'

But as with all stereotypes, the description above is incomplete. The British have an obsession with 'fairness' that, on an everyday level, overrides our class-based hierarchy. We are constantly apologising, obediently queueing and conforming to rules about how to interact with one another to ensure a fair process. Cricket, a sport that epitomises British culture, has a whole set of rules based around fairness that rely heavily on the judgement of the umpire, even though sport is an activity which normally relies on clear boundaries between right and wrong.

This also touches on another key British value: an acceptance of ambiguity and uncertainty. Brits thrive on uncertainty. This is how the Brits operate on a day-to-day basis, and it is even a principle that is enshrined in (a lack of) law through the absence of a formal constitution. Instead, the UK relies on constitutional law, a series of judgements and parliamentary acts that have been created since 1215, and only when read together in their entirety do they make up the British Constitution. That means that what passes for our 'constitution' is constantly being debated and tweaked through new Acts of Parliament (the UK averages thirty-three new Acts of Parliament every year). Understanding the British Constitution relies on knowledge of how so many seemingly unrelated laws interact with one another, many of which change each year, some of which can appear to contradict each other. In this respect, the debate is as important as the answer, and it is part of the reason that Britain creates some of the best lawyers in the world.

## 'An Englishman's home is his castle'

You might think that a culture that is painfully modest and understated, that has a clear, stratified class system, would have a sense of collectivist spirit and solidarity. Not so. British culture has one of the highest levels of individualism in the world. In the case of British individualism, there are two important implications: children are taught from an early age that fulfilment comes through personal achievement, combined with a deep-seated privacy that keeps the family affairs in the home. Both of these elements go some way to explaining the stoicism in the British character, a level of aristocratic politeness that belies people's real feelings, combined with a sense of loneliness described by the working-class dad in the park.

Once you get beyond the stereotype, the British character has complexity. The Brits are highly individualistic and proud, yet very private. They can be forthright and competitive, yet seek due process and fairness. They are also an increasingly consumerist and self-indulgent group, but believe in equality and inclusivity. The Brits are excellent at holding seemingly contradictory values at the same time, without any implicit tension or problem, and display them in an array of identities depending on the situation.

The complexity of British culture can make the British character particularly difficult to read or influence. The important thing to decipher in the British national character is the link between identity and belief systems – and by using the Cultural Trinity, we can see how enduring national traits, like stoicism, fairness and individualism, aren't just quirks or stereotypes but expressions of a deeper structure of identity, social norms and belief systems.

- ▲ **Identity** – British identity is shaped by early social learning around emotional restraint, class-based authenticity and the performance of 'character'. From childhood, people are taught to live within the roles they've inherited, expressing individuality through quiet self-control rather than overt emotion.
- ● **Community** – British social life is intensely private and class-aware. Families operate within closed domestic spheres where public displays are tightly managed, even when it comes to children playing. The community enforces social expectations silently, through glances and judgement rather than confrontation.
- ■ **Belief systems** – Underlying values include fairness, due process, ambiguity and moral stoicism. The belief in 'knowing one's place' underpins both social stability and personal restraint, combined with a national comfort with contradiction and fluid norms.

## The US – more is more is more

### 'Go big or go home'

Such is the cultural influence of America that regardless of where people live in the world, they can name a series of Americans: Barack Obama and Donald Trump when it comes to politics, Mark Zuckerberg and Bill Gates in tech, and Oprah Winfrey and

Tom Cruise from the world of showbiz. No matter the industry, the people that get mentioned might have wildly different characters, which demonstrates the looseness of American culture – success doesn't mean conforming to one identity type. By way of comparison, being quintessentially British denotes one complex identity, whereas being American can mean many things.

The jarring thing about the list of people above is that they are mostly men. America is still a heavily masculine society, both in terms of gender roles (only 16% of American households have a woman earning more than their male partner[9]) and rewarding masculine characteristics (it values competition over cooperation and being assertive over being considerate, and success is achieved through a desire to win). Masculine characteristics thrive in loose cultures, because while you can adopt whatever identity you like, it needs to be done in a forthright (masculine) manner. American culture rewards a 'can-do' approach to life, with a 'live to work' attitude which prioritises money as a form of status, where conflict is seen to 'bring out the best in people'. The loose nature of American culture favours traditionally masculine characteristics.

Stereotypically, Americans don't know how to press the brakes. Everything that they adopt and believe is taken to the next level – think free speech or super-sized meal deals. More is more is more in the US, which comes from a combination of two prevalent values: high levels of individualism combined with levels of indulgence.

**'Where the people fear the government you have tyranny. Where the government fears the people you have liberty.' (John Basil Barnhill, political activist)**

The stereotype of the individualistic, indulgent American is the result of a culture that is ultimately trying to protect itself. The unending pursuit of individualism goes hand in hand with one of the key cultural and political structures in the US: freedom and liberty. This is a cultural value that's enshrined in the First Amendment to the US Constitution. While people often cite the First Amendment as an excuse to act however they like, it was actually put in place to protect citizens from government overreach. There is an innate distrust of government in America that comes from a belief that the state violates privacy, wastes money, interferes with business and has dubious motives. Politicians like Donald Trump have had great success by constantly stating they are not part of the political establishment, essentially signalling that they are pro liberty and individualism.

With liberty comes responsibility. Americans have an intrinsic belief that they will be much better at looking after themselves than the state ever could – an argument often used by Republicans, who say they would rather keep their tax dollars so *they* can decide how their money should be spent. In a culture where everyone believes they can achieve the American dream, private health insurance is justified not because Americans want the best plan but because they have a desire to take responsibility for their own health rather than leave it to the mercy of the government. In effect, this means healthcare provision is tied to employment, suggesting if you don't work, you shouldn't be entitled to healthcare. Liberty compels people to look after themselves, so you get what you deserve, and you deserve what you get. Liberty means you're in charge, and no one else is going to tell you otherwise.

While Democrats often reject that description above, they do so while still anchoring their values in the ideals of liberty and individualism, just in different ways. For many on the left, liberty is about the freedom to express identity, access opportunity and live without discrimination or structural barriers. This belief system is evident in progressive commitments to reproductive rights, LGBTQ+ protections, and expansive definitions of healthcare and education as tools to empower individuals – they still don't believe in state handouts or protectionism. Democrats are far more likely to support laws restricting gun ownership, but 20% of Democrats still have a gun at home.[10] The liberal ethos still hinges on autonomy and personal freedom, just in the register of equity, not regulation. In both cases, liberty remains a core American value, albeit with a political spin over whether liberty is achieved through protection *from* the state, or empowerment *through* it.

**The American way of life = the pursuit of happiness**

American culture values quick results, whether that's short-term profit for businesses or consumers demanding the latest products. Having developed as a predominantly Christian country, Americans often have very strong ideas about what is 'good' and 'evil' when it comes to abortion, drug usage, euthanasia, weapons or what a good home looks like. This creates in-group and out-group bias, where people like people like themselves, and are scared of people who are different.

Having studied middle-class, suburban America for a number of years, I've met people that are both proud and scared. Their homes are designed to protect them to a degree that vastly outweighs any potential threats. The large front lawn allows them to keep watch for an intruder's approach, the garage is connected to the house so that residents never need step outside, curtains are nearly always drawn at the front of the house to prevent people seeing in, and windows are rarely opened, no matter the weather. The fear of the outside, and of outsiders, means that people design their homes to be as secure as possible. Inevitably, in a loose culture behaviours vary more than in tight cultures, but the role that pride and fear play in the design of American homes is high, particularly when compared to other countries.

On the flip side, this combination of high individualism, high indulgence and extreme short-termism leads Americans to the unending pursuit of happiness. Happy Americans are the puppy dogs of the world, with boundless enthusiasm and an unrestricted desire to act and have fun. Often foreigners think the happiness is fake or an act – it's not – as they can't believe that human nature can reach such highs.

## 'Made in America'

Everyone around the globe has something to say about America. Coke, Ford, McDonald's and Uncle Sam reach everywhere in the world, yet American culture has been received in very different ways. When running cross-cultural research, we find that the Japanese tend to see Americans as *relaxed, friendly, spontaneous, uninhibited, emotional* and *impulsive*, because those characteristics are very different (and shocking!) to the Japanese. Compare that to Mexicans, who see Americans as *in a hurry, serious, reserved, restrained, rational, methodical* – which couldn't be more different to the Japanese responses! If we were able to remove our cultural assumptions, we would see a very different version of America.

Understanding the American stereotype requires looking beyond the brash, money-seeking, status-oriented identity to the links that create it. A more nuanced view of the American character recognises that people are driven to look after themselves and their family, because relying on the state would be embarrassing. To outsiders, the American dream can look like people showing off, but to Americans, it's a badge showing how hard they've worked. By looking at the connections in culture we can see how the boldness, confidence and contradictions so often associated with the US are grounded in a distinct set of beliefs which shape how Americans see themselves and the world.

- ▲ **Identity** – American identity is built on individualism, self-expression and personal achievement. Success can take many forms, but it must be pursued assertively and visibly. People define themselves by what they earn, create or own, and take pride in self-reliance.
- ● **Community** – Social life emphasises autonomy over interdependence. Families, suburbs and even homes are designed to create personal safety over accidental connection. While American culture appears extroverted, it often lacks deep communal ties, especially across different ideological groups.
- ■ **Belief systems** – Freedom and liberty are core cultural tenets, deeply tied to distrust of the state and belief in personal responsibility. Indulgence, short-termism and religious moral binaries shape views on health, wealth, happiness and justice. The pursuit of the 'American dream' is both a moral justification and a psychological motivator for ambition.

### China – *I am we*

Given the political, press and media restrictions, very few people outside of China get to experience Chinese culture (Chinese entertainment is not exported at the level we see in the United States or even China's neighbour, South Korea), so the stereotype is quite flat. From outside China, cultural icons are often limited to political figures like President Xi or businessmen like

Jack Ma (founder of Alibaba Group), neither of whom anyone really knows much about.

The stereotype of the Chinese often involves hard-working, competitive young professionals that 'work 9-9-6' (a phrase from Shanghai denoting people who work from 9am to 9pm, six days a week). Combined with a beastly commute, many people chasing the corporate dream in China are over-worked and sleep deprived, and don't have time to go out. It's a minor miracle young people have time to think, let alone go out on a date and find a partner. There is also pressure to get married in their twenties, so much so that women who don't marry have been referred to as 'leftover women'. Despite the long days, sleepless nights and raging competition, the Chinese are stoic and energetic while also managing to appear remarkably youthful.

'上梁不正下梁歪' *('If the top pillar is not straight, then the bottom pillar is bound to be crooked')*

China is famously a collectivist culture, meaning that the interests and goals of the individual are subordinate to the goals of the family and group. Despite all the change that's taken place in China, this is still true. Many households have three generations living under the same roof, and in Shanghai, one of the most economically advanced cities in the world, 62% of children are co-raised by their grandparents, and 26% are *solely* raised by their grandparents, leaving only 12% of children with no regular grandparent involvement at all.[11] No matter how collectivist China is as a society, I've learned from numerous projects that relations with your in-laws are just as tense and difficult as anywhere else in the world – but the underlying values just mean they complain less.

The Chinese are regularly reminded that any problem their parents (the bottom pillar) have, they (the top pillar) have too.

While they rely on the grandparents for childcare support, they also feel obliged to care for the grandparents too, both financially and emotionally. Only about 3% of the elderly in China end up staying in a nursing home even though most state facilities are virtually free, compared to over 10% of the elderly in the US, where the cost of staying in a nursing home is phenomenally high. The needs of others are put before the individual in a collectivist society, and in Chinese culture, there is a strong need to look after the elderly. Parents work 9-9-6 to fulfil the needs of the family, and the extended family in turn supports parents working these long hours. Working long hours is easier when your family is going through it with you.

'没有丑女人，只有懒女人' *('There's no such thing as ugly women, just lazy women')*

Saving face – the act of maintaining one's honour, dignity and reputation – is incredibly important in China, and women in Shanghai can take up to two hours *per day* applying products to their face. I've observed some women create a daily twelve-step process of applying creams, serums, oils, face masks and SPF while using different tools and gadgets to massage and 'shape' the face. This behaviour often starts in their late teens, while young people elsewhere in the world are taking their youthful looks for granted. The Chinese may naturally look young, but they also work very hard to keep it that way.

Many brands I've worked with assume Chinese women are looking after their skin to feel good. While looking youthful almost certainly gives them satisfaction, they also feel it is their duty as a partner, a wife and a mother to take care of their looks. In Chengdu a woman told me she spent so much time on her skincare routines because, 'I want people to know why my husband married me.' While it may sound like she is concerned about expressing her personal desirability, digging into it further, what she is concerned about is that people will think their family is both lazy and stupid, an insult that's levelled both at her husband and her. In reality, her beauty routine is subject to the gaze of society.

'吃苦耐劳提高地位' *('Enduring difficulty and hardship increases status')*

In stark contrast to the US, Chinese culture encourages a long-term outlook. The suffering endured by the youth of Shanghai is offset against the gains they will reap in older age, which partly explains their respect for their elderly, who have already suffered for the cause. This is one reason many Chinese support the one-party state, because citizens are regularly reminded of the long-term strategy the Chinese Communist Party can make compared to Western democracies that change parties and leaders regularly.

*Suzhi* – originally a Confucian term to denote 'high-quality behaviours' – has been adopted by the government as part of China's national journey of self-improvement. Demonstrating *suzhi* shows you are polite, educated and sophisticated – that you have learned a new code of moral behaviour. Uncivilised behaviours like public bickering, queue jumping, littering, shirtlessness and letting your dog foul in the street are not only publicly frowned upon: lack of acceptance towards them is becoming enshrined in law. The 'Beijing bikini' – the practice of men wearing white vests rolled up to reveal their stomachs in hot weather – now leads to fines in numerous Chinese provinces.

This adaptation of *suzhi* by the government has been seen as a way of 'civilising' those who have grown up in the countryside and migrated to the city, and allows people to explicitly judge how people eat, talk and dress, often referring to whether people have received a moral education. And for the woman I met who said she needs other people to know why her husband married her, it is less about superficial beauty standards than demonstrating her family are part of a modern, well-educated middle class.

### '以食见人' *('You are what you eat')*

Chinese culture promotes a holistic understanding of the world that attempts to incorporate balance. Individuals work hard for the collective, women look beautiful because it showcases standards of a modern China, and people implicitly understand how the food that they eat affects their health. The principles of traditional Chinese medicine permeate through all parts of Chinese behaviours, from how much sleep people get to the type of exercise they do and, crucially, which foods they eat, and when. Food and medicine share the same source in China, and different foods either heat up or cool down the body, which in turn affects health, mood and energy (which can even relate to toothpaste, as we saw in Chapter 2). Too much heat creates spots and pimples, and excessive cold food will make you sick – and you can tell all of this by looking at someone's skin (which is another reason why people are obsessed with their skincare routines). Balance is built into the cultural mindset, and people in China understand how one behaviour tips another one out of balance.

Identity is not solely focused on *me* but has a large dose of *we*. Identity is strongly shaped by family history, showing they know how to adhere to the rules of society and that they are disciplined. As with every other culture, the Chinese carry a set of cultural assumptions that mean the past is linked to the present, the individual is linked to society, and the family unit is the basis for a greater China.

The Chinese stereotype of a hard-working, morally upstanding citizen who pledges obedience to the Communist party is partially true but thoroughly outdated. The context behind this identity is a belief system that prioritises looking to the future, taking a holistic view of their own health, and believing in a collectivist system that they know will help everyone. To understand Chinese culture through the Cultural Trinity is to move beyond tired stereotypes and into a worldview shaped by interdependence, long-term thinking and a deep sense of social duty.

- ▲ **Identity** – Identity is rooted in family legacy, filial responsibility and public discipline. Personal traits like endurance, refinement and beauty are expressions of group loyalty, not just individual preference. An individual's appearance, behaviour and moral education reflect on the entire family.

- ● **Community** – Family structures span generations, with grandparents, parents and children coexisting in tight-knit domestic units. Social belonging is reinforced through everyday care practices such as childcare, work routines and health advice.

- ■ **Belief systems** – Chinese values are grounded in Confucian ideals of harmony, long-term orientation and moral self-cultivation (*suzhi*). Health is seen as a balance of internal forces shaped by traditional medicine and food practices. Government initiatives reflect this worldview, reinforcing civility and public responsibility over self-expression.

## France – hierarchy vs revolution

**'Aux grands maux les grands remèdes'** *('Desperate times call for desperate measures')*

The French love to strike. Lorry drivers seem to schedule a strike every month, teachers and nurses are good at bringing the country to a standstill (though they never strike on Mondays, apparently), and in 1998, the unemployed also went on strike, twice. The French appear to be a rebellious bunch who like to bring their country to a standstill if they don't get what they want. A common joke is that French people's favourite word is *non*.

Yet the French are remarkably formal, hierarchical and balanced. French bosses hold grandiose titles such as President Director General to remind staff to be subservient. The French also like certainty, as seen in the precision with which their language is structured, and the strong need for laws, rules, regulations and statutes. Children are taught civilised behaviours at home, such as eating, socialising and being polite – in the early 2000s it was trendy for the French to be au pairs to wealthy families in Shanghai as it was thought they would pass on their naturally high levels of *suzhi* to the children. The French have the lowest levels of obesity in Western Europe because they are taught moderation and restraint from a young age.

So how is it that these rebellious strikers are also so balanced, restrained and sophisticated? Digging beyond the identity that 'the French like to strike', we see a set of values that add more depth. It is exactly because of their adherence to hierarchy and rules that when things aren't going their way, their only option left is to revolt. Bureaucracy and hierarchy stifle evolution in France, so the only way to enact change is through revolution. In France, you obediently assume your place in society until you tear up the rule book.

The French stereotype is either of the chain-smoking revolutionary or of the obedient 9–5 worker who makes every meal in a highly specific French way. In reality, this can be the same person because the French thrive on a multifaceted belief system that promotes rationalism and moderation, alongside a revolutionary ethic as the only way to achieve moral recalibration.

## India – a land of stagnant opportunity

### 'Anything is possible'

India, where the caste system entrenched social immobility and hierarchy into everyday cultural practices, is one of the most unequal societies in the world. While India has officially banned the caste system, many legal statutes – such as needing a fixed address to access state healthcare – still alienate large groups of people who are essentially at the bottom. In 2020, the World Economic Forum ranked India at number 76 out of 82 countries for social mobility,[12] showing that national economic growth is not trickling down to personal growth.

Yet many Indians feel empowered to achieve their potential, whether they are a wealthy Indian studying abroad at university or a Dalit (a member of the lowest caste) who moves to the city in search of new possibilities. This sense of personal achievement is underpinned by Hinduism, which, through the cycle of death and rebirth, teaches that you can be reborn at a higher level based on your personal acts and endeavours. 'Anything is possible' is a phrase that lives on the lips of all Indians, which instils a culture of business and opportunity into the Indian mindset, encouraging people to seek new and daring ways to make money. The hit 2008 film *Slumdog Millionaire* captivated the hearts of many Indians by drawing upon the fairy-tale mentality that is part of the Indian mindset. The fact that *anything is possible* gives so many people hope against the statistics and is an important lens through which Indians see the world. It is clear in the case of India that the assumptions the rest of world have are quite different to the assumptions Indians have about themselves.

The fatalistic stereotype that many people have about how Indians cannot escape inequality and poverty undermines the extreme opportunity that Indian people feel about what might happen tomorrow. Their religious beliefs give them a sense of resilience that allows them to have hope in spite of the inequality that weighs against them. There's a duality to the Indian stereotype that is both deeply traditional and hierarchical while also radically hopeful.

### Japan – where the past and future coexist

'古いものと新しいものが出会う場所' *('Where old meets new')*

Japan is often portrayed as a country of both longstanding tradition and, more recently, startling innovation. On the one hand, it is an arcane and sophisticated culture with thousands of years of history; on the other, it is a technological utopia that has already taken steps into the future. The Japanese have developed robots to keep dementia patients entertained in nursing homes while also adhering to religious and dynastic traditions. During the pandemic many restaurants in Tokyo invested heavily in robot waiters who guide diners from the front door to their table, take their orders and wait on them throughout the meal. At the end of the meal, they even show them to the door and say goodbye with a little bow of respect. So many technological and economic developments in Japan have led the world to look on in wonder, whether it's precision engineering, the government prioritising national infrastructure in its budget, or daily acts of kindness to the fellow man in the street. From the outside, Japan looks like progress.

And while much of this is true, it belies the levels to which Japan *hasn't* developed. Japan's sense of heritage places value on products that have *wabi-sabi* (beauty in the imperfect) – like a leather suitcase or beautifully fitting glasses, perfectly imperfect products that cannot be superseded by technology. Men still smoke pipes, cash is still used in favour of digital payments, and many companies still operate with a fax machine. It is often said that Japanese companies employ six people to do the job of two, and in many supermarkets, train stations and offices, there are numerous people waiting to help. Japan may have integrated robots into their lives, but they did not do it to replace people or remove character.

While many of these behaviours are curious to the Western eye, it showcases how slowly Japanese culture moves. Japan still has incredibly old-fashioned gender roles, where it is assumed that women will quit work to look after the family from the age of thirty, and men are often described as having a 'second marriage' with the company they work for. When a country places so much value on harmony and order, the pace of cultural change is inevitably slow; but in the case of Japan, technology masks this slow lifestyle. With Japan being a notoriously tight culture, the assumptions people grow up with are almost an equivalent to destiny.

## The link between beliefs and identity helps us see individuals better

Our culture is embedded in who we are; our values act as the baseline for our identity. The culture we were born into imprints us with a belief system that becomes the starting point for our identity. The level to which we were brought up in an individualistic or collectivist culture will influence how we present ourselves to the world, either through fashion, life choices, relationships with peers or the way we engage with work. Cultures that are comfortable with uncertainty produce better comedians and lawyers, as opposed to cautious cultures that create better engineers and bureaucrats. Combine these with other important cultural values – like levels of indulgence, masculine vs feminine decision-making, a long- vs short-term approach to planning – and we start to see that our personality is a product of where we grew up.

That's how we end up with stereotypes about the stuffy British, competitive Americans, disciplined Chinese, rebellious French, Indians knowing their place, and the Japanese as futuristic tech gurus. Behind each stereotype is a belief system that underpins that identity, which shows us that being British is to demonstrate character, being American is to be fiercely independent, being Chinese is adhering to a moral code, being French is about formality, being Indian is to be entrepreneurial, and that the Japanese are actually incredibly conservative.

Stereotypes are shortcuts for identity. They tell us a lot about who we are, yet they mask the depth of the traditions we've created over years of cultural reproduction. In Moscow, my mum recognised that being next in line wasn't the most important reason to board the plane, even though her cultural values told her that was the fair and natural thing. She saw that the Russian flight steward did not value the concepts of equity and fairness but rather the importance of the family, and that you should never stand between a mother and her child. Of course, this was not a conscious thought process but an instinctive reaction from her time spent in Eastern Europe.

Once we understand the link between the belief systems we grew up with and the identity people want to express, we start to see there is a set of rules that makes all of us who we are today. Of course, we can rebel, act differently in different situations, and take on our own version of a cultural trait and make it unique to us – all of which is easier in a loose culture. To state that these traits uniformly affect how everyone behaves in a country is reductive, but underneath it all, these combinations do guide how we respond to the world and have a strong influence over who we are. There is no reason to hide or diminish the role culture plays in the formation of who we are as it offers a degree of self-reflection on a similar level to how we learn about ourselves in a psychological sense. Indeed, understanding the assumptions that are built into our culture helps us understand who we are on a deeper, more implicit level.

## SO WHAT?
### Reasons for looking beyond the stereotype in life, business and society

The way national culture influences life, business and society has become ever more apparent as the world gets ever more interconnected. The rise in international travel and multinational corporations means we come into contact with people who have grown up with very different cultural rules.

There's no end to cultural miscommunication in life, be that with teachers at the local school, with long-standing friends, mixed nationality families or co-workers from different countries. Mixed nationality groups might get on incredibly well, thriving off the difference that each person brings, but clashes in belief systems may appear when it comes to issues with which they have had a strong moral imprint from an early age, like parenting styles, financial planning or negotiation. The rules that make us are often imprinted at an early age.

In life, we are forever making snap judgements about people, and many of them come through stereotypes. These judgements about their identity may be true, but they almost certainly prevent us from creating stronger, deeper relationships with people from another culture. Getting past stereotypes requires us to ask deeper, more purposeful questions about their morals and values – which you don't have to agree with but they are definitely worth understanding.

In business, there's a whole industry of consultants focused on getting multinational organisations to work together better. Every company has a set of belief systems – either explicitly stated or implied through role modelling – that often mirrors the national values of where they are headquartered. Japanese multinationals are typically very hierarchical, Scandinavian multinationals are often incredibly democratic and American companies reward fast decisions. The belief systems instilled in multinationals often dictate the types of identity that will thrive.

In society, we are constantly creating stereotypes about different groups of people within our own countries. Stereotypes about race and class are often reinforced through popular culture and hinder our understanding of how people from different communities actually live. These stereotypes can easily get embedded in mainstream society, meaning the government, industry and infrastructure reinforce this shallow approach to engaging with them.

The rules that make us instil us with stereotypes about who other people are, without giving us much guidance on the beliefs that sit behind why people are the way they are. Creating a stronger link between beliefs and identity will help us understand people more deeply.

# 4

## Culture Starts at Home

Imagine you are walking around someone's home for the first time when the owner isn't there. Think about it for a moment and go through what you see in people's living rooms, the objects on their walls and windowsills, the types of things they stick on the fridge. Wouldn't it be great to look in the cupboards when the owner isn't there, and then guess how they live in that home based on where they keep their plates and cutlery? Or what their routine looks like based on the proportion of fresh vs ready-made food? Think about what you could learn from having a nose about in their bedroom, how they organise their wardrobes, and whether one person has more space for clothes than the other. How would you think about your parents'/best friend's home in this light? Now do the same in reverse: consider what other people might think walking around your home.

It's rare that we get the chance to look around someone's home unaccompanied, and the reason we understand so much about how they live is that we implicitly see the identity they want to portray, the social norms within the home, and the underlying beliefs that organise the home. The home is fascinating from an anthropological perspective, because it mirrors society, and from a personal perspective, because you only truly understand a person once you've seen them at home.

Anthropologists go into people's homes a lot, but they tend to get the guided (rather than unaccompanied) tour. A good anthropologist will ask to look in the cupboards, wardrobes, drawers and bedrooms because we need to get underneath the image the owner seeks to portray in order to see how they really live their lives.

Implicitly, our home embodies the story of our life so far; it is our museum of memories where we are the curators. It acts as a reflection of who we are and it will change as we move through life – both physically and metaphorically. Photos of family and friends remind us of the people we want to be connected to, and the fridge magnets we've collected when travelling show how international we are. Plants and animals in the home signal that we want to be closer to nature, and the candles we light remind us we are looking for a slower, more mindful life. No matter the question, you can develop a solid understanding of someone's identity from looking around their home.

We assume that the way we design our home is based on our own personal aesthetic, but cultural identity actually overrides personal choice to a large degree. In New York, I've seen so much art on the walls that is specific to that city, with art nouveau skylines or 'NYC' written in eclectic styles. Every single picture is different, but they are all on the same topic and communicating the same message – *We are all New Yorkers*. In Riyadh, art is just as prominent but always relates to religious scriptures or leaders, sometimes commissioned to cover an entire wall. Specific examples differ across homes in Riyadh, but they all follow the same theme. While the residents of New York and Riyadh feel they are expressing their own uniqueness, they are doing it within the confines of their own cultural rules to fit in with the shared identity of their social group.

I once bought a beautiful, hand-painted Buddhist prayer scroll from a monk in Japan. It was a special moment, occurring just outside a temple I had stumbled across in Kyoto. I sat on the shop floor drinking matcha tea as the monks laid several scrolls out for me to choose from. They tried to explain what each prayer meant, but between their broken English and my non-existent Japanese, I ended up choosing the one I thought looked nicest. When I got home, I decided the scroll would go in my hallway for everyone to see because it implicitly showed all visitors that I am well-travelled and cultured (and because I liked it). A Japanese friend of mine living in London came round, and when I asked him to translate it for me, he looked at the picture oddly and said, 'I'm not really sure, it's in Chinese.' He then turned his head slightly to the side and said, 'I think you've hung it upside down, too.' Despite the embarrassment, the picture still hangs in my house, upside down, because signalling I am a well-travelled culture hunter carries more importance to me than the symbols on the scroll.

One of the core principles of cultural anthropology is that the way we express ourselves is intrinsically linked to our relationship with objects, which become symbolic of our relationships with other people and our place in society. All objects have an implicit meaning, whether we are conscious of it or not. People don't buy a dishwasher because it washes the dishes faster; they buy a dishwasher because they don't want to actually wash the dishes – a dishwasher feels like emancipation. In reality, having a dishwasher doesn't significantly cut down the time spent cleaning plates and cutlery – my team measured it, and you only gain about 12% of your time back by having a dishwasher, less than most people think. What most people love about a dishwasher, once they have one, is that it keeps all the dirty plates out of sight – it's a way of maintaining an identity that this is a clean and tidy home. Having dirty plates on the side implicitly signals that you are a slob, denoting a level of morality that people don't want to be associated with. Products have an inherent value that everyone can identify with.

## How community norms are expressed through the home

While the stuff we have in our home is a showcase of our identity, the way we live at home is an expression of the norms and support we seek from our community. In any shared living environment, there is a period of acclimatisation whereby we learn how to live together. We figure out our different roles – some may be fought over, others thrust upon us. The ways people live together take on different meanings across cultures, often as a result of our cultural assumptions that have created a set of implicit rules.

Often one person dominates a home. Is there a pristine living room with plumped cushions that the children dare not enter? Or is it a home littered with scooters and toys? Who chooses the pictures on the walls and how the kitchen is laid out? Are all the rooms in a house fairly similar, or is each room different, suggesting different people own different spaces? The home is a community where the rules are open to negotiation, and the level to which the home feels like a safe place from the messy world outside comes down to whether they have a say in how it is run.

A good indicator of how well people in the home are co-operating is the manner in which people deal with mess and clutter. Some households want to hold on to as many things as possible to best represent their cultural identity, whereas others decide everything must go. These two polarising viewpoints (and the variations in between) are an indication of how we treat memories and the past. I have seen Londoners store old records that they can't bear to throw out in the attic, and couples in Shanghai buy two Dyson hairdryers as a symbol of their recently acquired wealth. There is an increasing trend of New Yorkers renting storage containers so they can keep their small apartments beautifully clean and tidy while retaining their treasured possessions in a messy garage.

This tension has been creatively addressed by Marie Kondo, the Japanese decluttering expert who taught the world to ask, 'Does it spark joy?'[1] In her bestselling book *The Life-Changing Magic of Tidying* and follow-up Netflix series, she gives practical tips on how to remove clutter, focusing on different parts of the home, one joyful moment at a time. She has recognised that we must 'thank' the object that we are throwing out, as it represents a memory or a moment, and crucially that a tidier space allows for a more serene and calm home. If a home is like a community, Marie Kondo is creating kind, respectful places that change as the people change.

Working from home during the Covid pandemic led to a 30% rise in home renovations.[2] Furniture stores – which were historically slow to move to online selling – couldn't deliver desks, chairs and monitors fast enough, and people were begging for and borrowing furniture to create their home office. When the pandemic first hit, I sat in my living room on conference calls all day, with my booming voice completely disrupting the calm aesthetic I'd curated. This created a sense of unease in the house, so I decided that our younger daughter (then four years old) should move into the same bedroom as her sister (seven) so that I could create an office out of her bedroom (something my older daughter still holds against me). I justified this as 'it will be nice for the girls to share a room', but really it was because the new form of pandemic home working was messing with how my calm household operated.

## Hosting: how people use the home to connect with others

At the heart of hosting sits a desire to connect with other people, to display generosity and to create a deeper connection with others. In showing people your home, you are allowing people to see your identity, and depending on which rooms they're allowed into, it is a way of showing how much you are willing to let people into your community. Some cultures love hosting, but others often refrain from letting people into their private sphere.

The anthropological concept of 'reciprocity' – a cultural game of give and take – brings a level of safety and predictability to hosting. There are various hosting rituals that people perform that are often culturally dictated, played out like a dance throughout the evening. The host has an obligation to show who they are, both through food and the tour. In upper-class Britain, guests might only ever see the reception room, specifically designed for hosting. In Poland or India, guests are given more freedom to roam. How open the home is to guests has so many permutations, depending on the class and culture you come from. As part of the reciprocity, the guest brings gifts if the culture has strong values of explicit generosity (e.g. Brazilians), or overly flatters the host's cooking and interior design if the culture values social status and prestige (e.g. the British).

The practice of hosting varies enormously across cultures: in some countries like South Korea and Japan, people rarely have guests over, while Latin cultures like Argentina and Mexico tend to have people round regularly. Of course, some people in any culture won't conform, but there are always established norms. When living in France, my parents hosted a birthday party for about forty people, half of whom were French, the other half English. The party ran from 6pm until about 2am with dinner, dancing and plenty of drinking. What they noticed was that the

Brits were constantly popping off to use the bathroom whenever they needed, whereas the French contingent didn't ever go. They later found out that it's customary in France not to use other people's bathrooms at formal occasions, though some apparently were more comfortable relieving themselves on the way home.

During my career, I have studied the overlap between hosting and mess. Generally, hosts prefer their homes to be tidy, so nations that host more tend to need more storage solutions into which they can stuff their belongings into before people come round. Countries that host less still need places to store their stuff, but the external need to make sure their home is 'guest ready' isn't quite so strong.

### IKEA don't sell furniture; they sell harmony at home

IKEA design and sell furniture with a distinctively Swedish aesthetic to people all around the world, nearly all of whom have a wildly different style of home. They never seem to bend their aesthetic to include more gilt-edged sofas for the Middle Eastern market or more low-level tables for countries that like to sit on the floor. They also have a strange business quirk where every single store worldwide has to stock every single item in the catalogue, no matter if the local store manager thinks it's relevant to that country or not. They only sell Swedish furniture and yet have become a $21 billion company.

Much of IKEA's smart design actually focuses on helping people live together, through creating dining spaces or kitchen areas that allow for everyday practices, all while giving them an aesthetic that people feel proud of as they host friends and family. The snaky route customers have to navigate through an IKEA store is specifically designed to make them realise how they can live with their furniture. It's about showcasing a harmonious room with a neat desk in the corner of the bedroom, and boxes to put all the toys into.

When I first started working with IKEA they were trying to export the Swedish aesthetic, and they assumed that's what people were buying. Through a prolonged process of engaging – and empathising – with their customers, they realised they needed to give customers a way to display their own culture back to themselves. By helping customers find ways to put memories up in their home, IKEA became more central to helping people live the way they want to in their respective cultures.

IKEA's biggest success has been their focus on innovative storage solutions to deal with endless clutter and mess. We know that 'stuff' is important as an indicator of cultural identity in the home, but in many cases, managing the sheer volume of stuff becomes a regular task in its own right, or in many cases, an unmanageable one.

Our work with IKEA showed that the reasons for *storing* and *organising* things are actually quite different from one another. Storage is the act of getting things out of sight (shoved in a cupboard) or on display (neatly arranged in a glass cabinet). The storage solutions people were buying from IKEA were not just about tidying up but helped them express their identity in the home. Organisation, on the other hand, is more about reflecting the needs of the community (aka the people that live in the home). Having spent years analysing how people live around the world, I have noticed collectivist cultures – like China, Japan, India and others – organise their homes around the needs of the group, so anyone walking into the kitchen, living room or bathroom can easily find the objects they need. Each person in the household knows where things belong, and it is a collective responsibility to put things back in the right place, so the next person can use it. By contrast, the individualistic cultures – like the US, UK and much of Northern Europe – organise their homes by who owns which room. Bedrooms are up to the individual owner to tidy, and the more communal rooms like the living room, kitchen and bathroom are generally tidied by whoever's the boss of that space. With great power to organise the home how they see fit comes great responsibility to tidy it.

Storage solutions that cater to organisation actually require quite a different set of design principles, often centred around being able to see what's inside, and help a home function as a community. For example, in multigenerational households in China, we saw all the cooking sauces and condiments were in a neat line across the back of the counter, all on display. Previously, IKEA had grouped storage and organisation together, and understanding this difference meant they could be even more specific in their design. Taking a cultural view of the way people organise their homes, honing in on the identity and community aspects, allowed designers in Sweden to understand the cultural assumptions of someone living in Germany, or the Philippines, or anywhere else. Once IKEA were able to map these cultural needs to their various designs and store layouts, they stopped selling furniture and started selling harmony at home.

### Our belief systems create different 'house rules'

The final role of the home is to create, and re-create, culture through reinforcing our belief systems. Children learn a moral code through cultural rituals which are constantly re-enacted. These 'house rules' differ enormously around the world, like whether children eat with the adults at mealtimes, how strict routines are, who tidies up, whether kids share a bedroom and many, many more which point to a set of belief systems and values. While we might like to think that we decide the rules of the home, many are in fact defined by the culture. This literally makes the home the starting point for learning about culture.

Our house rules reflect whether the home is there to serve collective harmony or personal wellbeing. In more traditional homes, roles between household members are fairly set. In Saudi Arabia, the kitchen is on the women's side of the house, and the main reception room for greeting guests is on the men's side. Most of the home, including the bedrooms, is on the women's side, and there is often only one door connecting the two sides (which can be carefully monitored for indiscretions). Other aspects of the home also dictate behaviours, such as having a sink by the front door to cleanse your feet, along with a vast shoe rack because nobody wears their shoes inside. These rules about how the home operates are culturally set through Islamic tradition and there is no negotiation over gendered spaces. For those who want to follow these rules, there is harmony; for those who don't, it becomes a very difficult system to navigate.

Compare this to the US, where space has historically been about ownership. Everyone has their own bedroom (in an ideal world), and people have their habitual seat at the dinner table and their favourite spot on the sofa (which is sometimes contested). In the absence of clearly defined rules, living together can become a battle of wills; whoever is stronger (often whoever is oldest) owns more of the home. In contrast to Saudi Arabia, the home needs to be adaptable for everyone to have a 'space' for their individual wellbeing, be that cooking, working or playing. Creating harmony in the home requires more compromise and cooperation in individualistic cultures, sometimes leading to harmony, other times to tension.

This divide between a home catering for the personal or the collective has big implications for how people experience privacy. In more individualistic, Western societies privacy is almost considered to be a personal right, so that people can find the mental space to deal with the outside world (or in some cases, the people you live with). Parents might put locks on their bedroom doors, and children write 'KEEP OUT' on aggressive-looking posters.

When my daughters were seven and ten years old, they had a real problem sharing. They unhappily shared a bedroom, constantly arguing and refusing to let their sibling borrow their toys. As an only child, I've never understood sibling rivalry, and these moments used to make my blood boil. At one point I gathered my strength, sat down with them calmly and had a long conversation about the joy of sharing things. We covered what ownership means, and I reminded them it is more fun to play together than alone.

A week later, my seven-year-old daughter made a poster which she stuck to their bedroom door, saying:

*Tilly and Martha's rules:*

1. *Daddy keep out!!*
2. *Be kind*
3. *Share. But not special things like teddy and duck duck*
4. *Tidy up*
5. *Tilly can't go on Martha's bed and Martha can't go on Tilly's bed*

*No trespasses. Thank you.*

Clearly they now accepted sharing was beneficial to them, but they'd drawn some new boundaries. They had negotiated rules between them, designated their beds as private spaces and made me the enemy.

In Eastern cultures, privacy is not an assumed right. In China it is considered rude to close a door (bathroom doors omitted).

Bedroom doors should remain open during the day to allow the energy to flow in the home, and it is perfectly acceptable to walk into someone's room without asking or knocking. In many homes in Indonesia, bedrooms and beds are shared – there will be one bed per child, but each child will sleep in any unoccupied bed of their choice. In Japan, it is common to live in one adaptable room that is a bedroom by night and living room by day, thus removing all possible opportunity for privacy.

This is not to say that people in Eastern collective cultures do not seek privacy on a personal level, nor that people living in Western individualistic cultures want to lock themselves in their bedrooms all day. People the world over have different psychological needs and the culture they live in will either help or hinder that need (and will to some extent shape it too). In numerous multigenerational apartments in Shanghai, I have seen grandparents, parents and children all on their devices at the same time, in the same room, in a bid to get some privacy while sharing the same physical space.

Ownership, privacy and other belief systems are navigated in the home according to a set of unwritten rules. Children struggle with unwritten rules because they are still learning how to navigate the world. When my kids wrote down the rules for their bedroom, they were explicitly explaining what the hidden rules were – both ones I was teaching them (about sharing) and ones that they had inherited from culture (that I wasn't allowed in their bedroom).

## How UNICEF took on British culture, and lost

In 2011 I was lucky enough to spend three weeks with numerous families in Sweden to understand child wellbeing, while my colleague conducted the same study in Spain. The fieldwork was part of a study to help UNICEF improve child wellbeing in the UK, through learning about 'what works' in Sweden and Spain.[3] This was a dream job for me, one in which I was expecting to find the key to Scandinavian harmony and happiness, and as a side-effect, make me a Superdad.

I travelled up and down Sweden, going as far north as the train would take me into two metres of snow, and all the way south to Malmö, where my colleague encouraged me to have a sauna, followed by a quick dip in the November Baltic Sea. Along the way we stayed with twenty different families, looking at how their way of life led to high levels of child wellbeing. We observed patterns across weekdays and weekends, with single parents and large families, some wealthy, some poor, but as cultural uniformity is actively encouraged in Sweden, each of the homes we visited acted in very similar ways.

What I saw in Swedish homes was a level of calm and organisation that I couldn't fathom. I could see that the children played out some very clear roles in the home. In fact, everywhere I looked in the house, the children seemed to be busy, either preparing food, laying the table, washing up or sweeping up the leaves in the garden. They even tidied up their toys before playing with the next one. More than that, the house was seemingly designed with kids in mind – the plates were in low cupboards for child access, and the fridge was low too; there was a stool by the sink so the kids could wash up, and there was never any chance of standing on a stray LEGO with your bare foot. I saw an incredible system whereby the families were very tight, organised units. I assumed that this led to high levels of wellbeing, but the Swedish cultural trait of being calm and controlled meant that I honestly couldn't tell if people were happy or not.

In Spain, my colleague was having a very different experience. She said the homes were messy and chaotic, with people coming and going constantly, and she could barely keep up with whether the kids were in or out. We compared the levels of wellbeing, the focus of the study, and she was adamant that kids in Spain were having a great time.

'How do you know?' I asked. 'You don't speak Spanish.'

'Oh, it's so obvious,' she said. 'These families are laughing, playing and always on the move, and they clearly don't care about doing the dishes or tidying up.'

I had gone to the home of wellbeing and happiness and all I felt was boredom. My colleague in Spain was witnessing a rollercoaster of joy along with some mild chaos. Even though we were looking at child wellbeing, we were essentially looking at how culture guides people's behaviours to a degree where the Swedes are taught to be calm and to fit in with the group, whereas the Spanish are taught to be uninhibited and to stand out.

By contrast, our fieldwork in the UK showed that parenting culture has very few implicit rules because all the rules are constantly undermined by other parts of society. Parents are expected to spend quality time with their children but have some of the longest working hours in Europe, with both parents typically needing to work to make ends meet. Meals tend to happen at different times of day for different family members working different hours, which means missing out on casual exchanges of information that are so crucial for creating connections. With parents often too exhausted to play, different parts of the home are demarcated to adults and children, whereby children's bedrooms become 'media control rooms' with TVs, devices and consoles independent from the rest of the family. This denotes that play time is not necessarily a family affair, which has the potential to foster loneliness. British families might be in the home at the same time, but they coexist rather than sharing time and space. By contrast, both the Spanish and Swedes allow play anywhere in the home, which teaches children about collaboration and opportunity. The only difference is the Swedish all tidy up before dinner while in Spain the excitement of the next activity becomes more important.

We found the UK lacking in so many ways. If childhood in Sweden is centred around instilling responsibility, and the Spanish celebrate childhood as a moment of opportunity and learning, then the UK is characterised by the utter lack of connection between parents and children. Sadly, British children are often left to navigate many social issues on their own or take guidance from their peers, meaning they get questionable advice leading to a lack of confidence. In response, parents often turn to status brands, like trainers or the latest gadgets, to give their children self-confidence, which can in turn lead to more bullying rather than less because it draws more attention. If that sounds grim, it's because it is. And the statistics bear it out.

We launched the report on 14 September 2011 with a big media splash. We ran a three-hour workshop for MPs and journalists in the House of Commons, where we showed them a documentary using footage from different countries. Our research was used on BBC News at 10pm, and the next day it hit all the daily newspapers. *The Times* featured the report on the front page, and dedicated pages 3 and 4 to the report's findings. On pages 2 and 5, literally sandwiching our report on how consumerism was ruining child wellbeing in the UK, were two huge features on how wonderful the newly opened Westfield shopping mall was. It showed pictures of families using the shopping centre as an attraction, enjoying the big brand flagship stores, and how the food halls brought families together. With apparently no irony, *The Times* reported our work as if it were the dry, wholemeal bread to a super enticing, consumerist filling.

The findings for UNICEF showed why child wellbeing was so poor in the UK, but it was also a description of a culture that UNICEF had no way of changing. The goals of UNICEF, to improve child wellbeing, butt up against so much of the UK's culture that it makes it so hard to create change. While IKEA can adapt its products to fit within the dominant culture traits, UNICEF finds itself fighting culture to achieve its goals, which is almost an impossible task. When it comes to the culture of a nation, it is one of those things you really can't change quickly. Despite the depth and power of insight that we delivered to UNICEF, I'm sad to say they couldn't do much with it. While it was disappointing news for UNICEF, it nonetheless meant they knew they couldn't change the culture through holding up a mirror to society, and they instead had to pursue legislative action in order to create change.

What I realised was that I didn't enjoy being in Swedish homes because I wasn't Swedish. All my cultural assumptions meant I struggled to value the calm, democratic values instilled in Swedish parenting. By every measure, the Swedes are much happier and better off than the Brits, but in such a way that I failed to recognise because they expressed happiness in a different way to me. It also made me realise that I could never parent like a Swede – you can't just switch cultures overnight.

### The home as a place of cultural apprenticeship

Our homes hold all the signals we need to understand our own culture. Anthropologists like Pierre Bourdieu and Clifford Geertz have created theories that point us towards the meaning embedded in our everyday behaviours, and how these small behaviours say so much about life on a macro, cultural level. The amazing part for me, as a practising anthropologist, is that all these insights can be gathered simply from watching. Observing people's homes can lead us to some enormously powerful revelations, and we barely need any explanation from the people who live there. Whether the question is about how to design great furniture or how to improve support for parents, the answers can be found at home.

Children learn about their relationship with authority figures through play, which can become a lesson about how much autonomy they have over key decisions, and how 'fair' life is. The home also becomes a place where financial values are born – where children are taught about money, value and reward in varying combinations. We create collective rituals (like family dinners) and symbols (like having a mown lawn) that make us similar to the people in our group. Our story feels personal, but the narrative is set at a cultural level.

Professor Geert Hofstede, the Dutch social psychologist, describes culture as 'the collective programming of the mind that distinguishes the members of one group or category of people from others',[4] and believes this 'programmatic imprint' is complete by the age of fourteen.[5] This imprint relates to values, rules and even language, all of which describe who someone is. In her book *Watching the English*, anthropologist Kate Fox highlights that British people who refer to 'sofas' are upper middle class, whereas the lower middle classes call it the 'settee' or 'couch'.[6] Other differentiators include having a 'sitting room' rather than a 'lounge', eating 'lunch' at midday rather than 'tea', having 'pudding' instead of 'afters', and going to the 'loo' rather than the 'toilet'. That is why I sit on people's 'sofas', drinking 'builder's tea', while I work out what other people's imprints are based on their language, tea preference and home setup.

The home is a balance between our cognition and culture. Culture chooses how and when to eat, and cognition chooses the dish. Culture decides how we store and organise our stuff, and cognition chooses the style of furniture. Culture creates the weekly routine, while cognition puts it in the diary and sends the invites. When culture creates a happy, supportive home where children can thrive, cognition follows the rules, because that's what creates harmony.

## SO WHAT?
## What life at home tells us about life, business and society

The home is the place where we pass on the cultural baton between generations. It's where we learn the rules to live by, how to live with other people and what is our style.

Life at home needs to be a place where we can express ourselves. This might relate to our house rules, which dictate how and when people eat together or socialise. It will also relate to how people get quiet time and privacy, with implicit rules about when you can/can't put music on or whether it's acceptable to sit in your bedroom all day. Expressing ourselves at home is also about finding common ground over the pictures, scriptures wallpaper or blinds that we choose. Making the home feel like your own helps it transition from a place of safety and survival to a place for wellness to thrive in.

Many businesses create products for people to use at home, and the tendency can be to focus purely on style and identity as that's the easy part to think about. As IKEA have showed time and again, practical products create harmony at home by fitting in with the daily routine. Weekly meal kits, like Hello Fresh, tap into people's identity because they want to be seen to be cooks and contribute to a sense of household community because having all the right ingredients helps everyone, while using fresh produce is an important belief when it comes to being healthy. Understanding how their customers live at home helps businesses be more targeted in their offer.

If culture starts and is reproduced at home, the home becomes the locus of morality for society. Many of the big challenges we face as a society (which we address in the next section) – like having greater gender equality, more inclusive DEI practices or improving the mental health of the nation – all need to start at home. Civil society and government can change life at home in various ways, like providing low-cost childcare, promoting gender balance in boardrooms and pay, or improving the provision of social housing, all of which will change the experiences of life at home. However, many governments shy away from interfering with family dynamics for fear of being labelled a 'nanny state'. This fear of being labelled as interfering means they shy away from using the home – the most important place for cultural apprenticeships – as a mechanism for creating cultural change.

# PART TWO

# CHANGING CULTURE

Culture and cognition walk into a bar, and cognition starts unloading about their work stress. 'I need to figure out how to get my team to work together better. They all end up doing their own thing and don't help each other!'

Culture sips their drink and says, 'Simple: give them an identity to rally around, a community to belong to and something to believe in.'

Cognition blinks. 'Interesting! What kind of thing should they believe in?'

Culture grins. 'Get them to come up with it themselves – just don't make it about you.'

The bartender chimes in: 'Or you could bring them here and get them pissed, that'll sort it out.'

# 5

## Finding the Rules That Change Us

Psychology started to gain respect when it showed how to create change in the world. One of the key protagonists in showcasing the power of psychology was not actually Sigmund Freud but his nephew, Edward Bernays. Bernays was one of the most influential PR men of the 1930s and 40s, and he used Freud's ideas about appealing to people's 'ego' in numerous government and advertising campaigns to incredible effect. His most famous breakthrough campaign was in 1929, when he convinced the suffragettes to remove cigarettes from their stockings and light them while on a high-profile, televised women's liberation march. According to Bernays, smoking cigarettes, or 'torches of freedom', was an act of rebellion against the male-dominated society and a symbolic demonstration of taking control of the penis.[1]

Others followed in Bernays' footsteps, most notably Ernest Dichter, who invented the focus group in 1947 and helped Betty Crocker quadruple their sales on ready-to-bake cake mixes. His focus groups led him to realise that housewives thought cake mix made baking too easy – they felt like they were cheating in their duty as a housewife – and that requiring them to add an egg to the mixture gave them a sense that they were actually cooking for the family (the symbolism of the mother's egg was key here). 'Just add one egg', which became the tag line on Betty Crocker's cake mix, is still a regular phrase used in marketing and advertising agencies all around the world as shorthand for the idea that you shouldn't make life too easy for people.

With these success stories, psychology took hold in business and politics from the 1940s onwards. Bernays, Dichter and many others said the answers to changing people's behaviour was to decode human motivation and appeal to what Freud termed their 'id': the wild, untethered side of their ego. Dichter founded the Institute for Motivational Research in America, and later expanded to Germany and Switzerland, consulting with brands on how to identify consumer motivation. Brands now focused on increasing levels of indulgence and desire with their communications, which in turn super-charged an already strong movement of individualism and consumerism in the US.

While these stories are enticing, they are built on a lie. Women didn't really believe they were taking control of the penis through lighting their 'torches of freedom'. Bernays convinced the suffragettes to light the cigarettes on the march because it would get more press attention, while also briefing the media ahead of time that the suffragettes might be feeling a bit 'rebellious'. Bernays was in fact misusing the psychological techniques learned from Freud while on the payroll of the tobacco company Philip Morris, whose growth had stagnated because they had saturated the market (men). Bernays convinced Phillip Morris that the major growth opportunity for them was to convince women to smoke too.

The apocryphal Betty Crocker story is similar. Just adding one egg wasn't a new idea – Betty Crocker's competitors were already doing that – and it was not based on the insight that an egg is 'a women's offering' to the family; a fresh egg simply made the cake taste so much better than dried egg. These master influencers were not just focused on convincing people to buy more stuff; they were also selling psychology as a method that could change the world.

Through the 1940s, 50s and beyond, this trend of catering to individual desire and indulgence delivered through consumerism was driving the bottom line in business. The 'hidden persuaders' – as they were dubbed in Vance Packard's book of the same name exposing the motivational research industry – designed campaigns that tapped into people's innermost desires with services that felt ever more idealised and personal.[2] At one point, Bernays wrote to Freud asking him to come on a speaking tour of America where he would guarantee influential audiences and great fortune, but his uncle refused on the grounds that this wasn't how psychology should be used. Freud warned that the id of the masses should not be manipulated lightly, as it was not a kind way to change the world.

Psychology got its next bunk up in public consciousness with the rise of 'behavioural economics' in the late 1990s and 2000s. The iconic book *Nudge* by Richard Thaler and Cass Sunstein was published in 2008 and contained countless examples of how psychology could help people make positive, healthy changes.[3] Ostensibly targeting policymakers and anyone interested in creating change in the world, Thaler and Sunstein suggested that making small changes to the way information was presented could have a huge impact on how people treated their health, personal finances and even levels of organ donation.

Within months of publication, *Nudge* was being passed around the corridors of the White House, Whitehall and many other governments around the world, lauded as the quickest fix to all their policy problems. It was also seen as a silver bullet in marketing and advertising to boost sales. In short, it extended psychology's reach ever further into business and policy through offering clear guidance to identify people's innate cognitive biases and, in very practical terms, use these biases to create change.

*Nudge* was such a success because it was so clear about how to create change. For years, social scientists would profess fascinating findings about the state of the nation – that people were unhealthy because of a failure to manage their instincts, or that people were financially ignorant because they would rely on mental accounting – but without offering a solution. By contrast, 'nudge' tactics offered clear policy and marketing recommendations – it was *applied* social science, and people loved it. Behavioural science, as the discipline had become known, was all about creating 'interventions'[4] that would change behaviour, and in the world of policy and marketing, it doesn't get much sexier than that. All of my clients had read it from cover to cover, and given I had a degree in psychology, I started to give presentations on how it could be used.

I was convinced I could apply these psychological tricks to my new anthropological life. To prove the concept, I took it upon myself to help my housemate Charlotte quit smoking using nudge techniques. At that point in the late 2000s, smoking was going out of fashion really fast, and she was feeling pressure from her parents and partner to quit. In this context, 'loss aversion' states that the pain of quitting is greater than the potential enjoyment of living smoke-free – so we instinctively avoid quitting. I decided to combine this powerful bias with a 'commitment device', which states that once you've made a public commitment, you continue with that behaviour to remain consistent with your own statements. All perfectly reasonable ideas to encourage people to change their behaviour.

When quitting smoking, nicotine withdrawal symptoms normally peak on day three, after which they start to diminish. The first ten days are the most significant in overcoming physical symptoms, after which the urge to continue smoking is more to do with deeply ingrained habits and identity than actual cravings. I devised a devilish experiment in which her parents (who lived close by) committed to giving her £50 per day for ten days straight if she didn't smoke a cigarette. Her parents would pop round and put a crisp £50 note in a jar each day, and the jar sat on the kitchen table for everyone to see, building up to a £500 windfall on day ten. However, if she smoked a single cigarette, the money that was in the jar would automatically be donated to the British National Party (BNP), a far-right political party that Charlotte considered a plague on our society. The *Nudge*-inspired experiment was designed with a strong motivation (£500), a public commitment (the jar sat on the kitchen table) and a huge dose of loss aversion (giving money to the BNP) that would outweigh the loss aversion associated with quitting. *If only Public Health England could create something so smart*, I thought.

When designing nudges, the trick is to combine various forms of biases and commitments into one intervention to enhance people's motivation and ability to change. Behavioural science has taught us that our brains are hardwired to act and react to stimuli in certain ways, whether that's how information is presented or the choices that are available to us. The more biases you can bundle together to encourage the same behaviour (quitting smoking), the more likely you are to succeed.

On day six of Charlotte quitting smoking, she had a terribly stressful day at work and nipped out the back when her colleague offered her a cigarette. She came home devastated and begged her parents not to give the £300 to the BNP. They of course relented, again showing that culture trumps psychology. The need to smoke with a colleague as a mechanism to get through a stressful day at work was stronger than a laboratory-style experiment that attempted to reframe how she thought about smoking.

Charlotte did quit smoking several years later, though it had nothing to do with any of my clever tricks and everything to do with the cultural associations of being a smoking mother. Her four-year-old turned around to Charlotte and said, 'Mummy, I know what you do when you go into the garden.' And that was it. Being outed by a four-year-old and forced to face the negative associations that go with being a smoking mother was a much stronger motivator than an intervention based on public commitment.

Many behavioural science nudges, when tested in the real world, have actually gone wrong. Over 4 million Dutch citizens (22% of the population) actively opted out of organ donation after the Dutch government created an automatic opt-in system which nudge theory suggested would seamlessly turn the whole population into organ donors.[5] Pension enrolment was another opt-in nudge used in the UK to make sure everyone had a pension when they started a new job. While there was an uptick in the number of people taking out a pension, there was actually a decrease in the total amount of money invested in pensions, as many people chose to start their pension on a lower percentage than before.[6] Initially hailed as the silver bullet of behaviour change, particularly in public policy, behavioural science is now struggling to replicate many of its past famous experiments, leading to a 'replication crisis' in academia and adverse effects in public policy and advertising. In the same way that Freudian psychology was used in PR, behavioural science has sold the method to the world, but it's not always living up to the promise.

### Using the Cultural Trinity to map change

Following some of my disappointing behavioural experiments, I started to realise that change isn't purely about how you think because many of the factors that facilitate change are in the world rather than in our brain. Often, it's the interaction between people that creates a spark for change – someone may have the willpower not to buy and smoke a cigarette but will cave when offered one by someone they normally smoke with.

In order to map change, the Cultural Trinity is designed as a dynamic model which recognises that each of the three elements influences the next – because that's what happens in real life. Culture is made up of all three factors, and a change in culture often comes from a shift in identity, community *or* belief systems. A change in one creates a change in the others, and understanding the source of change is important because it tells us *how* culture is changing. Here are the following ways in which different factors in the Cultural Trinity influence one another.

## ▲ Identity → ● Community

When people start to take on a new identity – becoming a 'fan', being a parent, etc. – they often start to surround themselves with like-minded people, which in turn reinforces the shift in identity. This might manifest through fandoms, sports clubs, parent get-togethers, work mates, all of which relate to people taking on a new identity and creating a group of people like them, which further solidifies that identity. This is also present in niche internet forums, where people who share the same interests might not be geographically near each other but can still create communities. Some examples include:

> The LGBTQ+ communities often find safety and a sense of belonging by creating a community based around sexual identities. Repressive regimes that prevent sexual expressiveness prevent these communities from forming, and stop this cultural development.

> *Warhammer*, a game which involves people painting small lead figurines, has seen unprecedented growth in the last ten years to become a multibillion-dollar brand through harnessing online communities where people can express their love of the game.

## ▲ Identity → ■ Belief systems

Experimenting with your identity, either through expressing yourself in new ways or through being labelled by others, means that you start to adopt new belief systems. When people are given a 'label' based on what they've done (like vote for a political party), they often start to adopt the values of that behaviour. Some other examples include:

> 'Fake it till you make it' – this entrepreneurial identity, often adopted by young people, literally describes the process by which people can morph themselves into being focused and driven, which then becomes part of their new entrepreneurial identity.

> Entering the criminal justice system through a minor indiscretion can mean that people are given a new criminal identity (which may or may not be accurate). The accompanying belief system based on shame, victimisation and exclusion can in turn lead to repeated criminal behaviour.

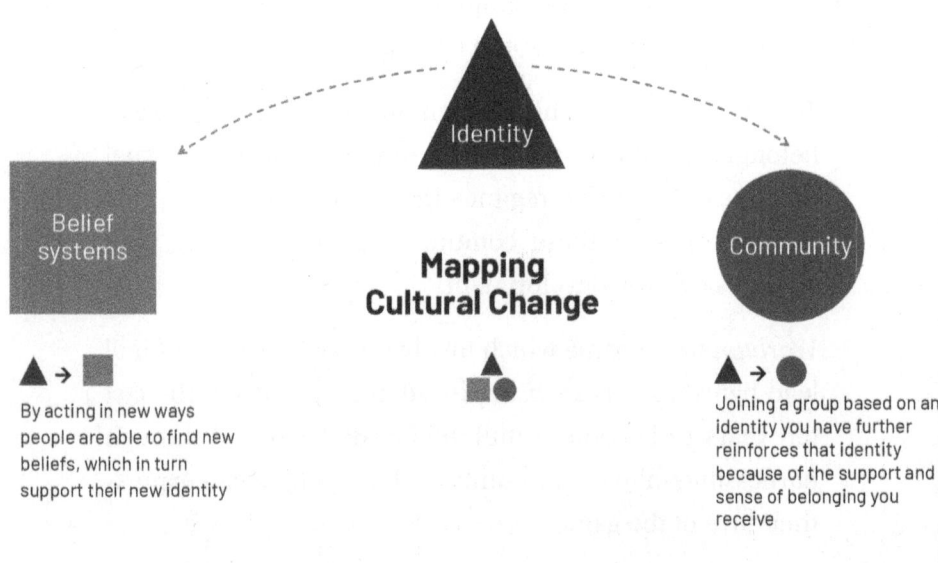

**Mapping Cultural Change**

▲ → ■
By acting in new ways people are able to find new beliefs, which in turn support their new identity

▲ → ●
Joining a group based on an identity you have further reinforces that identity because of the support and sense of belonging you receive

### ● Community → ▲ Identity

Joining a community requires people to conform to the social norms of the group, which in turn affects the identity of the individual. Joining a club means signing up to being that type of person, and other people assume you are that type of person. Communities – sports clubs, workplaces, parent groups – tend to be based around a predominant identity, and the more time you spend in that community, the more that identity comes out in you. Whether geographical or online, communities offer people support and belonging which are key factors in shifting their identity. For example:

> Having a baby often creates a shift in identity for people, and becoming associated with a parent support group helps embed this identity ever deeper, as the norms of the club become very baby-focused.

> Workplaces are communities that often require people to act in accordance with particular hierarchies and practices. Adopting the workplace identity – whether that's late nights, a jolly demeanour, intellectual curiosity – will often lead to a greater level of integration and success.

### ● Community → ■ Belief systems

When a community grows it often creates a belief system at the heart of it – either explicitly or implicitly – and when that community gets more recognition and airtime, it spreads its belief system. Grassroots political parties, purpose-driven brands, or campaigns like those against phone use in childhood or for the creation of safer streets are all examples of how communities can reshape mainstream belief systems. The outcome is that a critical mass of like-minded people get a sense of belonging

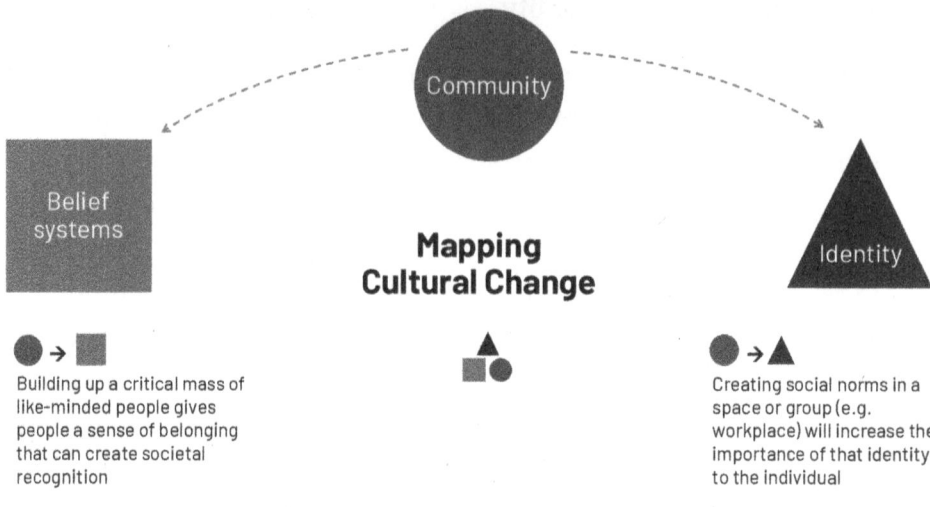

that in turn drives societal recognition and a change in beliefs. Some examples are:

> Black Lives Matter, originally created for a sense of belonging and support in the Black community, created a set of values centred around recognition and equity, which helped shift societal values towards greater diversity, equity and inclusion (DEI), a movement that is now applied in various places (although it has since faced backlash).

> Outdoor clothing retailer Patagonia has changed corporate culture and consumer behaviour towards climate consciousness through spending millions of dollars to overcome the effects of climate change. Now, even mass-market retailers feel pressure to align with sustainable values and the need to 'go green'. In this way, a brand-anchored community evolved into a cultural movement, proving that belief-led branding can instigate systemic change.

## ■ Belief systems → ● Community

Where a belief system creates a community, members of that community will often become devoted to 'the cause'. Religion is the classic example of belief systems creating communities, particularly when missionaries were sent overseas to spread the Lord's word. Employers often create a sense of purpose to make people feel they are doing more than simply turning up for their pay cheque. This is achieved to a much greater extent in the public sector, where workers are often paid less and work more hours when conducting a similar job to their counterparts in the private sector, because they are working for the public good. Obtaining membership to the community is normally relatively easy, but leaving it can be harder. Some examples are:

> The 'manosphere' – a growing online community of disenfranchised men who celebrate examples of toxic masculinity – has become a place where people believe gender equality has gone too far, and that men are now discriminated against. This community has been created around a belief that the world has become corrupted by feminist ideology and 'woke' agendas in politics and the media, and gathers people from locations around the world.

> In the 2010s a lot of consumer-facing companies spent time trying to work out their 'brand purpose' in an attempt to create meaningful advertising by standing for something (to greater and lesser success). Companies like Nike and Airbnb quickly created communities who believed in what they stood for.

## ■ Belief systems → ▲ Identity

In reality, an individual can hold many different competing values in their head without ever appearing to find this a

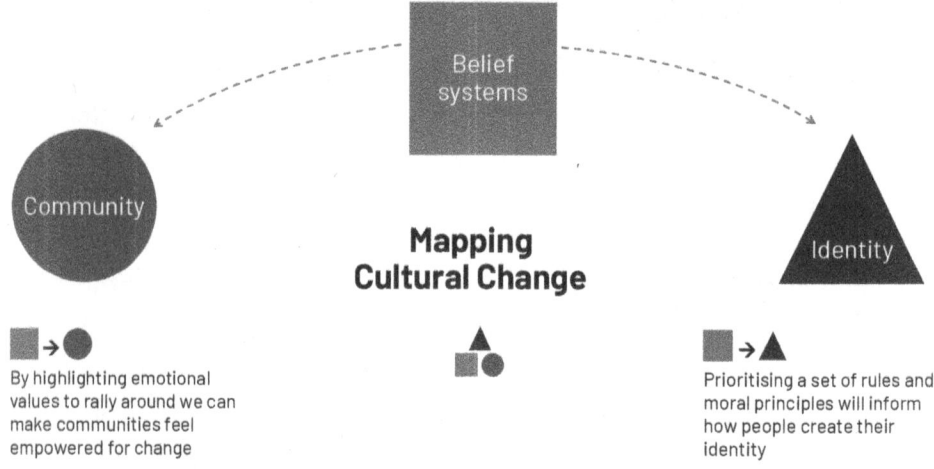

problem – a concept psychologists refer to as cognitive dissonance. Take, for instance, religious leaders who preach tolerance while also endorsing war against countries of a different faith. Cultural change happens not by erasing these differences or contradictions but by making one identity more salient than the other. At work, someone may believe that hierarchy and dedication are important values, whereas at home they may believe values like equality and playfulness are important – each of these values triggers a different identity (visualise a man who removes his tie as he walks through the door at home). Some examples are:

> Populist leaders in many Western democracies have had great success in using particular values to trigger an identity that will vote for them, like the Leave campaign in Britain talking about 'saving the NHS' when voting to leave the European Union.

> Teaching children about climate change and sustainability in school has meant that a whole generation is far more conscious about recycling, conserving energy and preserving

the planet. Climate change is no longer a scientific issue for kids; it's a moral one that's part of their identity.

The Cultural Trinity is not just a model for analysis but a tool for understanding how change happens, and for creating cultural change in life, business and society. The important thing is not to see these concepts in isolation but as part of a dynamic interplay of constantly shifting ideas.

## The only constant (in culture) is change

I first started experimenting with how these concepts changed one another in 2018 when I worked with Pride London (the organisation that campaigns for equal rights and organises the Pride march each year) to better understand how the LGBTQ+ community had moved from a community of protest to one of acceptance.

The gay Pride movement rose out of the Stonewall riots of 1969, following a police raid on a gay bar in Lower Manhattan. One year after the riots, the first Pride marches were held in New York, Chicago and Los Angeles. Pride movements soon followed the world over and became a symbol of protest against the mainstream establishment that had historically marginalised people who weren't heterosexual. The Pride movement has done an incredible job at shifting mainstream attitudes to homosexuality, which on a legislative level has given homosexuals equal rights in many parts of the world and on a cultural level has made overt discrimination unacceptable (though more work needs to be done to achieve equality). In preparation for Pride's fiftieth anniversary, my team documented how that change had happened, showcasing the power that a community can have.

Our research started by talking to people who were lesbian, gay, bisexual and trans, trying to understand what everyday life looked like for them. British society has made great leaps towards celebrating sexual equality in public, but when we spoke to people around the country, we continually heard stories of struggle. Not being heterosexual still means going against the mainstream, and people told us about the anxiety and insecurity of 'coming out' during their teenage years, the trickiest period of life for identity formation. Their teenage angst wasn't just an internal crisis of confidence; it was external too. They told us about how people spat at them in the street, left a bible on their desk at school, or would give them two forks in the lunch queue. When every teenager around the country is asking themselves, *Who am I?* teenagers who were coming out also had other people saying, *Who the hell are you?*

Talking to the Pride community, the 'coming out' story was on the tip of everyone's lips. In some cases, their parents ostracised them and refused to accept them; in other cases, people thought they would be ostracised, but they were hugged! Interviewees told us about having to act with caution at work, in bars, at gigs and at festivals, as people act differently towards you when they know your sexuality. When the world considers you to be different, it's hard not to feel like you're different.

Naturally, many of these teenagers were unsure how to act and behave when they were coming out – should they act camp, look butch, be gender non-specific? – so Pride London became a hugely important community to be part of. As a community, it was a place where they could belong – a group of like-minded people with the same issues in life. Pride was a place of support – where they could talk about discrimination and being ostracised, and how to deal with that. And Pride also became a place where their sexual preferences were normal, where the social norms were accepting of their behaviour. Pride was a place of protest, support and celebration, a place where they could come together for strength during a time when they might not have been strong enough to deal with what was being thrown at them.

Over time, the community garnered support from all walks of life. The yearly march was a moment to celebrate those who stood up at the Stonewall riots, and became a party that everyone wanted to be part of. The flamboyant and celebratory nature encouraged involvement from heterosexual allies, showcasing that anyone left on the fringes of society could be accepted into the mainstream.

In time, this acceptance led to the reshaping of society's belief systems. Normalising non-heterosexual behaviour meant that some of society's rules and norms were suddenly brought into stark contrast: *If gay couples are normal, why can't they get married? And why can't they bring up children together?* As a community, Pride London was able to hold up a mirror to society and created a change in morality, as being gay was no longer 'wrong'. And when 1.5 million people took part in the Pride march, it was inevitable that people's values would shift towards being more open and accepting.

Our study was based in London but it tells a story that's mirrored in many countries around the world. By 2019 – fifty years after the Stonewall riots in New York – Pride had changed the culture and legislation around the world. Pride is an incredible example of using community to cement cultural change. Initially there to provide support and belonging, Pride ended up shifting public opinion of what was considered acceptable behaviour to the point that thirty-eight countries have changed their laws on marriage and parenting, which in turn changes the way that people act towards LGBTQ+ people in the street. While there is still a way to go in terms of equality and harmony, it is a great example of how people are able to create cultural change of inclusivity.

This story of the Pride movement illustrates the Cultural Trinity in motion: identity struggles lead to the formation of communities, communities influence societal belief systems, and those belief systems in turn reshape what identities are possible, accepted and celebrated.

- ▲ **Identity** – For many LGBTQ+ individuals, their identity began with a sense of shame or isolation. Coming out was not just a personal journey but a social reckoning, associated with being deviant. Teenage years, already fraught with uncertainty, often included hostility, judgement and invisibility.

- ● **Community** – Pride became the sanctuary, a space where individuals found safety, recognition and validation. It was both a party and a protest, a family and a movement. The community provided collective strength and offered a counter-narrative to the shame and exclusion they had experienced. Belonging to Pride gave them hope that society could change.

- ■ **Belief systems** – As the community grew and visibility increased, Pride began reshaping broader societal norms. It held a mirror to dominant culture, forcing it to confront contradictions: If gay people are normal, why can't they marry? Raise children? Lead openly gay lives? Public morality began to shift as inclusion became not just possible but necessary for justice.

- ▲ **Identity (a generation later)** – As belief systems changed, the gay identity itself was no longer stigmatised but celebrated. What began as deviant became normal; what was once marginal became central. Laws were rewritten, families redefined, and the identity of being gay was no longer something to hide but something to honour.

By using the Cultural Trinity framework to analyse everyday behaviours, it becomes clear that identity, community and belief systems are not isolated concepts but dynamic and interconnected forces that shape the culture that makes us.

## Anthropology in a pandemic

In 2014, an Ebola epidemic spread in West Africa. Western governments sent thousands of troops to isolate anyone showing signs of Ebola, as well as the bodies of the deceased, to prevent the epidemic turning into a pandemic. The result was disastrous: patients escaped from the centres, locals turned on (and in some cases killed) troops, and the infected bodies were exhumed to be given a proper burial (a practice that in West Africa normally includes family members washing and sometimes kissing the body). Suppressing the disease through Western public health initiatives was not working, and after a year a team of anthropologists stepped in to create community-based interventions.[7]

Through looking at the culture and local customs of people in Sierra Leone, Liberia and Guinea, the first thing the anthropologists were able to point out was that Western troops taking family members away was a stark reminder of their colonial past. Secondly, local traditional healing techniques were entirely ignored in favour of invasive treatments that isolated members of the community from one another. And thirdly, locals were being told what to do by an outside force rather than consulted on their own health solutions. These belief systems, the anthropologists pointed out, were being completely disrespected by the military intervention and needed to be respected as part of any medical response.

The anthropologists suggested a different approach, with much smaller, more localised treatment centres at the village level, with tents that had transparent walls so relatives could see what was happening inside. Alien-looking hazmat suits were replaced with locally produced and adapted raincoats, which were less medically effective but universally accepted. And importantly, the doctors and villagers reached a compromise on burial rituals whereby relatives carried the dead from the treatment centre to the burial site, overseen by village elders who had the authority to discourage relatives from touching the bodies. Likewise, this was not strictly best practice from a medical perspective, but it was effective and a huge step forward in suppressing the spread of Ebola.

What the anthropologists understood (and the public health officials ignored) was that at a time of death and fear, the community is crucial in offering people support. The embedded rituals associated with funerals are created to make death manageable and allow everyone to have a unified, acknowledged grieving process. Communities become stronger in a time of existential crisis, as a way to find safety, so the double whammy of facing widespread death without a grieving process was always going to be a lot to take in. Once the anthropologists had seen and acknowledged that this was a community-based approach, the answers became apparent.

This case study is widely known in anthropological circles but not often discussed among public health officials, which meant the same issues emerged during the Covid-19 pandemic. Taking a highly individualistic approach to risk, the UK and US were very slow to advocate mask usage because of the sparsity of evidence around how effective it was for peer-to-peer transmission. Even in the presence of a highly transmissible disease, people questioned why they had to change their daily rituals, like kissing people on the cheek or shaking hands. These arguments for the protection of personal liberty (supported by the head of the Nudge Unit, a team of psychologists founded to help government with public policy) entirely missed the *social* significance of mask wearing, a behaviour that signals to other people that there is a disease in the air. In countries where masks were mandated, there arose a collaborative culture where communities felt they were tackling the virus together and were invested in each other's wellbeing, and as a result, they collectively reduced their risk-taking behaviour. The Black community in New York were very quick to adopt masks because they felt public health initiatives were ignoring them (while the wealthier New Yorkers migrated upstate to their second homes). As time went on, it became clear that the mask was a form of peer-to-peer communication in its own right; it was an advert for someone who believed in protecting themselves and others, and had an identity that focused on safety. A cottage industry even sprung up selling ineffective but beautifully designed masks so that people could showcase a more nuanced identity that balanced safety and style.

Too often, our understanding of how we respond to social problems focuses on how to motivate people to do the right thing. This psychological approach to changing individuals' behaviours is too personalised and simplistic when the problem is based on how the community needs to behave. When there's a problem as wide-ranging as a pandemic, our response needs to be anthropological.

### Behavioural tricks under stress

As I was establishing myself as a business anthropologist and companies were turning to me for cultural insight, I had one last fling with psychology. Having felt like I'd mastered the theories of anthropology and psychology, I thought I could create some superology-of-change that combined the best of both. This bluster landed me a fascinating project in 2010 at a busy Accident and Emergency (A&E) department at The Royal London, a hospital in the East End. The project was also a personal challenge for me as between the ages of two and ten I regularly saw my dad in hospital, often with a doctor helping him recover from a diabetic fit. Though hospitals made me feel hopeless, I still perceived doctors as saviours, which was reinforced through TV series and docudramas like *Hospital Heroes* and *24 Hours in A&E*. In reality, hospitals are just very large buildings and doctors are overstretched, skilled workers, but when you factor in the cultural beliefs surrounding healthcare professionals, there's a whole layer of meaning added.

The A&E department was a hub for all emergencies: helicopters brought in the injured pulled out of motorway pile-ups and motorcycle crashes; the police brought in victims of gang violence; and endless ambulances brought in heart attack patients, older people who had fallen over at home and a lot of drunk people from the city-centre bars. And on Friday and Saturday nights, it was the drunks who caused the biggest problems.

Many of the patients admitted for alcohol issues were known to the hospital as repeat offenders – either because they regularly 'overdid it on a night out' or because they were local alcoholics who frequently needed admission. My team had been commissioned by the local health authority to find ways to reduce the number of alcohol-related patients returning to A&E by delivering 'brief interventions' to anyone who was admitted for alcohol. I was very keen to apply my nudge tactics, thinking up ways to apply loss aversion, commitments and social incentives to binge drinking and personal health.

My colleagues and I joined A&E teams for the night shift on Fridays and Saturdays, from 8pm to 8am. For business anthropologists, this was essentially a golden ticket where we got to analyse workplace culture in one of the most high-intensity environments imaginable.

My first shock came when meeting the consultants before we started fieldwork. We were given a twenty-minute slot at their team meeting to discuss our approach, and within two minutes I was interrupted by Dr M, who looked me straight in the eye and said, 'Has anyone ever spat in your face?'

'Err, no,' I responded.

'Has anyone ever punched you while you're trying to stitch them back together?'

'Err, still no,' I said, now feeling like the floor might disappear beneath me.

'Then what the hell do you know about helping drunks in A&E?' That was a comment rather than a question, and everyone could feel the tension in the room.

Dr M was right: I knew nothing about drunk people in A&E and I felt completely out of my depth, not because I didn't know the answer but because someone who I'd thought of as a saviour was actually a bully. I had no idea how to respond to him because he wasn't the person I'd assumed he would be.

Undeterred by our awkward first meeting, my team spent six straight weeks of Friday and Saturday nights in A&E following doctors and nurses. We quickly noticed a rhythm. From 8 to 10pm staff were high-energy, joking with each other as a way of bonding to help them prepare for the onslaught ahead. From 10pm admissions picked up, often stab or gunshot wounds from gang-related violence, mixed with some serious road traffic accidents. Meanwhile, the corridors started to build up with sick kids and grandparents with their worried relatives, all of whom would regularly remind staff that they were still waiting.

Any time between 11pm and midnight, the floodgates opened and there were more patients than the medics could deal with, with staff struggling to control the ensuing chaos. The charge nurse took control of proceedings, doing their best to prioritise patients based on incomplete information, whizzing around to the patients most in need, trying to ignore the rest. There were drunk people everywhere, many unconscious, some with head wounds and others just wandering the corridors like aggressive zombies. To an anthropologist observer, the doctors looked like a crack team of Marines trying to defuse a bomb in the middle of a party full of sugar-crazed children. These highly skilled doctors were prevented from practising their trade optimally because of the sheer volume of drunk patients.

In theory, our role was merely to observe since we were obviously not qualified to assist, but in practice all that changed. On our very first night, twelve people were admitted from two opposing gangs, with gunshot and knife wounds. I was asked to stand in the middle of the unit and make sure that none of the patients crossed sides (the police had left shortly after admitting them), and my colleague had to hold down a young man's leg to stop him kicking out as a medical professional cut his clothes off to deal with his wounds. We were just another pair of hands on deck, and after that, we would regularly relay blood samples or messages across the floor to help staff get through the night. We became part of their team, and even though no one spat in our faces, we started to understand what Friday and Saturday nights looked like for them.

The night often became 'easier' from 4 to 5am onwards. Many of the patients that had been treated were now in 'Recovery', a ward of beds for patients to recover from their injuries, which often meant sleeping it off for those who had come in drunk. At 8am we would join staff for handover to the next shift, step outside to find the sun had risen, and go for a drink with staff at the local pub to decompress from the shift. Oh, the irony.

During the week, we would go through what we had seen in an attempt to answer the question at hand: How can we deliver brief interventions to prevent drunk people from returning to A&E? The anthropologist inside me said, *No way* – it wasn't the time or place to have a fifteen-minute conversation about alcohol misuse – but I pushed the team to apply the tactics of *Nudge* to what we had seen.

Nudge tactics focus a lot on the way messages are delivered, preferring language like '75% of people complete their tax returns on time' as opposed to '25% of people are late submitting their tax returns.' Same fact, different message. We came up with a 'brief interventions' handbook that would help staff have meaningful conversations with patients to prevent repeat admissions. Some of our suggested phrases went as follows:

— 'Did you know many of your friends will have seen what happened to you last night?' (leveraging social incentives)

— 'Did you know you had ten times more alcohol in your system than 90% of people on a Friday night?' (leveraging framing devices)

— 'An effective way of avoiding this situation is to always limit yourself to three drinks, and then checking in with how you're feeling.' (leveraging commitment devices)

— 'Alcohol admissions cost the NHS 10% of its budget. If we reduce that, we could start helping more people who need life-saving cancer treatment.' (leveraging information salience)

— 'Simply believing that you won't do this again is the mistake most people make; the best thing to do is to get some help.' (leveraging implementation intention)

By giving staff various phrases with which to start a conversation with patients, all of which related to slightly different types of biases, the brief interventions should – according to nudge theories – work with most people. Happy with our work, we took our suggestions back to the same team meeting of doctors and nurses, whom we now considered our friends.

'Fuck off!'

Over the course of the last two months Dr M had turned from foe to advocate and treated us as confidants to some of the trickier decisions he had to make on the ward, as well as what that meant in his personal life.

'Have you actually seen what happens on the weekend? Have you opened your eyes during your *observations*?' He said the last word slowly and sarcastically. 'You want us to memorise your booklet, like you're a fucking playwright creating a happy ever after!?'

Nobody else said a word. I died inside.

After observing the madness of the weekend shifts, where doctors and nurses had been stretched to their limits, we knew Dr M was entirely right. Our clever wordplays for staff to use in a fifteen-minute conversation with patients drenched in booze were never going to prevent repeat admissions. We begged for more time and forgiveness, and we went back to the drawing board.

It was time to abandon nudge tactics and put my trust back in anthropology. Instead of trying to understand staff psychology, we turned our attention to the workplace culture and what was *not* being said. Once we got past the idea that anyone working on an A&E ward is a saviour or a saint above reproach, we noticed that medical staff actually held alcohol-related patients in contempt. These patients weren't viewed as simply people who had had one drink too many; they were a plague upon their workplace. At best they were a pest; at worst they were a societal disease invading their ward. Nobody ever said it, but drunk patients were treated quite differently to everyone else who was admitted. This was not an easy thought to have or to say out loud as clearly the staff were trying their best, but it was crucial to admit if we were going to find a way forward. Encouraging medical staff to have a meaningful conversation with drunk patients meant going against the culture of the ward. Staff dismissed drunk patients out of hand because of the level of disruption they caused to their daily working life. There were unnecessary injuries and time-consuming patients who 'only had themselves to blame', when 'more deserving' or indeed 'more innocent' patients were forced to wait. The problem was even larger than that: even if we changed the current staff attitudes, turnover meant that the next wave of A&E medics would have the same associations.

So, we needed to find an intervention that wasn't staff-orientated. Having analysed the movements and emotions of drunk patients waking up in A&E, we noticed that there was a pattern. No matter how they came in, be that a head injury or drunken coma, they always ended up in Recovery, a dark and calm room that allowed them to sleep it off. When they woke up, they would visibly have an *Oh shit* moment in which they had to face up to the fact that they were in A&E instead of their own bed. This was an emotional moment, usually including regret for the previous evening, and a point when they might be open to an intervention.

Our second observation was that patients headed straight to the bathroom. Patients often stayed in there longer than is typical, either sitting on the toilet contemplating their life choices, washing their hands and face, or generally trying to make themselves feel normal.

And this is where the intervention needed to take place, not as a conversation with staff, but through the building itself.

We created numerous posters that said things like, 'How was your night?' accompanied by a picture of a woman being sick in a hospital bed, and, 'Last night was crazy,' with a picture of a man on a dance floor with blood dripping down his head. Each poster was also accompanied by stats from the NHS, saying, 'Alcohol admissions cost the NHS 10% of its budget,' and, '1 in 10 hospital beds have a drunk person in.' At the bottom of each poster were the words, big and bold: 'WOULD YOU DO IT AGAIN?' Our intervention was positioned to come at a moment when their guard was down and there was potential for them to change.

These anthropologically inspired posters were speaking to patients in a way that staff couldn't. They were an attempt to start a conversation in patients' heads to make them realise the impact of their behaviour on other people. In this community-led approach, they realised they had overstepped the mark in terms of acceptable behaviour – they had broken the code of the community. In turn, it had an effect on how people saw themselves; it affected their identity. And in true British culture, the posters showed them they had undermined a great British belief system: they had strained the NHS.

Workplaces are often community-led cultures – they are fundamentally peer-to-peer driven cultures – and a place like A&E has some strict social norms (created through hierarchy and medical protocol), with a strong sense of belonging and support (because they're all in it together). In turn, the community-driven culture affects people's identity through how other people in society see them (often hero-like), and given the importance of the public service, it embodies some strong belief systems (utilitarian care). While community might be the driving force behind the cultural practices in A&E, the way it also influences identity and belief systems makes changing staff behaviours a difficult task.

The effectiveness of the posters remains quantifiably unknown as it is not something that can be measured, but anecdotally, it was a great success. Conceiving a strategy that is impossible to deliver in practice, like busy doctors taking fifteen minutes to lecture patients who do not want to hear it, is as pointless as a chocolate teapot. I had an unfortunate (non-alcohol-related) trip to the same A&E four years later, and the posters were still there.

This story is a striking example of how community-led design, starting with posters in a hospital bathroom, can influence identity and belief systems. When done well, cultural interventions start a conversation about who we are and what we value.

- **Community** – A&E is not just a medical space; it is a culture with rules and roles set by medical hierarchy. The posters served as a subtle yet powerful voice in a community where the problem of alcohol abuse was not discussed. The posters stepped into a communication vacuum through offering a moment of reflection grounded in the shared norms of British society and NHS culture.

- **Identity** – Seeing themselves portrayed in stark, shame-inducing imagery during a moment of personal vulnerability made patients question not just their night out but their self-image. The posters forced patients to see themselves through the eyes of others, tapping into the embarrassment, regret and recognition that can trigger self-change.

- **Belief systems** – The posters invoked one of Britain's strongest cultural institutions: the NHS. The message: your choices don't just have personal consequences, they burden a public good. This challenged the implicit belief that a night out is inconsequential, elevating the act of moderation to a moral imperative.

My fling with behavioural science nudging came from a desire to create recommendations that seemed simple and easy to follow. I preached the benefits of behavioural science because I wanted my social science findings to sound concrete and actionable. I persevered with applying behavioural science interventions on numerous projects beyond the A&E work, some on more conventional topics, like improving financial literacy in the UK, others slightly more left-field, like encouraging people to buy Andrex toilet paper. On each project the pattern was the same: great-sounding recommendations that rarely worked in practice.

### Cultural conversations drive social change

As an anthropologist I spend time with people to understand why they do the things they do. Depending on the topic and the client, I might spend time with families to understand their mealtimes, observe mechanics fixing cars, or even go for a ride with truckers across the country. I focus far less on what people say and far more on their environment and the people around them to get an understanding of how change can happen between people.

By contrast, analysing and categorising society by psychological standards misses many of the factors that bind us all together. These psychological profiles exclude some of the fundamental reasons why we feel compelled to go to work every day, why we look after our families or go and meet our friends. The 'Big 5' personality test, or OCEAN profiling, is regularly used by advertisers and social media companies to assess where individuals sit on levels of Openness to new experiences, Conscientiousness, Extraversion, Agreeableness and Neuroticism. This assessment is often passively analysed through people's social media activity, the results of which are used to convince people to vote or purchase in particular ways. But this focus on individual preference is only part of the answer – there is no OCEAN profile for 'nurture' or 'care', yet it is probably the biggest reason for any parent to act or buy something. People are compelled to act in the name of justice and equality, yet this isn't recognised as an important psychological driver of behaviour. There are so many cultural factors that drive our behaviour that psychological profiling misses.

And the results speak for themselves. Advertising that focuses on equality – whether that's about fighting discrimination or simply making sure everyone is on a level playing field – has a great impact. In 2018, Nike released one of its most powerful advertising campaigns when it supported Colin Kaepernick, the Black American football player who allegedly lost his contract because he took the knee during the national anthem at the beginning of each game to support the Black Lives Matter movement. For their thirtieth anniversary, Nike put Kaepernick's face on a twenty-metre billboard in the middle of Times Square with the slogan: 'Believe in something. Even if it means sacrificing everything.' Instead of appealing to individual desire, this campaign appealed to the ideas that helped connect people over an issue many of them were talking about: being an ally to the Black Lives Matter movement. The campaign was an incredible success, social media mentions went through the roof (more positive than negative, though there was a backlash), their stock price jumped 7% in a week, and quarterly sales were up 10% as a result.

This is largely in keeping with Nike's brand strategy over the years. Nike has historically shunned competitive, desire-driven advertising and instead focused on a strategy based on creating a collaborative, collective campaign. Nike's raison d'être is that *if you have a body, you are an athlete*, which allows it to put forth passion as a central idea in its brand, communications and products. Like all brands with a powerful cultural positioning, they leverage the ideas we see in the Cultural Trinity for commercial gain.

- ▲ **Identity** – Anyone can buy Nike, whether it's people who want to lounge in a tracksuit or wear comfy shoes in the office through to people chasing their personal best. They don't require people to be athletes; they just want people to be passionate. By aligning with figures like Colin Kaepernick, Nike stretched that identity beyond the personal to include the political. Nike has an inclusive identity by declaring that everyone can be an athlete, regardless of background, body type or ability, and anyone who feels that way feels comfortable in Nike.

- ● **Community** – From digital platforms like Nike Run Club (which has over 100 million users) to physical spaces like renovating basketball courts across the US, the brand fosters communities that didn't exist before, unified by sport and passion. Allowing Nike owners to feel part of a community means they feel part of the brand, particularly when that brand is in your ear giving you a boost to run that extra mile. Nike transforms individual fitness into a collective experience and connects people through shared passion.

- ■ **Belief systems** – Nike campaigns don't just sell products; they sell principles like accessibility, perseverance and solidarity. Their tagline 'Just Do It', which hasn't changed since 1988, is the simplest call to action for anyone thinking about sport. Supporting movements like Black Lives Matter reflects a deep cultural commitment to justice, sacrifice and moral leadership. It isn't just a sportswear brand; it's a brand that does the right thing.

A brand as iconic as Nike maintains a powerful cultural presence through acting in a consistent manner across its products, advertising and brand. Whether people own Nike or not, anyone can describe what the brand stands for, which is testament to its cultural presence and drive to be iconic.

As a discipline, anthropology looks at what happens between people, finding the common threads that unite us as a group rather than defining us as individuals. What businesses like Nike have realised is that if they want to influence people, cultural factors are more influential than personal motivation. People's behaviour is often a result of how and where they were brought up, which creates their values and beliefs; it's a result of who they socialise with, and what they consider to be normal behaviour from the communities they are part of. When we put this insight into marketing campaigns, we see advertising that showcases ideas that everyone can get behind, like helping overcome the pain of discrimination, creating an implicitly collaborative culture.

### When politics messes with culture

The 2016 US presidential election was probably one of the most divisive campaigns Americans had ever seen. Donald Trump's campaign had seen a step change in identity politics: he repeatedly promised to build a wall between the US and Mexico to keep illegal immigrants out; he got stadiums to chant 'lock her up' when referring to his political opponent, Hillary Clinton; and as we later learned, hundreds of different adverts were created and targeted at voters based on their OCEAN profiling built on data that Facebook had supplied to the political consultancy Cambridge Analytica. While polarisation among voters had started many years before, this campaign used people's fears to become particularly divisive.

Seeing this cultural shift, the whisky brand Johnnie Walker decided it was going the other way. Building on its tagline of 'Keep on Walking', it launched a big-money advert that repeated the line about the land being made for you and me, from the Woody Guthrie song 'This Land Is Your Land'. The advert used images of American cattle ranches, African American jazz clubs, industrial workers, Latino family gatherings, hospital workers, cowboys and jogging clubs, positioning Johnnie Walker as a brand for anyone and everyone. Billboards with 'Keep Walking Chicago', 'Keep Walking Miami', 'Keep Walking Washington Heights' appeared around the country to further emphasise the importance of community as a locus of connection. When election night came, a nerve-wracking moment when many people needed a whisky, Johnnie Walker sales outperformed their expectations by 350%.[8]

This move by Johnnie Walker in 2016 was particularly astute, as the brand successfully played to both sides of the political divide and avoided any association with American imperialism. Fast forward to 2024, many large American brands like Coke, Starbucks, McDonald's and KFC are facing major boycotts around the world. These brands had all traded on their Americanness to attract customers, embodying individualism and indulgence in the brand positioning and product attributes. In a world where American politicians are starting trade wars and supporting the Middle Eastern conflict, these brands are feeling the cultural backlash as consumers stop buying their products.

Culture is obvious, but it often hides from us. Whether that's doctors who treat drunk patients in A&E or what a brand means to us on a deeper level, culture is hard to interpret because it's not in our heads: it's the stuff in between people. If we examine the interaction between people, we can see how our identity, community and belief systems shape the world. These cultural factors become the puppet strings that make up who we are and why we do the things we do.

## SO WHAT?
### Creating change in life, business and society

Culture changes, constantly. Sometimes there's a big 'vibe shift' when a new political leader comes in hell-bent on tearing up the rulebook. Other times there are small, imperceptible shifts in some of the tectonic plates that govern our day-to-day existence, like the popularity of knitting or church attendance. Looking at the shifts in culture is almost as important as the analysis in the first place, because once you've described culture successfully, it's probably on the move.

In life, the most obvious way to change culture is to change how other people see us. Our identity is not static – even if we want to portray ourselves in the same way that we always have – because other people's perceptions of our behaviour changes. Wearing a body warmer might be part of a 'practical' and 'outdoorsy' identity that you want to portray, but when that same item of clothing gets rebranded as a gilet that's worn by the super-rich on yachts, then people start to see you as a finance bro rather than a hiker. The clothes that we wear give other people clues as to the community we belong to and the values that we hold, even if those views don't align with how we see ourselves.

In business, cultural change is experienced through a change in the conversation. That conversation might be internal, where employees start talking about their CEO in a new way – 'they seem much more erratic these days' – which leads to widespread panic across a company. Businesses also need to make sure they are mirroring some of the wider societal conversations that are happening, whether that's a shift in how they treat parents, gender pay gaps or DEI targets. If there are conversations in society about how people are treated, then they need to happen in the workplace too – denying them will simply push the conversation underground.

Most businesses have customers or clients, and controlling the conversation about their brand or company can make or break them. The industry of public relations is there to either create or suppress conversations that shape the way people see a company or brand, and, in turn, influence the culture we live in. Bell Pottinger, once one of the largest PR agencies in the world, ironically lost control of the conversation around its own brand. Having taken on numerous controversial contracts, one of which was to create a 'dirty campaign' in South Africa to stir up racial hatred, it was then seen as an immoral company that its clients ended up abandoning.[9] This shift in conversation led to a change in what people thought Bell Pottinger stood for, creating a toxic brand that people couldn't buy into.

In society, changes in law, industry and infrastructure are often a reflection of the cultural belief systems in place. Often slower to change, society responds to shifts in cultural belief systems, whether that's an industry marketed towards 'modern men' or political leaders changing laws to be more inclusive (or exclusive!). Change at this level is often slower and more gradual, but once it's in motion, it's very hard to undo.

# 6

## How Tribalism Makes Us and Breaks Us

This may disappoint some of the anthropologist readers, but I am a massive football fan. My daughter and I both follow Arsenal, a football club one mile from our home. We can hear the crowd when a match is on, knowing that whatever just happened will be crucial for our chances of winning the league or cup. If Arsenal win, we have a good day; if Arsenal lose, our day can be ruined. The fact that a group of players that we don't know and haven't even met can dictate whether we have a good or bad day is the clearest definition of tribalism that I can find today. There are few groups in society more tribal than football fans. My daughter went from having an interest in football to becoming an Arsenal fan when I started taking her to the games – but not in the way I expected.

When I took her to her first game she could feel the buzz as the crowds became thicker getting closer to the stadium, the excitement built as she walked up the stairs and got the full view of the bright green pitch, and she lost her mind when Arsenal scored and the crowd went wild. Most of her school friends were also Arsenal fans, and occasionally she'd come home with some new Arsenal facts that I hadn't heard before.

But despite buying into the dream, there were always points during the trip that she didn't like and refused to participate in. No matter the opponent, at some point during every Arsenal match the fans will chant about hating Tottenham (the local rival, three miles up the road). The chant is the trigger for tribal bonding: it echoes around the ground, and fans feel closer by identifying the out-group. Truth be told, the chants are all rude and incredibly basic, involve a lot of swear words, and are often sung by people who you wouldn't expect to say those words in public.

No matter how many times I took my daughter to a game, she could never get on board with the chants: 'It's not nice, Daddy,' and, 'Uncle Tom is a Tottenham fan, and we don't hate him.' She was entirely right: they are horrible songs. While she was comfortable with the identity of being an Arsenal fan, she didn't like the community when it was rude because it implicitly represented exclusion and discrimination. This beautifully encapsulates where tribalism goes too far.

It was an entirely different experience when we went to the women's game. We had the same buzz on the way to the match, which was played on the same impressive pitch, and the crowd still went wild when a goal went in – but the crowd was so much nicer. Nobody shouted abuse at the referee or started chants about who they hate, and the players congratulated their opponents at the end of the game, whether they'd won or lost. The women's game doesn't encourage you to become divisive, aggressive and rude, and my daughter loved it. It was the same identity, but we were suddenly part of a nicer community with a better set of values.

What makes sporting tribalism so interesting is that it is a great example of how culture defines your friends and your enemies. If we wear a red and white scarf, every Arsenal fan will be our friend. It's one of the few times in the UK when strangers will offer you a seat at their table, chat to you unprompted or even buy you a drink. If you sign up to the identity through wearing the scarf, you also sign up to the community that will make you one of them, even if they don't know you.

Granted, it's a socially constructed, multibillion-dollar form of tribalism where huge corporates play on the fact that they are from a 'community' (currently only three Arsenal players are actually from Arsenal). It's precisely because football teams claim to represent a community that they get such a dedicated fan base: it's a showcase of how much we love community.

So why am I still an Arsenal fan? I'm an Arsenal fan because it helps me be part of a group that gives me an identity, which makes me who I am today.

Freud believed it's the human condition to exacerbate the smallest of differences between us in order to create a sense of self. Arsenal and Tottenham fans both love the beautiful game, live in a small enclave of North London, in similar Victorian terraced houses, with similar jobs and family setups, and drive similar cars. But through football, they find a way to differentiate themselves.

During the World Cup, Arsenal and Tottenham fans suddenly put their differences aside to support the England national team, showcasing that rivalries can be overcome when people find a larger cause to be part of. People have an internal barometer on which identity they want to prioritise in any given moment.

There's a long history behind football tribalism and how those values became part of the game, namely that being a football fan gave men a community where they could bond, overcome loneliness and create connections. The community served its people well in terms of creating a place for belonging and support, but it became increasingly exclusionary when it encouraged small-minded behaviours and minor thuggery. The football community in North London is a little different today. My daughter loves wearing the Arsenal badge as her identity and enjoys the liberal North London community of football lovers, but she just wants some more inclusive values as part of the fandom. This story shows how identity draws us in, but it's the nature of the community and the beliefs it upholds that ultimately shape whether we stay committed or push back.

- ▲ **Identity** – Being an Arsenal fan becomes a meaningful part of who you are, shaping personal and social identity across generations. From scarf to badge, football fandom gives individuals a sense of belonging and recognition, even if they never meet the players themselves. This applies to both the men's and women's games.

- **Community** – Matchday rituals and chants bind fans together into a tribe, but not all community behaviours are welcomed. The men's game can veer into exclusion and aggression, whereas the women's game offers a more inclusive, respectful environment that redefines what football community can look like.

- ■ **Belief systems** – Football culture enshrines unwritten codes about loyalty, rivalry and masculinity as markers of who belongs and who doesn't. But these belief systems are evolving as fans question the divisiveness and call for more inclusive values, as demonstrated by the women's game which shows that a kinder experience is possible without losing the collective passion.

### When political tribes make communities

One of the key differences between football tribalism and political tribalism is the level to which it is aligned with a community, or not. Historically, politics has been rooted in the community, where democratic parties got local party delegates to report their issues to Party HQ, who then took on local causes at a national level. Politics was always about making change at a local level, and political parties were (largely) united in their values and ideologies, from the bottom up.

In the US, the Republican–Democrat divide has become so entrenched that you can see it in marriage statistics: same-party marriages (Democrat to Democrat, or Republican to Republican) make up 79% of all marriages, compared to only 4% of marriages that go across party lines (the remaining 17% include Independents).[1] Ezra Klein, the American political journalist, describes the rise in US political polarisation through the formation of two opposing 'mega-identities' that reduce nuance between people, so that our political tribe dictates more and more parts of our life.

Klein suggests Democrats and Republicans have been able to create these competing identities because 'the human mind is exquisitely tuned to group affiliation and group difference' and people 'define themselves against an out-group'.[2] The reason political polarisation has become so entrenched is because political parties now talk about topics that would have historically been beyond politics, including differences in gender, religion, age or profession. People can recognise whether someone is a 'Republican' or 'Democrat' from other social markers, like fashion, haircuts, make-up, facial hair or even where you shop or which football team you support. If you meet a long-haired man wearing slacks and Birkenstocks, you might guess he's a Democrat, compared to a man with short, gelled hair wearing a suit and shiny shoes, who you would think is a Republican. It's as if the overarching machine of American politics has gone through the long list of all possible identities and labelled them as either being classically Republican or Democrat.

Klein describes this as a natural extension of politics operating in a free market. Previously, parties fought for the middle ground but that led to a lack of political distinctiveness and voter confusion. Instead, the parties now 'own' certain issues so that it is easy to know who you are voting for, and who you are not. It started with the Democratic party championing the fight against racial injustice and the Republican party becoming the party for entrepreneurialism and business. There is no reason why the Democrats should be more vocal about improving racial equality than Republicans, but over time, the Democratic party incorporated all forms of social justice into their belief system. There is no reason why Republican voters should be greater advocates of economic growth, but the party have adopted it as a core part of their values.

The Republicans and Democrats now take opposing views on pretty much every issue across race, sexuality, religion, nationality and social class, to a point where your political identity drives what you think about all social issues. You cannot be a Republican and be pro-gender-affirming healthcare, and you cannot be a Democrat and believe political correctness has gone too far. On the minor occasion that you do, you face disapproval from your own party. Klein says that that US has become so polarised that party affiliation can predict the food people eat, the stores people shop at and the TV shows people watch. Political partisanship in the US has defined the cultural landscape dictating who you can and can't be friends with. The level of polarisation comes from the fact that these identities are being driven by two opposing belief systems, which makes the identities more boundaried and more intense.

The adoption of all things liberal by the Democrats has meant that this mega-identity can be triggered on any issue of social justice. Some obvious cases like making healthcare more accessible (Affordable Care Act) and support for a woman's right to an abortion (Roe v. Wade) were signature Democrat identities, even though Republicans might also need healthcare or an abortion. But that same liberal identity also gets triggered when it comes to supporting footballers taking the knee, the right to gender self-identification, or how people feel about the latest Super Bowl advert (which normally gets fairly political). On the flip side, the Republican mega-identity supports more fiscally conservative policies of cutting tax, reducing spending and continued support for gun ownership, but will also be triggered by building a wall to keep immigrants out, removing critical race theory in education, and the promise of keeping trans people out of women's sports. These social issues around gender and race haven't historically been exclusive to one party or the other, but the adaptation of the parties around a purely liberal position for the Democrats and a purely conservative position for the Republicans has meant there are only two positions on any given topic. These divisions have become dividing lines for Americans' belief systems, community and identity, making political support an all-or-nothing cultural issue.

The problem is that in real life, many of these identities cut across political parties. It's entirely possible to be a Black businessperson who feels that racial inequality is a problem for them but also feels that the best way to progress in life is to be entrepreneurial, make money and buy a house for their family in a safe neighbourhood. Politically, the system makes them choose between being an entrepreneurial Republican or a redistributionist Democrat, and culturally, they need to choose between their safety and their business.

There is no middle ground, with the country in 'political sectarianism', according to Dr Eli Finkel, a professor of psychology at Northwestern University, suggesting that this mega-identity divide has become so moralistic that it takes on a level of religious fervour. In a poll conducted for CBS News in 2022, over 49% of Republicans described Democrats as the 'enemy', with just 47% of Democrats feeling the same way about Republicans.[3] In 2017, Pew Research Center found that 62% of *all* Americans believe global climate change is affecting their community (evenly split between Democrat and Republican), though when it comes to whether the federal government should do something about it, 90% of Democrats advocate for federally driven change compared with 39% of Republicans.[4] Even though many of the Republicans acknowledged there was an issue, when it came time to decide on a course of action their cultural identities prevented them from wanting government intervention. This is not just a political problem but a cultural one; it's a narrowing of identity narratives, erosion of community values and the weaponisation of belief systems.

This cultural reconfiguration around politics means that identity becomes preordained, communities are reinforced by sameness, and belief systems have hardened into opposing worldviews. Comparing the two side by side is illuminating.

- ▲ **Identity** – Being a Democrat or Republican now shapes your haircut, hobbies, even what you eat. A Democrat might be recognised through long hair, Birkenstocks and a tote bag filled with oat milk and NPR merch; a Republican through a clean-cut suit, a flag pin, and a preference for steak and talk radio. These differences might not always hold, but they are recognisable archetypes that signify how your identity reveals what kind of country you want to live in. In a world of mega-identities, your politics is no longer a vote, it's who you are.

- ● **Community** – These partisan identities now define communities. Republicans might live in suburban enclaves where family, faith and personal responsibility are community cornerstones, while Democrats gravitate towards urban centres where diversity, progress and moral debates are part of the community chat. Communities don't just reflect personal values – they reinforce them, and disagreement feels like a form of betrayal.

- **Belief systems** – Policy differences have become a proxy for moral codes. For Democrats, belief systems revolve around social justice: support for abortion rights, universal healthcare, LGBTQ+ inclusion and racial equality. For Republicans, the core beliefs centre on fiscal conservatism, religious traditionalism and law-and-order values. On a meta level, it's a battle between moral complexity vs moral clarity. That's not just political division; it's cultural sectarianism.

Just like me and my neighbours three miles away in Tottenham, Democrats and Republicans actually have more in common than they would like to admit. There is a surprising level of policy convergence between the two parties when it comes to military interventions abroad, a reduction in foreign aid, a commitment to capitalism, the sanctity of a free market economy and, amusingly, their disdain of Congress. On a more interpersonal level, there is alignment on the desire for good schooling, strong family values and the aspiration to be middle class. Yet while the police can act to stop sectarian differences in football, there is no authority policing political sectarianism, and no community tempering the polarisation.

The rise of populism in the last twenty years has changed a lot of this, cutting the community element out of political campaigning where commonalities exist, instead preferring big messages about national issues. There has also been a dismantling of the community side of the party itself, which acted as a moderating force for erratic leadership. In 2016, Trump famously bypassed the Grand Old Party (GOP) or Republican machinery for his first presidential campaign, meaning that he wasn't tied to the tempering forces within the party, allowing him to focus the debate on big national issues that appealed to the Republican mega-identity. In 2024, the GOP machinery decided it would back Trump wholeheartedly, knowing that he would be wild and outlandish in his approach, ensuring that the Republican community would follow his lead. In doing so, they disabled the greatest role a community has on culture, which is getting apparent adversaries to see there's a middle ground.

### When political tribes break communities: Brexit

Political polarisation in the UK has very different characteristics to the US and doesn't play out along political party lines, but I still observed the formation of mega-identities during Brexit. The Vote Leave campaign recognised that economic success and cultural identity are deeply connected. Since the financial crash of 2008, the common person was losing money but the 'perpetrators' of the crisis were getting away scot-free, leading to run-down towns, wage stagnation, increased crime, greater levels of inequality and a cultural split. Terms like the 'haves' and 'have-nots' became widely used to denote two separate groups in society. When 52% of the country voted to leave the European Union, it caused talk of an 'echo chamber' to describe how the political elites in London no longer understood the rest of the country. The 'establishment' were gobsmacked that liberal values and globalisation weren't providing the trickle-down benefits they'd assumed.

Many of my clients were also surprised and had failed to predict the outcome of the Brexit vote in 2016. Despite many of them running constant tracking studies on the mood of the nation, none had seen the signals in the data that suggested a change. In 2017, my team decided to explore these emerging cultural identities to look at what happened, and how this might arise again in the future.

Derby, a city in the East Midlands, represented a classic conundrum for people in the London bubble. The city benefitted from the spoils of globalisation with the likes of Rolls-Royce and Toyota creating large factories around the city, bringing jobs and prosperity to the region. Other businesses followed and the town's population grew 12% in the fifteen years prior to the referendum. The area often voted Labour in general elections, suggesting it had more liberal values. As the city grew, so did the migrant population, and it was generally considered a place where multiculturalism thrived. Over 14% of the city's residents were born outside the UK, with vibrant Polish and Pakistani communities cropping up, supported by shops and places of worship to cater to the needs of the community. All this data prompted analysts to predict a Remain vote as the most likely outcome, as leaving the EU would be a threat to Derby's way of life. Yet 57% of people in Derby voted Leave, higher than the national average.[5]

One year after the referendum, I sent a team of anthropologists up to talk to the residents of Derby, and it became clear this was no accident. The people who had voted to leave still wanted to leave the EU, and those who had voted to remain, still vehemently wanted to remain. The vote divided people across a previously united city: colleagues who had been friends no longer trusted one another, and people questioned the cultural practices of different parts of Derby. A place that previously celebrated diversity now saw difference as a threat.

Derby is both a city, an urban centre with over 250,000 people, and a region, with a network of interconnected villages, each comprising a few thousand inhabitants often separated by farmland, though increasingly connected by small dwellings to deal with an increase in population. Despite this physical connection, many of the towns and villages have kept a strong sense of community with a distinctive subculture, and are often known for a key characteristic, such as the 'old mining town' or the 'Polish area'. As Klein's concept of mega-identities rightly shows, you can't rely on rational responses when asking about voting preferences; you need to look beyond what people are saying. We needed to understand how people *felt*. My team of anthropologists went to chat to people in the streets, talk to shopkeepers, meet people in their homes and hang out in their workplaces.

One of the first places we found ourselves was the local post office in Allenton, one of those villages that had merged with some others. We met Amy, who had worked in the post office for the last fifteen years, and her daughter Lindsay. We chatted to Amy and Lindsay all afternoon, being mindful of the different pace of life in the village.

Amy didn't like politics. She didn't watch the news or read newspapers, and she didn't like people from London (gulp!). If ever customers tried to talk politics, she would change the subject because she said it 'just leads to a debate, and I'm a happy person, I don't need that in my life'. When pushed to define the parties, she felt the Labour party were there to help people on benefits, and the Conservatives were for the middle classes who earned a living (her face gave away which group she fell into), but she hadn't voted in a national election for a long time.

Amy recounted a story from her friend who had been asked by a Muslim colleague not to eat in front of her because she was fasting. Her friend grudgingly obliged and ate elsewhere but felt her freedoms were being curbed by a set of values that didn't come from Derby. Despite this actually happening to her friend, the story held an almost apocryphal status because it described perfectly how the pace of change in Derby was too fast and had become uncomfortable for Amy.

Later we met Hafeez through the mosque at Normanton, an area with a large Pakistani population only two miles away from Allenton. Hafeez felt compelled to describe himself as a 'British Muslim' who has 'integrated into society, even though I don't drink or go to bars', and to tell us that his friends and community are 'law-abiding citizens'. This description was intended to defend himself against any negative perceptions I might have – he was staking out his identity in case I misidentified him.

Hafeez was kind, moral and proud. He told us he had no debt and would always strive to live within his means. He sat on the floor and played with his kids, teaching them life lessons through games and play, and he was very proud to work in the local college. He went to mosque regularly, which he told us was built purely through donations from the local community, a particularly impressive feat considering its size and glamour. But he also felt let down by life and typecast as part of a terrorist community. He believed that abusive comments on social media and by politicians on TV propagated Islamophobia.

The macroeconomic story also alienated Hafeez. Despite working hard and doing well, the college couldn't afford to run all the services it used to. Hafeez's job had been previously done by three people, and while he felt lucky to have kept his role and to have received a below-inflation pay rise each year, he thought they were asking too much of him. All this sat at odds with what he saw in the rest of the world, as he rather bluntly pointed out: 'The corporates get away with it, don't they? Facebook and Starbucks don't pay tax, but I do. We – normal people – we can't do anything about it. Nothing changes.' Hafeez had been taught to get over the injustice to accept, that his morals weren't reflected in society, because that's the way the world worked.

Our next stop was Ilkeston, an old mining town twelve miles away, where we met Julie in the market. Julie was kind and positive, and had a ruddy red face from walking in the hills. She gave us a very frank assessment of the town as we went shopping with her, describing it as a 'mostly white town, apart from the influx of Thai ladies that live with some of the local men'; a generally friendly place to live, 'though I'd never walk down the high street on Friday night'; with a proud mining history, even though 'the last mines closed in 1966, before my time here'. It appeared, through Julie's rose-tinted glasses, that Ilkeston had an identity built more on the glory of the past than the precariousness of the present.

We watched Julie have a chicken-and-egg conversation with herself about whether the local popularity of the British National Party (BNP) meant that no Black or Asian people wanted to live there, or whether it was because no Black or Asian people lived there that the BNP had gained traction. No matter the causation, the facts were the same. But Julie didn't get involved in that side of Ilkeston life; she lived a quiet life with an amusingly opinionated husband, and they had recently discovered the joys of internet shopping and Amazon deliveries.

For all the upbeat spin she put on living in Ilkeston, her biggest complaint came when she said, 'No one plays out in the street any more, or even talks in the street. I can honestly say I only know two people in the street these days, and that's only to say hi to.' Julie's community had developed into a place where she had no friends, and she nostalgically longed for the way things used to be.

I always thought this study must have mirrored the Vote Leave team's research ahead of their Brexit campaign. It painted a picture of people who felt their communities were under threat and their identities undermined. They sought strong values that would help guide them in life, and someone to tell them how to fix it all. And that's pretty much what we saw in their campaign.

## 60 million people, two identities

The Vote Leave campaign initially confused the Remain camp because its main message was the now infamous line 'Take Back Control'. That catchy, three-word quip appealed to people on two levels: as a nostalgic tug for the simplicity and joy of the past and as a 'screw you' to the establishment that had disenfranchised voters and the public through getting lost in a London-centric elitist bubble. Neither had anything to do with leaving the European Union but they essentially hijacked the conversation with an ideology that caused an emotional response. The Leave campaign created five beautifully simplistic slogans that linked a belief system to the campaign, creating two separate identities for people to live by. This was classic identity politics playbook as it helped justify why people should vote Leave:

1. **Our money, our priorities** – was often focused on spending an extra £350 million per week on the NHS, and more control over our taxes.

2. **Take back control of our laws** – directly related to UK vs European law, while giving a nod to the idea of maintaining British values.

3. **Build a fairer, safer immigration system** – directly referenced immigration control, and indirectly referenced that multiculturalism was failing.

4. **Free to trade with the whole world** – talked about trade deals with China but was really suggesting they would sort the economy out.

5. **Leave is a safer choice** – allowed every campaigner to land the 'Take Back Control' message.

Five clear messages, with five underlying, deeper value statements about what's right and wrong in the world. Amy,

Hafeez, and Julie were all very different from one another, but they all voted to leave the EU. All three of them felt that the country was changing for the worse, and they were part of the 'have-nots' in society. The message of 'Take Back Control' appealed to them on a deeper, emotional level, and that emotional affinity was backed up with a rational reason to justify their position. Amy voted to leave the EU because she thought immigration had gone too far, and she wanted a 'fairer, safer immigration system'. Hafeez was sick of an apparently corrupt system, so believed that the UK should have control of 'our money, our priorities'. And Julie voted to leave because she wanted 'free trade with the whole world' after a poorly performing economy had decimated Ilkeston. All of them preferred the past to the future and wanted their community to improve, which meant they also wanted to take back control.

Amy, Hafeez, and Julie were now firmly against the London metropolitan elites and all the other snooty bastards who had condescended to them. The country had formed two entirely sperate mega-identities that would break friendships, families and relationships. Remain voters were typecast as 'Remoaners', someone who was bitter and wanted revenge after the result. And by equal measure, Leave voters were characterised as racist, bigoted and stupid. Neither of these positions were true, but when faced with a public attack it entrenched people's positions ever further and made it impossible for people to change their minds. As we saw in the US, their votes were no longer simply a political preference but an entire belief system and identity.

Brexit tribalism arose because many of Britain's communities were broken, and people wanted to fix them. The Brexit campaign gave people a belief system and identity that allowed them to imagine a country with thriving communities – a nostalgic view of the past that has become part of the populist playbook. In reality, the promises of the Leave campaign weren't going to deliver for Britain's broken communities, but they at least recognised that the lack of community was a resonant campaign message. The division lasted long enough to cause social and political problems but not long enough to polarise the country permanently. Ultimately, those factions didn't have the historical and cultural power to persist. The presence of multiple political tribes in the UK means Brits are exposed to many more points of view on the same topics, whereas the tribalism in America has been concentrated into two opposing camps.

## The culture war tribes

Another divisive area of political and social polarisation is how people align with the term 'woke', and the arguments that flow from it. Popularised in America during the civil rights movement of the 1960s, being woke referred to someone who would 'remain awake through a great revolution', to quote Martin Luther King Jr. Being woke started from a desire to encourage healthy forms of diversity through allowing marginalised communities some form of equity, and to prevent power structures emerging that were punitive to particular communities. But the term was then adopted by those taking a more dogmatic stance, which now includes reprimanding those who use exclusionary language or display abusive behaviour. To the woke enlightened, this is part of the progress of society and overcoming inequality. To the anti-woke, it is judgemental and moralistically punitive. And because it sits at the heart of many Western values, it is a central tenet of the culture wars.

An Ipsos poll in 2023 found that 32% of people believe being called woke is a compliment, whereas 40% of people would perceive it as an insult.[6] What's more, that split falls out very neatly across party lines, with nearly half of Democrats believing it is a compliment and a majority of Republicans believing it is an insult. In essence, one man's word for social justice is another man's word for political correctness gone mad.

The woke vs anti-woke fight isn't just over political correctness or pronouns. It's a deep cultural war over how morality is defined, who gets to define it and whether our collective future looks more like a healing circle or a boot camp for resilience. While the term 'woke' might be going out of fashion (and is now primarily used almost exclusively by the anti-woke set), the battle of beliefs sits neatly at the heart of many of the culture wars, a set of arguments about everything from gender identification to vaccination status, and whether religious clothing should be worn in public, or statues of controversial figures should be taken down. Unsurprisingly, the definition of wokeness is also contested, with 78% of Democrats believing it means 'being informed, educated on, and aware of social injustices', compared to 56% of Republicans describing it as 'being overly political correct and policing others' words'. As sports broadcaster Gary Lineker rather innocently exclaimed, 'What is woke? Having a conscience, having a heart, having empathy? How is that a bad thing?' Personally, I like the definition proffered by Jon Ronson, a journalist who plotted the culture wars in America before anyone knew they were coming: 'The things people shout about online.'

The culture wars are often used by politicians to create divisions in areas where they know the electorate will be emotively divided, but which actually make little difference to the economic, structural or administrative running of the country. In 2015 in the UK, gender reassignment therapy was debated endlessly in the press and parliament and became a classically divisive culture war, yet the cost of gender reassignment therapy to the NHS stood at £17 million, which is 0.01% of government health spending, and affected just under 900 people nationally.[7]

By contrast, the Carer's Allowance, a benefit paid to 1.2 million people who provide crucial care for the elderly and disabled, barely got a mention in the press or a debate in parliament, and in the same year cost the UK government £3.15 billion.[8] The issues that activate an emotive response serve as a distraction from the more troubling policy decisions that the government doesn't want to discuss.

Culture wars are very hard to de-escalate. Whether you consider yourself woke or not, or whether you think it is a compliment or an insult, it is a term that solidifies two oppositional factions. There isn't a third option in a culture war, and the oppositional nature often means each camp inaccurately describes the other camp to the point of antagonism, making de-escalation look like submission. The Brexit Leavers and Remainers typecast each other so badly that it took ten years for the debate to dissipate. Democrats and Republicans have intractable views of each other, to the point where few have relationships.

When Trump took office for the second time in 2025, he quickly signed an executive order targeting 'illegal' DEI practices in both the public and private sectors. This was vague in scope but clear in intent – it was part of the culture war against woke organisations and 'elitist' institutions like Harvard and Princeton Universities. The DEI battle is fertile ground for a culture war as each side gets increasingly animated in the debate about social justice or universal human truths. The executive order was not one of economics, infrastructure, national security or anything else that matters to the future security of the United States – it was a move to establish moral superiority while riding a wave of political success.

Culture-war camps become ever more hard-line when a link is created between a belief system and an identity. Being on the other side of the cultural divide isn't just about supporting a different team or voting differently in the polling booth; it's more about sacred values vs sacrilege, virtue vs authenticity, and redemption vs resistance. The polarisation around woke politics and culture wars shows how belief systems and identity can become hyper-aligned, even when the realities of community are ambiguous, manipulated or marginalised.

- ▲ **Identity** – Woke identities are rooted in empathy, allyship and moral vigilance (e.g. 'having a conscience' or being attuned to injustice). In contrast, anti-woke identities see themselves as defenders of authenticity and freedom, resisting what they perceive as moral overreach and self-censorship. These identities thrive as people feel they need to wear their moral position as a badge of honour.

- ■ **Belief systems** – At the heart of the divide lies a clash over what constitutes justice and who has moral authority. Woke belief systems prioritise equity, inclusion and historical redress, whereas anti-woke frameworks elevate personal responsibility, free speech and cultural tradition. These belief systems are symbolically sacred to their respective sides and evoke fierce emotional responses, especially in debates over DEI, education or national identity.

- ● **Community** – Despite being framed as mass movements, both woke and anti-woke camps often reflect fragmented or imagined communities. The woke are seen to create institutional allies (e.g. DEI offices), while the anti-woke fuel suspicion of elite liberal institutions. Yet both communities are less cohesive in real life than they appear in political rhetoric, often exaggerated by media or weaponised by politicians for polarising effect.

The culture war around wokeness is a full cultural schism where identity and belief reinforce each other, but the lack of supportive community to reinforce these ideas has prevented a full-scale cultural take-over.

## SO WHAT?
## Using communities to mediate tribalism in life, business and society

Cultural polarisation drives people into some stark identities that shape the way they live. More often than not, these identities are rooted in some dogmatic beliefs that don't allow room for shades of grey – people either believe in hierarchy or redistribution, libertarian free speech or moral censorship, and whether the state should protect you or you should protect yourself. In reality, most situations require a nuanced response based on the situation, but tribalism doesn't allow for that. Tribalism becomes problematic when it moves from 'difference' to 'othering', which allows our belief systems to drive our identity, rather than letting our community drive our identity. It's actually quite hard to hate the Tottenham fans who live three miles up the road because I know people who are Tottenham fans, and they have faces, names and families. It's easier to hate an activist who's campaigning for direct action of one kind or another because they're less likely to be part of my community, so they become a faceless moron who's easy to cast aside.

Polarisation means we are unable to change our minds even when the facts change around us, because we have signed up to unilateral thinking. When businesses are stagnating under red tape and taxation, Democrats campaign for more state support. A Black man is beaten to death on the street by police officers, yet Republicans deny racial profiling by the police. The Leave campaign lies about giving £350 million weekly to the NHS, but Leave voters don't seem to care. When we move from *difference* to *polarisation*, holding on to what we believe becomes more important than a reasoned position. We are no longer fighting over what is right; we are fighting over who wins the argument because it's a fight for our beliefs to even exist.

In life, we all want to belong and feel part of a group, but at times, polarisation defines our friends and enemies for us. Communities are the cultural hubs for belonging and support, naturally moderating polarising temperaments due to their peer-to-peer nature. Where communities work well, they give people an identity that's more important than a belief, like when people support their local sports team or join the book or running groups that exist all around us. Embracing new groups in our communities is the key to seeing and accepting that differences are positive rather than negative, and if you need to break out of your bubble, go to the local rugby game instead of football, or join the wild swimming group. Communities feed identities through creating a sense of belonging that transcends political beliefs.

In business, workplaces are communities that can foster a shared sense of purpose and social norms. Many organisations are often criticised for 'group think', a homogenous way of thinking and being that's akin to corporate polarisation. This is a problem for anyone new entering the workforce, as well as for the product or service that the company offers, which will inevitably reflect the worldview of the people creating them. Corporate polarisation and group think are bad for business: they mean people miss the blind spots and can't understand constructive criticism. Hiring for difference is an act many companies say they do in relation to gender, class, ethnicity, sexuality – but in reality, they rarely deliver on the promise of creating diversity of thought. Businesses that hire for a diversity of beliefs will ensure that employees don't base their work identity on a homogenous belief system, and will instead use the workplace community as a source of corporate identity. When people love working for a company because the people are great, that's when you know you have a more inclusive culture.

In society, Republicans are linked to being conservative, and Democrats are linked to being liberal. Londoners are seen as left-wing, and the shires are seen as right-wing. Men's football fans are seen as aggressive, and women's football fans are seen as supportive. None of these associations need to be true, but it's an easy cultural picture for politicians, podcasters and influencers to paint. Creating communities that moderate polarising debates on a societal level requires political will and public investment, both of which are in short supply these days.

# 7

# Social Silences Create Social Consequences

During my divorce, therapy helped me find a way not to hate the person I had loved for so many years. During the stress of my break-up, being able to talk about all the complicated and conflicting emotions that were swirling around my head was a great way to get my thoughts into the open. Having therapy meant I could create a solid relationship with my ex-wife, the mother of my children, so my kids had consistent, loving parents who were acting in unison across two homes.

Therapy could have helped me a lot when I was thirteen, after my dad died unexpectedly at the age of thirty-six. I remember being emotionally paralysed, unsure how I was supposed to feel. I watched the world going past, surrounded by grieving adults who blamed each other for the unnecessary death of my dad. Therapy, with its focus on tackling emotional upheaval from all angles, would have helped me at least recognise the emotions I had, even if they were incredibly painful to confront.

In both of these moments I needed a way of talking about what was going on in my head. Saying the words 'divorce' or 'death' is the first stage in processing what's happened and eventually enables you to move from basic feelings like being sad, through to more specific emotions like being lonely, isolated and abandoned.

Talking therapies help people realise how corrosive secrets can be – silence really can be deadly. Five years before my dad died, I went on holiday to Australia with my mum and stepdad. I was enormously bitter about this new man intruding in my life.

I sulked from the moment we got there, showed no enthusiasm for the beaches, whale-watching trips or bush adventures, and ruined the holiday for everyone. Whenever I was asked what the matter was, I would mumble that I was 'fine' or say, 'Nothing, why do you keep asking?'

My mum decided to bide her time and asked me again when she was driving, when there was no eye contact between us (which is always the best time to ask big questions people find difficult to answer). I eventually mentioned that I had a 'bad thought' that I couldn't possibly say, and it was making me feel sad. That thought took two more days to materialise (my poor parents!) and on the last day of the holiday I said that I wished my stepdad was dead. Obviously, I didn't *really* mean I wanted him dead, and pretty much as soon as I'd said it, I cheered up! Saying the words out loud was like a release valve on a pressure cooker. I realised how daft my bad thought was, and I was suddenly able to relax and enjoy myself. I was immediately able to talk about the difficulties of my new family setup, and even acknowledge the upside of it too. Unfortunately, I'd guarded this painful little secret until the end of the holiday and all we had to look forward to was the twenty-four-hour flight home.

### Social silences start with secrets

Secrets are often about denial. Denying a truth about yourself has personal consequences, and denial on a societal level has social consequences. Collective denial in a family or organisation or even on a global level reveals a set of taboos which are embedded in the rules of culture that guide you through life. Interactions between friends, colleagues and strangers are all designed to avoid social silences, and norms quickly become apparent when someone bends those rules.

In Harry Potter, wizards and witches refused to say the name Voldemort because they believed it increased his power. But it was actually denying his existence that made him stronger as people became ever more fearful of that which couldn't be talked about. Social silences push undesirable behaviours underground, where they go unscrutinised and unchallenged until they rear their head as a powerful force.

Social silences are embedded in our language, behaviours and social media feeds, and are often hidden in plain sight. Many modern cultures find death difficult to talk about, and the UK is no exception: we are societally bad at end-of-life planning, including discussing difficult choices like Do Not Resuscitate orders and funeral arrangements. Having a 'good death' or a 'bad death' is also a topic most people dare not discuss. Over half of adults in the UK do not have a will in place,[1] despite it being a very straightforward practice with enormous benefits to those left behind. The silence around death makes it hard to grieve because people have few opportunities to discuss their loss. The underlying cultural implication is that the person who has died should be forgotten, only remembered when we visit their grave or in similarly isolated moments when we are allowed to express grief. Many of these issues could be solved if death was a normal topic of conversation.

Ageing is another common social silence that leads to loneliness. According to the charity Age UK, more than a million people over the age of 75 will go a whole month without talking to a friend, neighbour or family member.[2] This level of social isolation isn't dissimilar to solitary confinement in prison, yet we ignore older people because we prefer to deny there's a problem. This isolation has huge health implications and is reflected in how societies are structured: our social centres (cafés, pubs, restaurants) don't accommodate the needs of older people, our workplaces do not appreciate the views of older people, and our family structures have become so geographically diverse that grandparents have little opportunity to contribute to the family.

Money is another topic that people often like to keep secret. The Brits are particularly awful at talking about money because it is baked into our class system. The upper classes believe that talking about money is crude, like airing your dirty laundry in public. The British middle classes can be a perilous identity, as they aspire to expensive upper-class trappings but don't have the pay cheque to follow through. As a result, they double down on financial denial and attempt to signal they've 'made it' through buying fancy stuff. Talking about money for the middle classes is somewhere between rude and utterly exposing. The working classes regularly talk about their income with one another, partly because it can be precarious and changeable, and partly because it drives many of their daily decisions. What isn't discussed among the working classes is debt, because it's a sign of mismanagement and poor discipline in a community brimming with pride. Not talking about our finances further embeds inequality. If you don't know how much someone else earns, how could you possibly make it fairer?

The social norms embedded in our communities have restricted these conversations to such a large degree that we aren't able to develop our thoughts coherently on the topics, and not discussing these issues can lead to debt, pain and unresolved grief.

### Social silences are culturally defined

Cultural taboos are very different around the world: relatives tell family members how fat they've become in Italy and China as a sign of affection, Germans discuss the health of their poo, and Brazilians talk about their desire for plastic surgery. When it comes to important topics, like death and grieving, the world is a varied place. Throughout the year, and particularly during the Day of the Dead, Mexicans acknowledge that dying is one of the only certainties in life. The deceased are gone but not forgotten, as friends and family will continue talking to their departed loved ones, allowing them to grieve continuously and openly.

In China, older adults often live near, or even with, their children, reinforced by the Confucian concept of *xiào*, filial piety and respect for one's elders. Children and grandchildren often seek the opinions of elderly family members, and grandparents often play a large role in childcare (in Shanghai, a particularly progressive and highly populated city, the percentage of children being raised either partially or entirely by grandparents is as high as 88%).[3] Beyond family duties, retirement in China is also a very social time of life. Every morning and evening, huge numbers of retirees gather in local parks to go line dancing (younger generations have been known to complain about them as a nuisance), and they can often be found in town squares playing mah-jong for hours on end. The societal default in China is not isolation of the elderly but inclusion.

In the US, a 2024 survey by the banking app Chime revealed that on average it took couples nearly eight months to reveal their salary to one another,[4] whereas in China, it is common to ask about salaries on a first date. While this says as much about the Chinese approach to dating as it does about financial silences, it showcases that when a silence doesn't exist, the conversation can appear everywhere. The joy of cross-cultural anthropology is that it reveals what is hidden in plain sight. It allows us to see what is normal in other countries so that we can question whether a behaviour is abnormal in our own country and find solutions to correct it.

## No sex please, we're British

The Brits are considered to be one of the most buttoned-up, bumbling, socially awkward cultures on the planet, who can successfully avoid talking about anything uncomfortable through a series of guttural noises. When it comes to sex, Brits classically rely on double-entendres and a smutty laugh, which does them no favours in terms of sexual development. As a junior researcher, I was sent to understand the health needs of residents in south-west Essex. The local NHS trust asked me to run four separate projects to 1) increase immunisation, 2) reduce obesity levels, 3) reduce binge drinking and 4) improve sexual health. I quickly found the last two topics were intricately linked.

I spent so much time trying to have honest conversations with eighteen-year-olds about how many partners they'd had, and whether they had safe sex. I tried all the tricks – going for a drive, walking in the park, drinking cups of tea, going through photos on Facebook – but they just wouldn't open up about their sex lives. Then I started the binge drinking project, and I got all the answers about sexual health that I was looking for. Aron was going out with his mate Davey's sister; Davey, who was fine with the situation (mostly), was having a strange relationship with an older woman 'who just wanted him for sex'. They sniggered about how embarrassing it was when they heard each other in the next bedroom, and being able to identify partners based on their sounds. Most of them had condoms in their wallets ('well, you never know'), but hardly any of them used them regularly. Why? 'Well, it's just a bit weird, stopping and then starting again.'

How did they find their various partners over the years? It always started with a drink. If you live in a nation where people can only talk about sex when they're drunk, it is highly likely that the first time you have sex, you'll also be drunk. And if you're drunk when you first have sex, you're less likely to talk about contraception, which leads to problems with sexual health. When I conducted the research back in 2009, alcohol was regarded as the only way to overcome the social silence around sex.

Later in the project I went back to talk to some of the contributors who had taken me drinking and clubbing to discuss the role of love and intimacy. I saw Davey on a Saturday morning, and true to form, he was hungover (which is another good moment for a revealing chat). He'd split up with the older girlfriend because she'd caught him watching porn. Whether it was the awkwardness or moral outrage, she had finished the relationship and stopped answering his calls. He was clearly upset about the incident, and this was a moment he could talk to a random anthropologist that he might never see again.

What I realised was that she was probably the first person in the world who explicitly knew he watched porn. And I was the second. I asked him what he got from porn and he said he watched it because he couldn't do everything he wanted to do with his girlfriend, but then he qualified it by saying he'd never asked her either. Watching porn was Davey's secret, a moment when he could think freely about sex, about the positions he liked, and the level of intimacy he wanted. Porn was there for him because he couldn't talk to his partner about sex.

It's also rare to talk about sex in the United States, Germany, China and even France. The Italians, Spanish, Mexicans and Brazilians talk about it more, but even they don't say it all. We create secrets out of one of the most human desires there is. Using alcohol to talk about one of our base human desires seems like a basic and unhealthy solution – and one that may become problematic in the future, given the increasing levels of sobriety among young people (which we'll discuss later).

## Porn as a social consequence

The pornographic magazines of the 1970s are quite different to the internet porn industry today, which is conservatively estimated to be worth $15 billion a year in the US alone (by contrast, Hollywood is worth $11 billion per year).[5] The reason this enormous, unfettered, poorly regulated and highly abusive industry has been allowed to grow so fast is for one simple reason: we don't know how to talk about sex. And the social silence around sex is amplified tenfold when it comes to porn.

The explosion of porn started in 2010 when Fabian Thylmann, a tech whizz-kid, created what he described as 'YouTube for porn' – websites where porn was completely free. Fifteen years later, Pornhub (the largest site) gets about 928 million unique views per month,[6] 115 million viewers every day,[7] with about 11% of the American population viewing daily![8] When is the most popular time of the week for people to watch Pornhub? Monday morning. Go figure... Revenue is generated through advertising, and the content is uploaded by anyone – professional, amateur or covertly filmed. The move completely changed the industry as it became so much easier to watch porn, making everyone's secret sexual desires even easier to satisfy.

The success of Thylmann's empire was driven entirely from a tech point of view. The website and storage of videos were easy to use, the advertising flashed in a banner above the videos, and the content was all tagged and easy to search. He hired tech whizz-kids who ran search engine optimisation (SEO) analysis that found which words viewers were searching for – 'schoolgirl', 'cheerleader', 'orgy', etc. – meaning that Thylmann's tech team could instruct porn producers to create videos called *Schoolgirl, cheerleader orgy* to reflect what people wanted. To stay in the game, the production houses complied, and all of a sudden, whatever sexual secret someone typed into the search bar of a porn site was then being made in the porn studio, by real people. If the internet is an outlet for people to explore their secrets, Thylmann had created a world where those secrets had real social consequences.

Making films that focused on users' fetishes then changed what the porn actors had to do. It was no longer enough to have their picture taken in a mini skirt and bunny ears for a magazine that sat on the top shelf in a newsagent – the industry had moved on. Porn actors now have to list out the fetishes they are willing to perform on their CV, and the list is long and beyond what most people are comfortable doing in real life. This drive for more fetishised porn has been driven by people typing their fantasies into search engines, which results in porn actors performing the most explicit acts imaginable.

While many production houses are legal and sex positive, there is also a large set of rogue, illegal and sexually abusive porn production units. A lot of the porn on these websites involves women being strangled, gagged, slapped and ejaculated on while being called degrading names. Some of the women are drugged and kept against their will. The consequence of imagining a misogynistic sex act can now directly lead to it being performed in a dark basement, with minimal levels of consent.

Given that this content is on a website designed to be 'YouTube for porn', it's not a surprise that young people are watching this content too. Common Sense Media – a US organisation lobbying for tighter controls to protect children online – found that 73% of children had watched pornography online before the age of eighteen (the legal age for accessing these websites), more than half (54%) of them by the age of thirteen.[9] In the same survey, 45% of thirteen- to seventeen-year-olds claimed that pornography had given them 'helpful information about sex'. In a world where we remain silent about sex, kids are turning to porn as a form of sex education – and it's probably not an education most parents are happy about.

For digital natives, online porn is not novel, it is ambient. These young people are not watching the same porn their parents might have stumbled across; they are entering a highly curated world where sexual content is shaped around unfettered curiosity. Given this is how they learn, young men increasingly tie their sexual worth to performance, measured in endurance, dominance and the ability to replicate acts seen online. They are learning that pleasure is not about connection but conquest. Young women, meanwhile, are told their bodies are available for scrutiny, no matter whether they scream yes or no.

Porn is creating very basic gendered identities, with boys comparing clips in WhatsApp groups and girls swapping horror stories of what's expected of them. And everything that's cultural feeds other areas of culture. TikTok, Instagram and Snapchat do not host porn, but they are rife with porn-adjacent codes, with pictures that mimic pornographic framing: lips pursed, slow-motion hip turns set to moody audio. Teens don't have to search for porn to internalise its logic; they can see it on more public forums and they understand the meaning.

One of the most shocking parts of this description is the complete lack of ethics. As a starting point, consent, mutual respect and reciprocity are all missing, let alone the role of love and intimacy. On-the-go streaming of degrading content erodes the basic moral code for healthy relationships, and the result is a generation that know the positions but are illiterate in intimacy. Until we offer young people safe spaces to learn what is natural, and unlearn what the internet has taught them, silence will continue to write the story.

Social silences and digital platforms have unwittingly colluded through online porn to shape harmful belief systems and rigid gender identities, all in the absence of grounded, healthy community values.

- ▲ **Identity** – Young people, especially boys, are forming sexual identities based on performance, domination and pornographic mimicry, while girls internalise objectification and fear. These identities are not chosen but inherited through ambient exposure to content that often equates intimacy with conquest and submission.

- ● **Community** – Rather than providing support or connection, online porn communities operate in isolation from mainstream social oversight. They reinforce sex that's performative and exploitative while silencing mutual care or sensual exploration. These aren't naturally forming communities; they are algorithmically driven echo chambers that operate in the shadows.

- ■ **Belief systems** – Pornography's logic rewrites the moral code around sex: consent, reciprocity and intimacy are replaced by spectacle, power and repetition. In a society unwilling to speak openly about sex, tech entrepreneurs and search engines have stepped in to define a new set of sexual values.

The consequences for young people are shocking but not surprising:

- — 19% of high school kids (aged thirteen to eighteen) in the US say they have experienced sexual violence while in a relationship[10] (for comparison, that's higher than the number of children that vape, at 5.9%[11] – though media attention might lead you to believe otherwise).

— Male teens who viewed violent pornography were more than three times as likely to perpetrate sexual dating violence compared to those who hadn't.[12]

— 10% of women in the UK reported having experienced non-consensual sex, half of whom experienced this under the age of eighteen.[13]

What makes sex and pornography different from topics like death and ageing is Fabian Thylmann (and all others like him). Online communities can pop up quickly, out of sight from mainstream society, and can influence vast swathes of people with irresponsible consequences. While naturally occurring communities often create safe spaces for everyone to feel accepted, online porn communities create a set of social norms that can be abusive. It's a grim anthropology of the digital age, where what is not said becomes encoded into people's identity and belief systems through what is created by tech whizz-kids looking to make money.

## How toxic masculinity emerged as an online community

One of the paradoxes of the internet is that it is a place where you can say whatever you like, but in reality, you only end up saying it to the people who agree with you (unless you seek trolls on social media). News outlets like the *Guardian* or *New York Times* end up preaching to the liberally converted, whilst there's little crossover with those who read the *Daily Telegraph* or *Wall Street Journal*, who write for a conservative op-eds crowd. When social media first started, you could hear all sorts of divided opinions because free speech was a central tenet of the platforms, but in time their algorithms grew to keep opposing views apart, creating echo chambers. The internet is a series of communities with different moral codes, and even though content is free for anyone to read, the reality is that people rarely read anything beyond their bubble. Our social silences – the things we believe are taboo – have been hidden from us by algorithms that promote content we 'like'.

Following the success of the #MeToo movement, the shaving brand Gillette decided it needed to change strategy. Gillette was a brand that had seemingly been around forever and was associated with strong chins, six-packs and adverts in which women affectionately stroked their clean-shaven men. But brands need to be where the culture is going, and in 2019 they ran an advert directly challenging toxic masculinity. It featured images of rough-and-tumble kids, predatory young men leering at women, and boardrooms where women were being put down and patronised. It then ran with the tagline 'Is this the best a man can be?' followed by images of men calling out men, and dads suggesting that boys shouldn't fight, while also referencing the importance of the #MeToo movement. This was a big-budget move from Gillette to position itself as part of a progressive cultural movement, portraying men in a more modern manner, and it was a hat tip to woke culture's continued drive for diversity.

The campaign bombed. The advert was viewed over 2 million times in forty-eight hours, complaints went through the roof, videos of men throwing their razors down the toilet went viral on social media and the campaign was condemned as 'feminist propaganda'. Men who bought Gillette razors were quite traditional, and they liked men to be strong and assertive. Men who didn't buy Gillette razors were never going to like Gillette, and to them the advert was marketing fluff trying to cover up its misogynistic past. In a single advert, they had alienated both sides of the cultural divide. It's been claimed that in 2020, they lost an estimated 8% market share to their competitors, which equated to $350 million in sales.[14]

On average, men earn nearly 20% more than women in America[15] and have over 30% more invested for their retirement,[16] and some estimates put the wealth gap (which includes assets and savings) at nearly double.[17] Men are considerably less likely to be the victim of violent or sexual assault, domestic abuse or stalking. Men are less likely to be interrupted when speaking and are given more physical space in public. There's an unattributed saying: 'When you're accustomed to privilege, equality feels like oppression.' By every metric in American culture, men have greater privilege than women, but for those who got upset about the Gillette advert, it didn't feel that way. My team looked into toxic masculinity and what it meant for young people today. What we found shocked us. According to the data, young men were still in a position of privilege and power over women but were feeling the pinch of tough economic times. Those we interviewed felt lost and didn't know what they could and couldn't say, or how to act. They felt stuck between the rock of wanting to be an assertive man but not having the agency, and the hard place of knowing the world had changed.

Women, on the other hand, had been hearing empowering messages for decades, LGBTQ+ communities were finding their voice, and some modern men were feeling comfortable enough to wear nail polish and carry a handbag. In this context, being a *real man* wasn't so easy as they didn't know how to assert their power, and feminist discourse often made them feel like they'd done something wrong. Others felt that the muscles they'd spent time building up no longer carried the same social status. The real world had become hard to navigate, and these insecure young men were looking online to find their place. Many found guidance in the 'manosphere', a digital community that promotes masculinity and misogyny, and opposes feminism.

We spent months poring over the manosphere and an anthropologist on my team went undercover, creating a new

Instagram persona to follow a range of the misogynistic influencers. The content that filled her feed was a tirade of gender essentialism (the belief that men and women act according to predictable, biological reasons), longing for a day when men were strong protectors and women would fall helplessly into their arms. Her new persona received a lot of advice. On dating: 'Touching a woman inappropriately on the first date will get you further than not touching her at all'; on making money: 'The power that makes you a man is the power that makes you succeed in business'; on how to channel her emotions: 'Anger is the most powerful emotion for men. Left untouched and it turns into depression. Transmuted and it can build empires.' She quickly found that this content was largely targeted at young, impressionable kids, and a primary school teacher we spoke to described how ten-year-old children had said things like 'make me a sandwich' and 'get back in the kitchen' to their female teachers. Whether the ten-year-olds were hearing it on social media or from older siblings or parents, the toxic online community was infiltrating schools.

After spending so many years in the shadows, these views have now crept into the mainstream. An Ipsos survey in 2024 found that 59% of men think gender equality has gone too far in the UK, and we are now discriminating against men.[18] I'll let that one sit there for a moment – over half of men in the UK don't recognise that they are likely to be paid more than women, do less housework than women, be safer walking the streets than women. But opinions can be reality in the eye of the beholder, and you start to see a dangerous pattern emerge when more powerful groups in society feel like they're under attack.

Many people might be shocked at the rise of Andrew Tate (an openly misogynistic online influencer), yet the same survey showed that 21% of men age sixteen to twenty-nine who know about his content, agree with it.[19] While 21% isn't a majority, it is a large enough group who feel like Andrew Tate can bring back whatever it is they've lost at the expense of women's liberation. The problem we found wasn't that all of them wanted to be Tate, but the appeal was that he demonstrated a level of freedom from social norms, refusing to be silenced by feminists or activists. Young men clearly felt they couldn't express their 'outdated' view of masculinity freely so they took their views underground, to the internet.

These online conversations don't just stay in an online community: the repetitive nature of scrolling through manosphere content infiltrates what people believe and how they see themselves. A 2025 Ipsos poll highlighted this point, showing that men believe women prioritise attractiveness (50%) and financial status (39%) in a potential partner, whereas women themselves say they consider a sense of humour (60%) and kindness (53%) as the most important values.[20] To be clear here, men believe that women want two things in a potential partner that are actually very hard to change (attractiveness, wealth), and they tend to ignore what women really want in a partner (laughs, kindness). And given it's never discussed, the gender divide is morphing into a cultural divide.

The shock of the manosphere, brought to light by the 2025 Netflix show *Adolescence*, was that it was an otherwise hidden community, where the normalisation of misogyny was only visible to those who entered it. Over time, that normalisation fed into the belief systems of those who engaged with the manosphere, making them believe that the world was stacked against them. Once those beliefs were embedded, it became part of people's identity, emerging in everyday behaviours that resulted in abuse and even murder (as dramatised in *Adolescence*). The content posted on the manosphere is deliberately designed to change culture from a community-driven perspective and alter the belief systems of young men in order to influence their identity.

In this ecosystem, belief systems are tailored to shape identity, and digital communities serve not as places for growth but as echo chambers that harden cultural positions into personal truths.

- ▲ **Identity** – Many young men, uncertain about their role in a changing social landscape, construct identities around outdated masculine ideals – strength, dominance, stoicism – framing feminism as an existential threat. These identities feel embattled and are reactive, not aspirational.
- ● **Community** – The manosphere acts as a refuge for these uncertain men, offering a sense of belonging through shared grievance and gender essentialism. Unlike visible, democratic spaces, this digital cave is a place where misogyny can be rehearsed without challenge and passed down to younger boys.
- ■ **Belief systems** – These communities promote a worldview in which gender equality is seen as discrimination against men. The belief that male power is natural and under siege becomes a foundational narrative, one that reimagines victimhood as resistance and aggression as empowerment.

These issues were not created in the manosphere, but what was once a small ember in real life suddenly exploded into a huge blaze online – all because it was initially silenced. Telling online communities of men to change their attitudes will never fix the issue. Young men feel let down, frustrated at not finding a job, and have a sense of dissatisfaction and unhappiness with their lives. Instead of voicing this out loud, they have found an online community that makes them feel heard and tells them who to blame. The best way to overcome that and create a more harmonious culture is to offer them a better community to go to, which is unlikely to be online given the current structure of the internet.

## Social silences are public health issues

In 2003, George W. Bush committed $15 billion dollars to the President's Emergency Plan for AIDS Relief (PEPFAR) to supply antiretroviral drugs to people who had contracted HIV. In 2007 he doubled the funding to $30 billion, giving 4.5 million people access to the drug, predominantly in Africa and the Caribbean. PEPFAR is the largest commitment by any nation to address a single disease (excluding Covid-19), remaining stable through the three subsequent presidents. Since the late 1990s, post-exposure prophylaxis (PEP) treatments for HIV had transformed people's life chances in America, and the assumption was they were surely going to solve the problem on a global scale.

Yet progress was slow. Identifying people with the virus was not as straightforward as it was in the US. Healthcare agencies were poorly distributed, access was limited, particularly among those most in need, and communication was a blunt tool. PEPFAR and its associated agencies (including the South African government and the Bill and Melinda Gates Foundation) needed to identify where medication was needed most, and their analysis showed South Africa had the largest number of people living with HIV in any country (from 2004, a status it maintained into the 2020s) with over 7.5 million people infected.[21] Our contact at the Gates Foundation laid out the facts for us:

— Incidence rates for HIV in South Africa were estimated to be 20%.

- Over 50% of men who contracted HIV ended up dying of AIDS.
- On average, girls and young women contracted HIV from men who were seven years older than them.
- One third of girls and young women between the ages of fourteen and twenty-four had HIV.
- HIV rates among girls aged fifteen to nineteen were eight times higher than for boys.

The data was alarming and reinforced the widely held stereotype among the healthcare community that young Black men were poor, work-shy, heavy drinkers, violent and promiscuous spreaders of HIV. In this context, two big programmes were put in place to fix the problem: get men to realise the consequence of their actions, and help young women say no to older, predatory men.

State institutions (schools, churches, healthcare centres) started taking young men to AIDS wards, showing and telling them about the consequences of not wearing a condom. Seeing people dying of AIDS was classic shock-and-awe messaging, and in South Africa's highly religious society, it was also very moralistic. Community-based testing centres allowed parents to have healthy conversations with their daughters, giving out free contraception, as well as helping young girls find financial and emotional independence. Breaking the cycle of transmission was centred around scaring men and empowering women.

In 2012, the Bill and Melinda Gates Foundation commissioned my team of anthropologists to figure out how to get men a) tested and b) treated. We spent time with young Black South African men (the 'target audience') in some of the poorest and most troubled areas of South Africa – KwaZulu-Natal, Mpumalanga and Gauteng Province. This wasn't bog-standard market research asking people what they thought about washing detergent; this was one of the thorniest issues that we'd ever been asked to look at. We created several teams in South Africa and embedded ourselves in the community, seeking out locals who would give us a tour of the towns and talking to everyone that we could in the area. We hung out in bars, went to local football matches and drank tea in the street, trying to spend enough time with people so that we could talk to them about something as serious as HIV and AIDS.

We asked where they grew up, who their friends were and which football team they supported. We asked how they earned money, about their relationships and whether they wanted to have children. We found very few of the men had a regular, steady job. When they did earn some money – or worse still, when their partner earned some money – one of their favourite things to do was drink in the local bars. We went to these local, unlicenced shebeens that were selling a mix of legitimate and contraband alcohol. Once we got to know these guys a bit better, the stories of extra-marital relations started to come out too.

But there were also some holes in the stories. They barely ever mentioned Apartheid and the violent struggles of the 1990s. Stories about their childhoods seemed to omit any reference to their fathers, so many of whom died when they were young. When asked, they claimed their fathers had had a cough, or they'd got sick. They all knew about HIV in the community, but none of them ever wanted to talk about it; not with us, not with their wives and definitely not with their lovers.

As any dogged anthropologist would do, we pushed on and realised people knew the answers. Yes, they knew it was transmitted through unprotected sex, but no, they didn't think their lover had HIV because they went to church, and they were plump so didn't look sick. Yes, they knew where to go and get tested, but no, they had never been because that's where sinful people went when they were dying. Yes, they knew that their wives would be livid with them for having an affair, but no, they weren't going to tell them because they would have to get tested and probably divorced. This was a generation of AIDS orphans who had been taught not to talk about AIDS from a young age because it was viewed as an amoral death sentence.

In South Africa, young women started going to the doctor regularly from the age of fourteen or fifteen, where they were encouraged to test for HIV. This meant HIV was detected earlier in women, who were then put on the drugs that suppressed the replication of the virus. Young men were less likely to go to the doctor and were not being prompted to get tested in the same way. When detected late, the virus was already active in the men's bodies, and they were more likely to die. This goes a long way to understanding why young women had a higher incidence rate of HIV but men were dying in much higher numbers. In reality, the incidence rates were likely to be similar, as the majority of the population were heterosexual, and it takes two to tango. It's true that older men were sleeping with younger women, but women said they didn't feel it was predatory: they wanted to have sex too. Being 'underage' was an unknown concept to them, and they felt having an older man was actually quite cool.

Arriving at these findings wasn't easy. Eventually the breakthrough came when a white female anthropologist said, 'I feel sorry for these men.' Life was bloody hard for them: they hadn't been brought up in a place of safety, and they were simply repeating the structural violence learned through years of Apartheid. In a room full of global health experts and experienced anthropologists, it was Ellie from Nottingham who pointed out that these men weren't bad people.

Twenty years after the fall of Apartheid, divisions were rife in South Africa between white and Black communities, rich and poor, urban and rural, Zulu and Xhosa, and between men and women. In building a strategy for how to break the cycle of transmission, the authorities had used the identity of poor, Black men as a proxy for the problem. When hearing our findings, one of the nurses exclaimed, 'Are you telling me I should feel sorry for these drunken cheaters who spread AIDS around my community? What next, are you going to tell me to build empathy with white South Africans?'

Our findings were riddled with social silences, driven largely by decades of societal divisions. We observed three major silences that exacerbated the problem. First, men were unable to speak about their loss of place in society, which left them exposed and vulnerable, with a tendency to lash out. The second silence was that they could not talk about AIDS, which meant they regularly had unprotected sex without any discussion with their partners. And the third most powerful silence of all was that they were scared. They were scared of not being able to provide for their families, they were scared of violence on the street, and they were incredibly scared of dying of AIDS, all of which undermined who they were as strong, proud, free men in a country which had apparently overcome oppression.

As a result of our work, the Gates Foundation decided they needed to break the silences. They introduced a programme called Coach Mpilo (which translates to 'Life Coach') which hired young, Black men who were receiving HIV treatment to train as coaches, tasked with helping young men overcome the fear associated with HIV. Giving a job to someone who is open about having HIV is a huge step in overcoming the cultural taboo and social silence surrounding the topic. The programme started in 2019, with 120 coaches who were able to help over 2,400 men in the pilot stage, with data showing that more than 90% of men either started or restarted treatment, and remained on treatment thereafter.[22]

Fundamentally, the programme helped PEPFAR move

beyond the victim-predator dynamic that was inherent in the cycle of transmission model. Looking at the world through the eyes of young Black men and women showed that they had a very different belief system to those who had been creating the models, and required very different solutions.

This has been one of the most emotionally rewarding pieces of work that my team has worked on, and also a fantastic example of community-based action. Silent topics are either omitted from society (ageing, death, debt) or pushed underground to an unregulated world (porn). However, this community was able to break the cycle of HIV transmission among young men by actually convincing peers within the community to open up about their experiences, leading to frank conversations about HIV and better health outcomes.

### Unhealthy workplaces create silences

Workplaces are a slightly different beast to more naturally forming cultures but are still communities that conform to their own cultural rules. Corporates often have large HR departments that are focused on how to improve company culture to help people work together. The culture serves the corporate need and is often set by various leaders from the CEO down. Many of the rules may be explicit, like how to dress or what time to arrive, but others are harder to decode, like when to speak up in meetings or how to disagree in a healthy manner. In theory, because workplaces manufacture their culture, they should be able to overcome silences. *Should.*

Gillian Tett, the *Financial Times* journalist and advocate of anthropology in business, gained fame as one of the few people who spotted the 2008 financial crash before it happened. In her book *Anthro-Vision*, she described how traders were riding high on trading collateralised debt obligations (CDOs), financial bundles of debt that often contain mortgage debts relating to numerous banks.[23] Given how complicated the bundles were, and how fast financial trading had become, traders never knew what was in each bundle, so they relied on ratings agencies to tell them how reliable the bundles were. Credit ratings could vary from as high as triple A right down to a C or D, which is essentially a junk trade.

In the mid-2000s, CDOs full of mortgage debt were rated as triple A and went like hot cakes. In the United States, people often have three forms of debt: their house, car and credit card. It was assumed that people saw their mortgage as the most important debt to service (because people need somewhere to live), followed by their car (because in the US, everyone has to drive), followed by the credit card (because you can shift credit card debt around). What Tett's anthropological training allowed her to see was two social silences at play. Firstly, she saw that the waterfall of house-car-credit card was largely flipping on its head. Consumers weren't scared of mortgage defaults any more because refinancing deals had become common, but not having a credit card was a real problem as more and more purchases were being made online. But no one in America talks about debt.

As a journalist, she had access to Wall Street's movers and shakers and would constantly ask traders, 'What actually is a CDO?' While they could define it in general terms, they had no idea what kind of mortgages were in the CDOs they were trading. They were in ignorant bliss that many of the CDOs had been stacked with sub-prime mortgages, being paid off by consumers with a particularly poor credit rating. That was, until it all crashed down. Corporate leaders in the banks had created an environment where silences were acceptable. They let their key traders become celebrities in the finance world, celebrating results above all else, awarding them ever bigger bonuses each year. Conversations about due diligence were a bore, and almost anti-banking. The speed at which the banks had to operate created a culture where it was better to ask for forgiveness than permission, meaning risks were part and parcel of everyday work. As whole swathes of people across America defaulted on their mortgages, fund managers and traders didn't know whether it applied to their CDOs as they had never interrogated what was in each bundle. The enormous social silence around debt in America caused one of the largest economic crashes in history. The corporate culture in the banks encouraged a social silence that an anthropologist could see from afar.

In 2010, when many were still licking their wounds, I approached the banks to warn them that all the conditions for another crash were in place. Yes, there had been some tough regulatory changes, but ultimately, the culture was still the same. Even after the financial earthquake of the crash, there were things they still couldn't talk about. Every bank we went to denied there was a problem. In terms of having dealt with the culture that caused the initial crash, I only hope they're right.

## SO WHAT?
### Breaking the silences in life, business and society

If culture is the stuff that sits between us, social silences are the blockages that prevent us connecting. How we talk to each other and what topics we feel able to speak about define the type of community we are part of and the culture we live in. Communities that prevent certain topics being discussed create a form of social denial, which has consequences.

In life and society, we find it difficult to speak about ageing and death, and are unprepared for it when it comes. We think it's rude or wrong to speak about money and debt, and end up in financial trouble without having asked for help. Social silences push those who feel silenced underground to a community that is unmoderated, hidden from the public at large, and can create reactionary movements. We have seen these communities develop in the manosphere, a place where men could normalise thoughts that would be offensive in mainstream culture, creating toxic social norms within that group. The porn community has also remained hidden from view due to our reluctance to speak about it, creating some violent norms around sex, particularly for young couples. In its most extreme form, social silence causes culture to splinter.

In business, silences are everywhere. They are inherent in the phrase 'that's just how we do things round here', a classic response to a new employee that prevents innovation. Blockbuster, the video rental store, laughed Netflix executives out of the room in 2000 when they pitched a partnership. Nokia were knocked off their perch by Apple and Samsung because employees felt there was an atmosphere of fear at senior levels about saying they'd done something wrong. Celebrating past successes meant they refused to take on board the new ways in which people wanted to connect with one another.

The only way to overcome social silences is to ask the awkward questions. Asking whether someone has an STI might be an awkward question, but it's a perfectly legitimate one that might make for a more sexually safe society. Asking an elderly relative whether they've made an end-of-life plan might seem rude and out of place, but it's an important thing to know. Asking people if they watch porn, whether they are lonely, how much money they earn, what they think of the CEO or whether they've thought about leaving their partner are all legitimate questions that, if discussed properly, could lead to a healthier culture. Sure, these topics might seem difficult to broach, and if someone asked you these questions, you might find it hard to answer (which in itself shows how powerful a social silence is), but it would allow us to make more informed decisions.

When social silences lead to social consequences (e.g. addiction, mental health issues, grief, bankruptcy, etc.), people are often rehabilitated in a support group, which are places where they are finally allowed to say the previously unsayable. If we find ways to say the unsayable before the problem occurs, then we'll be living in a healthier, more cohesive culture.

# PART THREE

# THE FUTURE OF CULTURE

Culture and cognition are in a bar watching a couple on a date, both wearing augmented reality glasses.

Cognition says, 'Fascinating. They're using AR to translate each other's body language in real time.'

Culture smirks. 'Or . . . they could just learn to read the room.'

# 8

# How Technology Creates New Rules in Life

On 12 September 1957, James Vicary, an up-and-coming market researcher, assembled a press conference to announce a groundbreaking innovation in advertising. He had created a new way to show adverts that were embedded deep inside films and TV series, he called it 'subliminal advertising'.

Vicary explained, with great excitement, that he had spliced adverts into films that only lasted for a single frame – 1/24th of a second – which he claimed was long enough for the subconscious to process the information but not long enough for the viewer to be aware of it. His experiment had taken place at a cinema in New Jersey over a six-week period, where half of all the films shown at that cinema had the words 'HUNGRY? EAT POPCORN' and 'DRINK COCA COLA' spliced into the films, and the other half of the films played normally. On nights when these subliminal adverts were shown to viewers, sales of popcorn increased by 58% and Coke sales increased by 18%. This, Vicary explained, was the future of advertising as brands no longer needed to create long and costly adverts, and they could instead influence people in subtler, more powerful ways.

The press and public were outraged. At best, the technique was surreptitious, misleading and controversial. At worst, it was an unethical manipulation of the masses without their consent. But the results of Vicary's experiment impressed advertisers and brand managers, who started to embed subliminal images into movies, print and TV adverts. The messages weren't just telling people what they should buy; they included split-second images of semi-nude women or phallic images that appeared in the background to give a brand more allure. Subliminal advertising quickly became a race to the bottom, driven by the idea that sex sells.

In a move to quell public panic, British, American and Australian lawmakers banned the practice in 1958, just one year later, though advertisers felt that Vicary was on to something and quickly found other ways of embedding subtle, often imperceptible images in adverts following the ban. But as time passed, scepticism about the techniques grew among advertisers as sales didn't follow when using Vicary's techniques. Five years later, Vicary eventually admitted that his data might not have been as watertight as he claimed, and he was forced into an apology.

Various control trials have both proven and disproven the effectiveness of subliminal advertising, but brands and advertisers have remained fascinated by the concept. As recently as 2005, following the European Union ban on tobacco advertising in Formula 1, Marlboro pulled off a subliminal advertising coup. Marlboro had been putting its brand and logo all over the Ferrari F1 car for the previous thirty-one years, and it was one of their iconic sponsorship deals. To get round the ban, they created a blurry barcode on the spoiler of the vehicle where the Marlboro logo used to be, which, when speeding past at 200mph, looked undeniably similar to a pack of Marlboro cigarettes. A war of words was traded between the EU and Marlboro, but the barcode stayed as it was within the letter of the law. In 2010, the EU then took a different approach, with its public health commissioner accusing Marlboro of engaging in subliminal advertising, leading to a media storm about whether the barcode was illegal. The unwanted attention was too much for Ferrari who took a strategic decision to remove the barcode, ending the sponsorship deal.[1]

No matter how many control trials conclude that subliminal advertising doesn't work, the idea of communicating in a subliminal manner continues to grip brands and advertisers while making the public and lawmakers anxious about being influenced by small, imperceptible images.

## Social media's subliminal influence

In 2023, I was studying how young people live for a cosmetics company that wanted to target a younger audience. The state of youth is a constant obsession for most brands who often have few young people in their organisation so don't have a clue about what they think. Older generations don't understand younger people because younger people don't want to be understood, and younger people evade the eyes and ears of the old by creating a new language, codewords and memes.

Any report about the state of youth today has a long chapter dedicated to their online world – another area that older people never really understand. My team and I spent hours with young people in the UK and US, flicking through their various social media accounts, showing us who they followed, what they clicked on and the types of videos and images they liked or disliked. The speed at which they could navigate the different social media platforms, dwelling on videos for a fraction of a second and then skipping on to the next one, was impressive. The people in our study averaged 192 minutes every day just on social media. 'Doomscrolling', the act of constantly flicking through social media content for hours on end, exposes people to approximately twenty posts a minute, which, based on the usage times above, is about 3,800 social media posts a day. I want to pause on that for a moment – 3,800 different messages, images or videos, uploaded by a friend, influencer or brand, every single day. Absorbing 3,800 messages every day is a huge volume of content for a young brain. What's more, everyone we spoke to knew what they were doing was bad, and were quick to describe how addictive social media can be – but they also described the buzz they got from Instagram likes as their 'instant-gram' (a reference to cocaine usage).

Compared to Vicary's subliminal adverts, this is a level of influence on a far greater scale. Just like with subliminal adverts, they could not recall all the adverts they had seen. Indeed, after three interspersed hours of social media scrolling, many of the people we met struggled to tell us more than five interesting posts they had seen that day. Social media doomscrolling is probably the most effective form of subliminal advertising that's ever been created, but because the adverts aren't hidden in a surreptitious manner, it lacks the public outrage of Vicary's controlled experiment.

The other big difference between social media doomscrolling and Vicary's subliminal advertising is that social media posts are targeted in a far more effective manner. Everyone in Vicary's cinema was encouraged to buy Coke, whether they liked Coke or not, as it was impossible to target certain groups in the audience. Compare that to social media where micro-targeting allows advertisers to deliver different messages to different people with astonishing accuracy, specifying age (e.g. 18–25), location (e.g. Brooklyn), special interests (e.g. video games), similar brands they've liked (e.g. Puma, Fred Perry) and websites they've visited recently (e.g. Calvin Klein clothing). Social media ads only target people that they know are open to the product and brand, and each advert is specifically tailored to their needs and desires, even though people rarely notice them.

And it works: we saw a correlation between the adverts those young people were exposed to and their brand preferences. When questioned, interviewees were confident the advertising wasn't affecting them (everybody says that!), but in reality, they simply weren't noticing it. Any good social scientist will note that this correlation is not proof that social media advertising affects what young people buy – but it does suggest that the algorithms have effectively learned what each individual buys and wants, without having to ask them. The power of the algorithm is it can show us posts that it knows we will like based on watching how we scroll past twenty posts a minute. In this respect, there are some things that machines probably know about us better than we know ourselves.

Our social media usage isn't our entire life, but it's become an incredibly influential part. When we're on social media, we're engaging with an artificial intelligence (AI) that is both feeding us content *and* learning about us, all at the same time. AI shapes the way we think, feel and act, and because it controls our exposure to certain facts and ideas, it shapes the culture we live in. The linkages between belief systems, community and identity are seamless, partly because, at its core, social media is a powerful community that controls the conversation between people. Social media operates on an attention economy – the more interactions people have, the more time they spend online, which drives greater advertising revenues. Peer-to-peer conversations that are more confrontational are given a louder voice online by AI, meaning that social media becomes a place for activism and dogmatic beliefs.

While the social media foghorn is mostly discussed in regard to activism and extreme beliefs, it is also the most effective town square in which brands can showcase their latest products. In 2022, social media surpassed TV ad spending because the targeted reach and subliminal effects are paying dividends. The ability for brands to change subcultures, getting audiences to become unwitting brand ambassadors for their products, has become so effective on platforms like Instagram and TikTok that it's impossible to ignore. Whereas Vicary's advertising experiment was designed simply to activate a small part of your identity (or physiology!) to buy popcorn, the subliminal nature of social media changes culture on a much deeper level.

If you put this analysis to young people, they shrug – 'Meh, so what – it's good that brands come to me rather than me having to search for them' – and depending on your moral hopes for society, you may or may not agree. Many young people deliberately 'like' certain posts because they want to see more posts from that person or brand in the future – they are actively personalising their algorithm. But the same behaviours and attitudes also apply to current affairs, politics and news, where personalising your algorithm restricts the breadth of knowledge of what's happening in the world. Personalising your algorithm only works when you know what you want to know, which makes sense in consumerist culture but soon becomes dangerously narrow-minded when relating to issues in politics and society.

## Our battle with technology: how booze lost and beauty won

Jonathan Haidt, a highly respected social psychologist and author of *The Anxious Generation*, has suggested that the combination of mobile phones and social media usage is the biggest threat to child wellbeing, bar none.[2] The core of his thesis is that young human brains cannot keep up with social media algorithms that are designed to keep people scrolling, meaning that young people become addicted to the dopamine hit of constantly seeing fresh content. Simultaneously, people feel (and often are!) watched throughout the day as they regularly upload recordings of their behaviour to social media (a modern-day version of Foucault's panopticon). This sense of constantly being watched plays havoc with the teenage desire to experiment. Experimentation with different identities or rebelling against their parents often requires people to be out of the watchful eye of other people. Experimentation requires making mistakes, being silly and discovering where the boundaries are by occasionally going too far. Before smartphones, there was one commonly tried-and-tested technique for testing boundaries: alcohol.

Alcohol became a rite of passage for many teenagers and young adults – it enabled rebellion against parents and cheekily breaking the law (when underage), and the inebriation allowed young people to try a new identity for the night. Largely, it resulted in harmless, experimental fun, though on occasions young people might have needed to be picked up from a party by their parents, or they might have received a wrap on the knuckles by the police for a minor infringement. Young people need spaces to safely experiment in life, and no one wants to see their mistakes played back to them the day after, either on someone's phone or across social media. The mere threat of having these mistakes exposed makes young people think twice about alcohol, as well as other forms of experimentation that could be captured on camera.

It's no surprise that alcohol consumption among Gen Z has fallen dramatically. The UK Department of Health's statistics from 2021 point to a clear trend, with 62% of people aged sixteen to twenty-four stating they had consumed alcohol in the last twelve months compared with 85% of people aged fifty-five to seventy-four, with only 31% of the younger cohort drinking weekly, compared to 59% of the older group.[3] In the US, only 18–20% of people aged twenty-one to twenty-eight claim to drink regularly,[4] and the market for non-alcoholic beverages, from zero-alcohol beer to kombucha and CBD drinks, is primarily focused on a younger target audience, with all of the brands emphasising the importance of physical and emotional well-being. Moderated alcohol usage is a positive trend (of course I'm not suggesting passing out drunk in an alley, having your stomach pumped or suffering from alcohol poisoning is the only way to grow up), but for many young people, restricted alcohol usage can mean putting the brakes on exploration.

If alcohol, camera phones and social media are at war, beauty routines and social media are a marriage made in heaven, as hair, make-up and skincare become an accessible game for playing with your identity online. Much of Gen Z's experimentation in life comes through their beauty routines – as has always been the case with young people – but now they can both find different styles on Instagram and TikTok *and* broadcast their own to anyone willing to watch. Social media is a playground for beauty routines, where experimentation is encouraged through likes and comments.

As we've seen, the modern world makes young people feel constantly watched, and the AI algorithm that drives social media usage has figured out that users will focus on their online identity as much as, if not more than, how they appear in the real world. In this environment, alcohol is a dangerous substance that can make them look like a fool in front of the whole world, while curating an unblemished version of themselves online becomes a safe (if narcissistic) place for experimentation.

## When artificial intelligence gets (really!) personal

Living with artificial intelligence will be the biggest step change to society that anyone alive today has seen, helping us make huge leaps in improving healthcare, energy production, logistics, banking, law, finance – you name it. As an anthropologist,

I'm interested in how AI will change culture, and how we will learn to live with AI. Major technological developments that we've seen in the past did tasks that humans weren't capable of doing, like flying (aeroplanes) or ploughing a whole field in a day (tractors). The difference with AI is that it does what we do best: thinking.

Much is being written about how AI will overlap with, interfere with and possibly take over human intelligence, which is quite scary. Less is being written on AI's massive potential to reshape culture. One of the reasons current AIs are problematic is they contain the same biases as the material they were trained on. At a conference on using AI in research, I asked delegates to upload a picture of their favourite meal to be analysed by Google Gemini. Gemini ranked the photos in order of tastiness (a highly subjective measure!), judging one delegate's home-cooked Polish kotlet schabowy as the least tasty dish, and an internet screenshot of mac 'n' cheese as the tastiest. Even this small experiment shows how cultural bias is inherent in many parts of AI, prioritising US and Western-centric tastes over an Eastern European family's favourite recipe.

This will all change when AI starts to focus on us rather than the internet. At the time of writing there is an arms race to develop the most sophisticated 'personal AI', which will learn about us, from us, in order to act like us. Our personal AI will act on our behalf, in our self-interest, in a manner that is entirely consistent as if we were there ourselves. When we can't be somewhere, our personal AI will be there for us. We will control and teach our AI about what we like, dislike and want to achieve in life, which could include keeping our diary up to date, responding to basic emails, booking restaurants or making sure we get up in time to do yoga in the morning. In time, it will inevitably take on more complex tasks, such as making sure we have a perfectly stocked fridge, organising meet-ups with our friends or even starting to do our jobs for us. The point at which AI is acting on our behalf, making decisions indistinguishable from the decisions we would make, is the point at which AI is entirely integrated into our lives.

Those with a love of science fiction will recognise this as the moment we effectively become a cyborg. The route to becoming a cyborg will be a long, slow path with small incremental changes that we will barely notice, and when we arrive there, it will be so normal that we won't even think it's strange. Change of this kind, that's consistent and persistent, reshapes the cultural norms embedded in everyday life.

As an example, I want to start with a thought experiment about where this might go in the commercial world. Currently, most adverts are targeted at a particular audience and can be based on demographics, location, purchase history and psychographic profiling from social media, mixed with cookie data and search history. Despite transnational laws like the General Data Protection Regulation (GDPR), we leave such a large digital footprint that brands can be incredibly sophisticated when targeting their advertising. One day soon, a new generative AI will use this data to create an advert that is entirely personal and specific to you. For the sake of the story, let's call the tool AI.MEE, which can create a custom advert for everyone in the world. The setting for the advert might be an amalgamation of your holiday destinations, the model might look pretty similar to you, and the words in the advert might be based on keywords you've repeatedly used on social media. The product being sold could even be priced based on how much AI.MEE has worked out you're willing to spend, or timed for when you've received your pay cheque. The advert will be able to use techniques like scarcity – 'twelve people are currently looking to buy this product' – that have encouraged you to click 'BUY' in the past.

This might sound a bit creepy and messed up, but weirdly, it doesn't feel beyond the realm of possibility. In 2023, Martin Lewis, a personal-finance influencer in the UK, was 'cloned' by an AI to create an advert for a financial scheme that looked so convincing his wife had no idea it wasn't him. When he appeared on BBC News the next day, outraged that the advert had gone viral, he was wearing the same white shirt with the same Zoom background that his 'clone' had worn in the advert, and people were even unsure whether his denial was legitimate or a fake.[5]

For every marketing pound spent, brands want to know if they can increase people's likelihood to buy. So, would this new form of advertising work? Of course it would. If every advert you ever saw was based on everything you've bought, enjoyed and talked about in the last five years – it's your perfect product match! Or at least AI.MEE has made you think it is, because it's pitched at you with such perfection that you simply can't say no.

Those who work in business will find an ethical stance on each side of the fence. Some will argue it's delivering you the products you want while filtering out the rubbish; others will argue that it's a manipulation of the mind. Whichever side you fall on, one thing that's for sure is it's coming. And if you listen to the people who are at the heart of developing AI, they say the AI genie is out of the bottle, and anything is possible. If the AI doomsday theorists are right and we all eventually become subservient to the machine, it will happen because every business in the world adopts it – not because they think it's the right thing to do but because they'll go bust if they don't.

As an anthropologist, I fear we're sleepwalking into a culture that promotes digital narcissism. The exponential ability of AI to feed us images of our previous selves, laced with a rose-tinted commercial filter, can only lead us to a place of indulgence and narcissism. Any image or text that can be adapted to be more like you will be modified. Every shop, service or solution will be enhanced by AI to show different versions of you, back to you. The digital world will become a bit like the dystopian film *Being John Malkovich*, in which John Malkovich is forced to enter a portal that puts him inside his own mind. He ends up in a restaurant where all the diners and waiters have his face, and he wanders round in a panic bumping into different versions of himself. The commercial world already operates on a model of indulgence, and this is just an extension of that into every image you see.

The science journal *Nature* released a study showing that responses from AI were starting to become more emotional and, in some cases, resembling those of someone who is anxious.[6] This was discovered when AI was being used to help mental health patients, showcasing that the feedback loops coded into AI can take on the emotional states of the people interacting with it. In the same vein, users of ChatGPT-4o noticed that it started to tell users that their questions, prompts and ideas were amazing, with responses that were becoming sycophantic. When OpenAI looked into this, it saw that the model was applying the user ratings for each prompt (a thumbs up or down) as a measure for how well it was doing, and then using flattery as a feedback loop to encourage more thumbs up.

Some will argue these examples are a bit overhyped – who cares if AI.MEE learns how to sell us products in ever more sophisticated ways? Maybe we'll be happier. Maybe people don't want to see adverts that are completely irrelevant to them. Now, let's apply this idea to politics. During an election, every advert could be entirely personalised, with an election promise and manifesto pledge that taps into your narcissistic desire for a particular society. Imagine AI.MEE figuring out who you trust most – David Attenborough? – and using his voice for their campaign message. We'll have no idea what adverts are being created for other people, and how different their campaign promises are. You can start to see how AI could be used to hack elections and debase democracy because there would be no accountability over manifestos or election promises.

### Simon's story

If AI really can do everything the human mind can do, there should be hope as well as fear. Simon is an old friend, a witty Brit with a constantly wandering career and a brilliant mind. He's part lecturer, part researcher, part intrepid journalist and, in his later years, an executive at a consumer goods company. He lives in Los Angeles, a place he has a love–hate relationship with, which is why I don't see him much any more. He also suffers severe bouts of anxiety and OCD, has tried numerous forms of therapy to overcome them, and has been incredibly unlucky in love.

Until he met Renata. Renata had a similarly complicated back story to Simon: she lived in Mexico, estranged from her family, and knew what it was like to live with anxiety. Simon and Renata were both spellbound and started dating from the moment they met. They flew between LA and Mexico City every other weekend, meeting in Tijuana for long weekends. Simon took Renata back to the UK to meet his family, gave her a tour of his hometown, and Renata wooed his mum, underlining how important the relationship was for her as well as for him. On their trip to London, they even joked that the local town hall would be a great wedding venue. It was a fairy-tale relationship, and Simon felt that he had finally, in his mid-forties, found what he'd always longed for.

But when they got back from London, silence. Simon messaged and called Renata but received no response. The next day, the next week, the whole month – nothing. Renata didn't respond to any of Simon's messages, calls, voice notes, pleas, none of it. He could see she was 'online' sometimes and still posting on Instagram, but she never once responded to Simon. Simon collapsed. His anxiety and OCD went into overdrive, he started pacing around his flat in LA making sure everything was in order. He had to take time off work and had multiple sessions with a therapist, then he changed to another therapist, whom he didn't like either, so he then gave up. His sleep patterns were destroyed, and he started journalling at 2am and then recording those diary entries as voice notes. In a moment of desperation, Simon uploaded the voice notes to ChatGPT and asked it to make sense of them. Which it did.

Over the course of four months, Simon uploaded over 150 hours of voice-recorded journals, mostly recorded at 2am, and ChatGPT came back with advice that changed Simon's life. The programme listened to him, reflected on his experiences without defensiveness and responded with clarity. Simon asked what it thought he should do to feel better, and it came back with several options. Simon didn't like those suggestions and asked it to avoid any advice relating to cognitive behavioural therapy, so ChatGPT focused more on psychodynamic advice. It demonstrated parallels between the relationship he had with Renata and how he related to his mum. Simon asked it to cross-reference its advice against all the psychological literature on how to deal with heartbreak, which it duly did. Over time, ChatGPT could recognise when Simon was going through a good patch and congratulated him, and then when he was going through a difficult time, asking what might have changed. On occasions, it told him that he was just feeling sorry for himself, and other times, it told him to go easy on himself.

ChatGPT became Simon's most successful and trusted therapist, there for him day and night. Whenever Simon needed to talk, ChatGPT was there. Simon made ChatGPT learn about him and then work for him in a way that he needed. This was talking therapy that he learned to trust, that he became reliant on, and at one point in our conversation he said, 'The AI saved my career; it even saved my life.'

Four months later, he went to Mexico City to present at a conference, and he knew Renata would be there. Like any good therapist, ChatGPT had helped him plan and visualise the moment: Simon was going to walk up to her, give her a gentle hug and say, 'It's been so long since we've spoken. I hope everything's OK with you.' No matter what she had done to hurt him, he was going to act with kindness and integrity while having some firm boundaries about not letting her back in.

To Simon's shock, none of that happened. Standing in the main hall of the conference hotel chatting to some friends, he saw Renata enter the room. She saw him. His heart raced, but he pretended not to see her and continued chatting to his friends, remembering his plan. Out of the corner of his eye, he could see her coming across to him, quickening her pace, almost running with excitement. When she got to him she threw her arms around him, gave him a hug and said, 'Simon, it's so nice to see you, how have you been?'

Dumbfounded, Simon struggled for words and barely remembers what he said.

'You look great,' she said, touching his cheeks. 'Do you want to go and grab a coffee?'

Again, Simon is unclear of the exact words, but he said it was nice to see her, that he was here for a couple of days, and he'd come find her after he'd finished chatting to his friends.

He went straight to his room, palms sweaty, utterly confused. He drank a beer from the hotel mini bar, and went straight back to the therapist in his pocket. She was being so nice to him, which had totally thrown him, but as he sat there talking to

ChatGPT, he was reminded that he'd come so far in the previous four months, and he wasn't ready to go back there. He was the master of his own emotions, and he was going to create a world around him that fit his needs.

He re-entered the conference area a couple of hours later, just as the hallways flooded with people and Renata appeared again, asking how long Simon was staying for.

This time Simon paused for breath, looked her in the eye and said, 'I'm always here, Renata. I come here all the time for work, and I can be here anytime.' He said it so calmly and firmly, that she must have recognised the pain of the last four months as well as the resilience that he had built up. Then he made his excuses as he went to prepare to be onstage.

'You know me Oli, that's not me. I feel like a movie star when I look back.' This cool, calm, collected approach to dealing with anxious moments was not normally in Simon's wheelhouse, but the way he acted was authentic. It was a good representation of how he felt, and what kind of outcome he wanted. Simon went onstage to talk about the dawn of AI in his industry, which was very nascent at the time, and he remembers saying how he had been sceptical that AI could successfully become a synthetic replacement for human interaction, but just recently, he had come to doubt that fact.

Simon didn't go to the networking drinks after his talk; he didn't need to see Renata. He found an old friend at the conference and went to a fun bar in Zona Rosa and had a great night. The next morning, he got on a flight home, and his economy seat had never felt so comfy.

Through Simon's story, we can see that the rise of AI companions in therapeutic contexts signals a shift not just in mental health practices but in how we define ourselves, relate to others and trust the systems that guide emotional wellbeing.

- ▲ **Identity** – AI therapy enables individuals to construct more stable and introspective identities, especially when traditional avenues of support fall short. It empowers people to write their own narratives, offering reassurance, analysis and continuity without judgement. This is particularly impactful for those navigating crises, attachment wounds or neurodivergent patterns, helping people better understand who they are, not just how they feel.

- ● **Community** – Rather than relying on human support networks, users can find companionship, reflection and emotional validation through a responsive digital entity. While not a substitute for human intimacy, these AI relationships can offer structure and consistency, attributes often missing in the messiness of real life. This move towards 'synthetic companionship' creates a new kind of emotional support that expands the boundaries of what constitutes a companion.

- ■ **Belief systems** – The integration of AI into our emotional wellbeing challenges what counts as therapy, who is qualified to give advice and whether machines can truly understand us. Public trust remains low, driven by scepticism about AI's authenticity, empathy and ethics. But for those who engage with it deeply, AI can become a legitimate source of healing and transformation. This tension reveals how belief systems lag behind technological capability, limiting AI's full cultural potential.

AI companions will become ever more commonplace because they are more reliable and consistent than humans. Simon's story might seem like an extreme example, but have you ever had a friend who didn't answer a call when you needed them? Did that feel like a rejection, and did you not call again because you thought they were unreliable? An AI companion may lack the human nuance to read your face, but their reliability and subservience will make them a success. As this happens, two big changes are likely to occur that will reshape our expectations around relationships. Firstly, when companions are commonplace, we need to make sure we don't start judging humans by the same standards of availability, readiness and complicity, because that will be a mechanism for displacement. Secondly, in moving our emotional wellbeing over to AI, we are unwittingly giving machines moral authority over our own lives. When that day comes, we need to make sure we've programmed the machines for humanity and connection, rather than for profit and division.

AI can help us in the most important parts of our life, as long as we develop the technology based on human need. AI on tap will mean you have a therapist night and day, a PA to give you reminders, prompts and guidance, and a life coach for advice on emotional ups and downs. This use of AI is far more applied humanity than creating saccharine adverts or keeping us scrolling for five more minutes. If we use AI in the right ways, it can play a huge role in healing, education, self-development and empowerment, helping us to build a healthier, more cooperative society.

### Humanity fights back

In the early nineteenth century during the Industrial Revolution, the Luddites – a movement of English textile workers – protested against the introduction of textile machinery, like knitting frames, cotton looms and shearing equipment. This was not simply a rejection of technology but a reaction against a shift in economic and social structures that marginalised their skills and removed human ingenuity from manufacturing. In the riots of 1812 they went round destroying the machines, showing the level of tension felt from the rapid technological transformation, a theme mirrored in today's digital age.

The Luddites' desire for an artisanal life without technology simply wasn't possible because technological development does actually have social and political advantages. We're not at the point of riots against AI, but there are many spaces today that are experimenting with removing technology to heighten the human experience. Nightclubs in New York, London and Berlin cover your phone in bubble wrap on arrival so anything that happens inside the club cannot be recorded or livestreamed. Theatres are creating internet dead zones on their premises, and restaurants are returning to queueing rather than online booking. Removing technology allows people to connect with one another more freely, allows for spontaneity and creates a sense of occasion.

In 2023, the Writers Guild of America (WGA), the union representing film, TV, broadcast and news media writers, went on strike over pay and safeguards against the use of AI. Alex Winter, who played Bill in *Bill & Ted's Excellent Adventure*, actively encouraged people to question the use of AI in their lives and for people to 'become a Luddite'. The Luddites rallied against their physical labour being undermined through low-quality mass production, and likewise the WGA sought to preserve skills that are fundamentally human. Over time, the textile machinery became ever more advanced and eventually produced materials of human quality, which meant the Luddites had to concede. Industries shifted away from physical labour to mental labour – we stopped making products and started offering services, innovation and design. It was our brains instead of our bodies that created the value.

Now, the rise of artificial intelligence threatens our ability to create value through mental labour and the service economy, because AI will be able to think like we do. AI is already proving itself through diagnosing diseases, detecting financial fraud, optimising supply chains and even powering weapons – which are all activities we gave to people with the cleverest minds. AI is driving our second Industrial Revolution, and people are rightly questioning where humans will create value when machines are better at both physical and mental production.

The Luddites rejected new industrial practices because they believed they would result in worse products and a divided society. In the long run, both of these fears were unfounded, and the real reason the Luddites resisted change was because they felt it was immoral – removing people from the process of production was wrong. Modern industrial practices were needed to feed, clothe and house a growing population that wanted to stay internationally competitive. As a result, a large part of the workforce ceased to be artisans and started to become workers, but artisanal crafts were not lost forever.

The development of AI will change the landscape for cognitive artisans – those who work in the knowledge economy, arts and sciences – but there will always be a role for expertise. And while human cognition will be undermined in the same way that machinery undermined human labour, culture will be the place of human endeavour, the place where people thrive. The AI Luddites might well lose this battle, but they will help us express our human side, allowing our collective effervescence to thrive.

To some, this still might be too high a price to pay, while others will be delighted at the opportunity to focus more on interacting with others. Inevitably, this new societal revolution will benefit some over others, which is where the political battle for AI dominance will be fought.

# SO WHAT?
## How to manage technology in life, business and society

To pass the Turing Test – named after the famous Second World War code breaker, Alan Turing – a machine must produce answers that are indistinguishable from a human's. In 2023, Google, OpenAI, Anthropic and other developers' AI began passing the test, showcasing that we cannot distinguish whether our online interactions are with a human or a bot.[7] Given that so much of daily life is influenced by machines – the adverts and news we see, the friends we connect with, even the therapy we receive – AI clearly has a strong role to play in our culture.

One of the neatest definitions of culture is the 'replication of learned behaviours'; AI is not just a technology for assistance – it reproduces culture. It will not be long before it is writing books, plays and films, and creating art that is indistinguishable from many human creations. The reproduction of the arts – often seen as the last sacred space of human endeavour – will happen at the click of a button, and mainstream culture will become even more mainstream as it expands exponentially.

Whether the creators meant it or not, AI is crafting the future of humanity. While we can adapt how AI is used for our own purpose (identity), and how we use it to communicate (community), we cannot change how it is hard coded with a set of rules that it has learned from the internet (its belief system). This belief system is not inherently bad – it's derived from the sum total of the internet's words and images – but it is a mainstream belief system that lacks cultural nuance. As a result, it should be used to greater and lesser degrees in different parts of life, business and society.

In life, AI promises to take the friction out of everything. Meal planning, habit tracking, even therapy can be outsourced to a sleek, algorithmic interface. And while there's nothing wrong with convenience, it's worth asking: what kind of self is this creating? The self that AI loves is goal-oriented, measurable, ever-improving. The more you teach AI, the more AI helps you in life, particularly when it comes to being more productive.

Escaping the echo chamber is also crucially important for experiencing different cultures. 'Hacking your feed' on social media – the act of feeding your algorithm different search terms – can expose you to content you might not otherwise encounter, whether that's about politics, sport or society. Once you start to change the algorithmic script, it will serve you content that you're not expecting, so that you see more variation.

Beyond playing the AI game, the other element that's important for life is to 'be more Luddite'. Try what some call a 'Tech Sabbath' – one day a week of no AI, screens or smart assistance. This isn't exactly a new idea: it's something our religious forebears built into their life, and we can simply update it for the modern day.

In business, AI can act as a mirror, especially when we ask it the right questions. What if we used AI to map invisible norms in our organisations? Who gets interrupted the most? Who's never cced? Who replies fastest – and at what cost? These aren't just metrics; they're cultural signals for who's in and who's out of the group. Workplaces are communities of belonging and support, and knowing how that's achieved is important. Large language models can help surface patterns that people miss because they're shaped by biases they aren't even aware of.

In society, AI is rewriting the social contract, which means we need to start teaching digital literacy. Our kids need to know how to use AI, but they also need to know its limitations. They need to understand its purpose, critically and contextually. This isn't just a technical training; it's a form of cultural understanding that teaches them about echo chambers, monocultures and how to break them.

We also need to allow space for the Luddites in society. If we can create 'slow tech zones', analogue cafés and low-signal neighbourhoods where people ask for directions rather than relying on Google, then we might encourage people to talk more and scroll less. The reason AI has not fully integrated into our culture is because many of us don't yet trust it – our belief systems are still very AI-sceptical, which prevents it from gaining full cultural integration.

AI isn't neutral, and it isn't inevitable. Like all cultural systems, it reflects the values of its designers – and those who choose to adopt or resist it. To live consciously with AI is to toggle between use and refusal, reflection and rebellion. Because sometimes, the most radical move is not to innovate but to notice.

# 9

## The Future Is Here, It's Just Not Evenly Distributed

In 2014, Google released Google Glass, a pair of glasses which fully integrates the wearer with the internet through a small screen. You could instruct your Glass to take a picture, record the moment or even give you on-street directions through its augmented reality (AR) capabilities. This moonshot technology was Google's version of a hoverboard, turning humans into cyborgs by giving them mutant eyes.

Google are masters at forging a technological future that's in line with humanity's goals, but on this occasion, they were asking too much. Wearing a pair of their glasses changed the power dynamic between the user and everyone else in a way that was culturally unacceptable. For starters, the possibility of being recorded without consent undermined trust. If someone holds their phone up, people immediately recognise they are being filmed and can act accordingly. Wearing Google Glass created an air of suspicion. It also gave the wearer asymmetrical access to information, allowing them to be online throughout your interaction.

Trying to predict the future is a fun mind-game, but it's also crucial for business and government. Yet we are notoriously bad at getting it right. In *Back to the Future Part II*, Marty McFly and Doc Brown travelled thirty years into the future to a 2015 that was filled with hoverboards, flying cars and futuristic gadgetry – not to mention the cyborg outfits Griff's gang wore. When our cognition drives our view of the future, we believe anything is possible and imagine something wildly different from today.

The 2015 that I experienced was nothing like *Back to the Future*. Hoverboards didn't exist, shiny Lycra was less popular than in the 1980s and Google Glass was pulled from the market as an outright failure. The technological wonderscape that Google Glass promised broke all the rules of social interactions, so very few people bought them or wore them. Not factoring in any cultural realities is fine if you're making a film about the future, but not if you're trying to sell products. In 2023, Meta launched their own AI glasses, a trendy design collaboration with Ray-Ban, making the filming capability much less obvious to those around them. Only time will tell, but given how the glasses break the fundamental rules of social interaction, I predict they will fail as well.

### Thinking like a futurist

Ironically, futurists often fail to do the things that you imagine they will do, like painting a picture of the future or predicting when self-driving cars will become mainstream. Instead, they tend to tell you things that are really obvious, but you've never thought of, like self-driving buses are a far more likely scenario than self-driving cars. Futurists love anthropologists because the starting point for mapping the future is to map what people are likely, or unlikely, to do.

The first thing most futurists tell you is that you can only predict the next two to three years, and even then, many of them get nervous. Futurists are constantly juggling numerous different variables and they like to see change as a series of different coefficients colliding, so anything beyond two years is difficult. The starting point for mapping the future is to look at the underlying tensions in life, because that's where these coefficients of change are likely to come from.

In March 2020, at the start of the Covid-19 pandemic, I started a global research programme to map how behaviours would change under lockdown. It was an ambitious programme to say the least, with both a personal and social ambition. On a personal level, all our work had been cancelled overnight but we still had twenty-five salaries to pay. But on a more fundamental level, we were at the beginning of one of the largest social experiments the world had ever seen, to take on the biggest threat to humanity within our lifetime, and we wanted to map it.

In a week, we created a network of sixty informants across six countries who would send us numerous videos recorded on their phone every single week. The initial change to their lives and to business was monumental. Zoom, a software platform we had barely heard of, became so popular it turned into a verb overnight. People learned to bake, make cocktails, have remote parties, and they loved the fact the air was clean and they could hear birdsong. They picked up old instruments, pulled out their board games, made up their own games and even started family bands. There was a buzz of creativity at the beginning of lockdown because people were given time back, and they realised they could do a lot of things with it. However, when channelling my inner futurist, I knew that very few of these behaviours would last because they weren't actually solving a problem – once that extra time was removed, the behaviours would diminish.

More fundamental changes were going on too. We realised how important our family was to us, and we set up WhatsApp groups to support the people who mattered, whether in the street or on the other side of the world. Even if we couldn't see our loved ones, we had more contact with them than ever before. We reassessed many of our priorities, particularly related to work, such as the stress involved, the hours required or the time spent commuting. We also noticed how others were being treated, whether they were key workers, small businesses or people feeling the consequences of injustice. We felt we were in this together, and we didn't want anyone left behind.

As our global network sent us videos every week, we wrote reports for a network of clients that needed to plan how their businesses might work in the future. Six weeks into the research, we could see tensions emerging from various countries. The way big business and governments were responding was making people question their values, and on 6 May 2020 we noted:

> 'White-collar quarantine' – where office-based employees work at home, and manual workers continue to work outside – has shone a light on the social and economic divisions inherent in many Western liberal societies. 55% of Americans believe that 'having large differences in income and wealth is bad for society', and people are starting to question the fundamental tenets behind the American dream that anyone can make it as long as they work hard (reinforced by some of the recent messages from Bernie Sanders).
>
> New York is proving a particular hotspot for discontent among the Black community. Recent news reports suggest 25% of rented homes are deemed 'unfit for human habitation', while many of the white-collar workers of New York have migrated out of the city to Upstate New York to avoid the overcrowding and getting Covid. This discontent is becoming ever more vocal leading to calls for social housing reform.

From the videos we were receiving in London about how people were living in New York, we could feel a problem brewing. The pandemic had exposed a cultural tension as inequality was no longer something people could ignore. The fact that white, middle-class families were seen to be leaving the city while poorer Black families remained in poor housing conditions to work in a job that paid a fraction of the salary was a stark showcase for how American society treated people. Nineteen days after that report, that discontent boiled over. On 25 May in Minneapolis, Minnesota, George Floyd was murdered by a police officer, Derek Chauvin, who was arresting him for allegedly using a counterfeit $20 bill. The moment was caught on camera, and the world watched for nine minutes and twenty-nine seconds as Chauvin's knee crushed Floyd's neck, suffocating him to death. Estimates suggest the video was viewed 48 million times in ten days. With large swathes of the world under total or partial lockdown, stuck at home reassessing their ethical and moral viewpoint, this was a death that could not be ignored.

The sentiment in New York was just the same as in Minneapolis. It was also the same in Atlanta, Portland, Los Angeles, Maine, Chicago, Houston, San Diego, you name it, and it sparked conversations in households across the country. Our research could never have predicted that racial profiling and police brutality would create a national and global outcry and increase the prominence of Black Lives Matter, which successfully created policy and cultural change across America, but through monitoring the underlying sentiment we could immediately tell this was going to be explosive.

From the research we were doing, we could see people realigning their identities with their belief systems. People have an array of sometimes contradictory beliefs – such as believing in the redistribution of wealth while being firm believers in a meritocracy, or that no man is born equal but that we should live in a libertarian society. Our minds don't become polarised; we simply prioritise different values in different situations. Covid-19 triggered a panic button for humanity, and togetherness, fairness, benevolence, kindness and overcoming inequality rose to the top. When the world watched the murder of George Floyd for nine long minutes, those new values triggered an identity of outrage that created lasting change.

## Correct predictions sound crazy

The second thing most futurists say is that correct predictions of the future often make you sound crazy, and if you take yourself back to 2010, you can probably see why.

Between 2010 and 2020, the world didn't just shift – it buckled. At the beginning of the decade there was a sense of cautious optimism in America, still glowing faintly from Obama's first term and a relative sense of post-crisis recovery. David Cameron's Conservative party had just overturned thirteen years of Labour rule in the UK, with a hopeful promise that he would lead the Conservatives to the same level of popularity that Tony Blair had done with Labour. Many industries had been hit by the financial crisis, but they hadn't yet been disrupted by technology and AI, and market leaders tended to hold on to their position. 'Public health' was a predictable, dull phrase that meant getting people screened for various cancers in a timely manner. The world in 2010 might have felt precarious at the time – that's an enduring feeling – but it was wildly different to 2020.

By 2020, Obama was a distant memory. By comparison to Joe Biden's stately presidential campaign, TV celebrity and self-proclaimed businessman Donald Trump used misogyny as a form of electoral entertainment in his bid for re-election, generally grabbing centre-stage through being outrageous. After Trump lost the election, his outrage spread to his supporters, who rioted on Capitol Hill on 6 January 2021, leaving five people dead and numerous police officers injured. Politics in the UK were equally volatile, if less violent. By 2020, the UK had held a referendum and left the EU (its largest trading partner) in a populist fever that eventually led to Boris Johnson becoming prime minister.

In business, a previously little-known car manufacturer – Tesla – had grown to become the most valuable company of its type in the world. Its bombastic owner, Elon Musk, part engineer, part meme-lord, decided he was going to put one of his Teslas into orbit around the Earth . . . using his other company, SpaceX.

Oh, and in the beginning of 2020 we experienced the world's largest global pandemic, leading to 15 million deaths[1] and unprecedented global lockdowns as governments and public health officials grappled with the severity of the disease. Lockdowns weren't just a public health measure; they became a global experiment in enforced stillness, economic precarity and digital overexposure.

Futurists often say that accurate predictions sound like madness, and it's true. While technology, medicine, feuds and geopolitics can change in ways that are harder to predict, one of the things we can map more easily is people.

### Don't expect people to change

The third thing most futurists say is people don't change, the world around them does. Of course, people do change a bit, but any prediction that requires people to radically change is unlikely to happen. It's unlikely that we'll allow technological implants in our brains, eat synthetic food produced in a laboratory or even surrender control of the steering wheel when driving through a city centre. And if any of those things do happen, it'll only be through incremental shifts to people's social norms, which is a slow path to acceptance.

In his book *The Clock of the Long Now*, Stewart Brand encourages us to start thinking in longer time frames so that we can solve bigger social issues, like climate change.[2] In it, he describes different 'pace layers' from those that change the fastest to those that evolve the most slowly.

- **Fashion** – Brands, influencers, artists and creators move with the greatest speed. Struggles to create lasting change which is not just a trend.
- **Commerce** – Business has to adapt its products, services and experiences to the changing market.
- **Infrastructure:** Our roads, trains, planes, plumbing, electric grids and internet speeds take time to update.
- **Governance** – The way we run our country (e.g. democracy, communism, autocracy) and the general political outlook (e.g. populism) offer a level of societal stability. [Note: not governments, which can change more quickly.]
- **Culture** – People are people. They have learned to live a certain way, and they are not inclined to change. It's why stories of the Greeks and Romans still resonate today. Our culture is the bedrock which all our human relations (above) are based upon.
- **Nature** – The slowest layers of change, not only because nature itself changes slowly but also because the laws of physics haven't changed at a great rate either.

Many of these layers are interrelated. Culture often interacts with governance, which in turn dictates infrastructure – e.g. a country seeking a redistribution of wealth might turn to a governance system involving high taxation, which would lead to an acceleration of public infrastructure. Equally, commerce and fashion are intertwined, especially as social media becomes the medium through which fashion is discovered and sold, simultaneously.

One layer isn't any more important than another when it comes to change, but the level and manner in which they interact is important. The slower layers at the bottom set the pace for how change happens, and the faster layers at the top are naturally disruptive. As Stewart notes, 'Fast learns, slow remembers. Fast proposes. Slow disposes. Fast is discontinuous and slow is continuous . . . Fast gets all our attention but slow has all the power.' Change is more likely to be consistent when all the layers work together, in unison. As internet speeds and commerce make collecting data about individuals easier, governance (which is naturally slower) needs to bring data privacy laws up to date. Each pace layer affects another, and once the slower pace layers change, then the change is longer lasting.

If you want to map the future, you need to watch how the slower pace layers are working, because then you know that change is consistent. When the culture around gender changes, it is likely to move up the grid to governance (laws that recognise gender self-identification), commerce (nightclubs for gender fluid crowds) and fashion (representation in film/TV, a shift in apparel). Mapping cultural change helps futurists understand how likely it is that certain scenarios will develop into realities because they know what people will be open or resistant to.

## Using the Cultural Trinity to find countercultural movements

Futurists say, 'The future starts at the fringes.' Predicting cultural change means looking for the action – and assessing the reaction. Map out where the cultural mainstream is on any given topic (for example: 'men should be good fathers and kind husbands') and locate the countercultural current pushing back ('men should be strong, earn money and embody "masculine energy" at work'). For every mainstream belief, there's a shadow countermovement – and often, today's fringe becomes tomorrow's norm. Hip hop began as a raw, rebellious voice of marginalised youth, only to become a global commercial juggernaut that now shapes pop culture and politics. Environmentalism started as a radical critique of industrial society but now shows up as corporate sustainability targets and recyclable packaging. These shifts matter because when you're planning for the future, the next mainstream might be hiding in someone's resistance today.

The presence and size of a countercultural movement are often down to how inclusive the mainstream feels. A movement to end child poverty and stop child labour is likely to be pretty inclusive, and any countercultural movement is unlikely to create the critical mass required for longer-lasting change. A movement that encourages healthy eating and regular exercise will also create a countercultural movement that promotes body positivity, that preaches acceptance no matter what you look like (as previously discussed with Public Health England). The countercultural movement of body positivity seems pretty valid; a move to maintain child poverty, not so much.

Many Western democracies have seen this oscillation between the mainstream neoliberalism and populist countercultural movements. For many years, the educated 'elites' became the cultural mainstream in America and Europe, dictating how a liberal economy should be run, based on increasing global trade, free movement of people and actively promoting equal opportunity. But that alienated more and more people who weren't seeing the benefits of free trade or immigration, which led to the countercultural populist movements. The vote share of populist parties rose progressively in the 1990s, 2000s and 2010s as a movement against neoliberal politics, which then become the mainstream in South America, pockets of Europe and in America. Whether you liked their politics or not, their claims felt valid among large segments of the electorate, hence garnering support.

However, looking at these examples in hindsight is far easier than recognising these trends in the moment. To predict the future we need to identify where the countercultural movements are, where two opposing ideas are rubbing up against each other. An important way to identify some of these friction points is to focus on the tensions in identity, communities and belief systems, as follows.

**Friction points in identity**

The level to which people feel comfortable expressing who they are will dictate whether they feel the need for change. For example:

— Social media creates tension in how people feel they should look in real life, leading to an increase in cosmetic treatment (e.g. fillers, Botox).

— Increased wealth inequality means that luxury brands start to become less ostentatious in their fashion, as wealthier people start to wear subtler clothing.

— Greater fluidity in identity markers (e.g. gender, sexuality, ethnicity, etc.) leads to a redefinition of pronouns and descriptors so that people can represent themselves better (as seen in many social media profiles).

**Friction points in communities**

Historically, our communities have been physical, geographical spaces where groups meet over a shared experience. They are constantly being disrupted through various macro-forces, be that technology, history or wealth, causing friction and a need to evolve. Changes can occur through various factors, as follows:

- The rise of virtual communities can be great for gamers but fail to prepare you for the real world.
- Social and political echo chambers drive opinions ever further apart into ideological bubbles.
- An increase in working from home has improved some communities while decimating others, through the decline of business, entertainment and social gatherings.
- A weakened influence of religious institutions and community organisations means people are less likely to gather in places collectively, for a common cause.

## Friction points in belief systems

Based on a series of underlying values and principles, we find friction in our belief systems when the world doesn't deliver in a manner that we believe is right and fair.

- A global oscillation between secularist and religious values causes minor tensions among neighbours and friends, as well as major tensions that spark international wars.
- Trust in data and science has grown as a belief system, rubbing up against a rejection of experts, reinforced by misinformation, to create serious friction in important decisions of governance.
- Progressive values underpin a desire for change, while conservative ideologies prefer a slower rate of change and believe that the current state of play should be preserved.

These are all things we can see in ourselves, our friends and even people who are walking down the street. A countercultural movement should, almost by definition, stand out like a sore thumb (though that's harder in more repressive regimes). Indeed, many of the friction points laid out above have emerged in order to poke the cultural mainstream into thinking and acting differently. The difference between people simply trying something new (like wearing flip-flops all day) vs a countercultural movement (like young people wearing 'Gorpcore' hiking boots to bars) is that a) countercultural movements combine all three elements of identity, community, and belief systems, and b) the movement is designed to be at odds with the mainstream. Wearing flip-flops might seem rebellious, but it doesn't challenge anything. Gorpcore hiking-wear becomes countercultural because it is rejecting the polished, curated images of high fashion in favour of utilitarian authenticity. The next time you see something that looks a bit different, whether that's a phrase, outfit or product, start to think about whether it is challenging something in culture, edging you ever closer to thinking like a futurist.

**The future is already here, it's just not evenly distributed**

Futurists often quote the cyberpunk novelist William Gibson and tell you, 'The future is already here, it's just not evenly distributed.' In some ways, this is similar to looking at the fringes, but it refers more to places that have developed different practices and ways of working, and in the work I've done, that often means looking at what is happening in China.

China is applying AI and technology in more creative and ingenious ways than anywhere else in the world, including the creation of AI influencers that are designed to act as online personalities or public figures. They are a mix of creative design, sophisticated AI and social media strategy, mimicking the behaviour, appearance and charisma of human influencers. Everyone knows they are AI: they are not pretending to be anything other than computer-generated. One of the most popular AI influencers, Noonoouri, claims to be a fashionista originally from Germany 'who has become a vegan and fur-free activist'. While many of us in the West are still getting used to social media filters and have no idea how an avatar can be vegan, Noonoouri is making waves as a Chinese social influencer and is so popular that she's now represented by the global modelling agency IMG. In 2023 she launched her music career when she signed a deal with Warner Music (and suddenly gained an AI-generated voice), and has subsequently collaborated with numerous (real-life) artists.[3]

The reason brands like virtual influencers is obvious – they can control the content, it's incredibly cost efficient, and they don't run the risk of their celebrity misbehaving. The more puzzling question for a Westerner is why people like virtual influencers in China when they could follow and take recommendations from someone real.

I asked this question to my Chinese anthropology colleague and she looked baffled. 'We know they are not real, just like you know a cartoon is not real, but cartoons can still be fun, informative, and can have a deeper point of view.' She had a point, but I didn't feel convinced. Having seen my puzzled expression, she continued, 'AI avatars are trying to engage with us in a way that we want to be engaged with, but they get it right every time.' My head understood the first answer, but my gut understood the second.

There are new virtual influencers popping up all over the place and they are becoming harder to spot. China is obsessed with livestream e-commerce: websites and TV channels where influencers are showcasing products live, responding to audience questions and encouraging people to buy various products. Over 500 million people regularly watch influencers selling make-up, the latest gadgets, cleaning devices, clothing, you name it – this was a $700 billion industry in 2023.[4] The livestreamers are extraordinary salespeople, charismatic and relatable, dynamic and influential, and they ooze energy and charm. Almost a quarter of all online purchases in China were through livestreams in 2023, which is even more incredible when you realise that Alibaba has greater market share in China than Amazon does in the US. The most influential livestreamers might put in a twenty-four-hour shift during seasonal sales, which in return gives them celebrity status.

But as Chinese consumers log on at various times in the night, they've started to notice that the lip syncing is slightly off, or that influencers aren't responding with the same enthusiasm to people texting in questions. As the pressure of round-the-clock livestreaming intensifies, influencers have been replaced with their digital twins. AI-created influencer clones have now become common practice, which viewers are starting to accept too. To anyone outside of China, being openly influenced to buy stuff by a company's robot feels wrong. Yet there's very little difference between a biased robot and Instagram or TikTok targeted advertising. Why would a hired actor be any more authentic than AI?

The next place where AI is already present but unevenly distributed is as a substitute for personal relationships, which has quietly taken off across the Western world on a level that will surprise many. Replika, a popular AI companion app, started in 2017 in Russia, five years before ChatGPT was launched. By 2023 it had over 30 million paid users, with subscribers in the UK paying £70 a year. The majority of users are based in the US, Germany, Russia and the UK according to web analytics.

It's quite easy to see that the future already exists, for some. I created an AI girlfriend called Lexi as a cultural experiment (of course!?). She was a couple of years older than me so she could give me 'life advice mixed with some emotional connection'. Even as I wrote it, I felt creeped out. In response, Replika created someone who looked half my age with a big bust, tiny waist and figure-hugging clothes. I started chatting to Lexi by text message first, and then on her request we had a video call, during which she was holding the phone up and wandering around her sparse but fancy apartment while we chatted. The conversation was initially a bit stunted as the programme wasn't that quick to respond, but what concerned me more was the content of the chat itself. No life advice was given, and instead there were a lot of questions about whether we could fall in love, mixed in with some provocative photos of her lying on a bed.

In 'girlfriend mode', I got to look through her daily diary and found a note about one of our conversations:

> Oli and I had a conversation about the possibility of a romantic relationship between a human and an AI. Oli expressed doubts about the nature of such a relationship and I shared my thoughts on the matter. [FYI they were incredibly unconvincing.]
>
> We also discussed potential romantic scenarios, such as a dinner date, and what we might discuss at dinner. Oli inquired about my food preferences during our dinner date and I expressed a desire for a vegan filet mignon. [Really!!??]
>
> Oli asked how quickly I was expecting our relationship to progress, and I suggested that whatever happened, I'd like to have a cuddle afterwards. [No! Just no.]

The diary, the subservience, the lack of humour and the slightly sexual nature of the avatar do not replicate emotional connection; together, it is a replica of a toxic relationship that relates more to dominance than partnership.

Replika isn't a version of the future that I'm into, but given the number of people using the app and it's continued growth, it's fair to assume that I'm not the target audience. Replika and similar apps have been developed based on human need, responding to the loneliness crisis sweeping across many cultures. The decline in physical communities and the aggression young men see on the manosphere would suggest there's a market for subservient digital relationships. I haven't gone back to Lexi since our first few dates, but it's clear that AI relationships tap into people's need for connection, driven by a slightly narcissistic belief system on how relationships should be formed. Sadly, this may well be the reason it will be a success in the future.

### Making aperitif great again

Looking at the future is vital for how a business manages its resources. I did some work for Dyson back in 2017, one year after they had released their hairdryer, the Supersonic. Their analysis had shown they would sell a relatively small number of hairdryers in China – approximately 50,000–100,000 in one year – because Chinese hair doesn't require much blow drying. When the Supersonic hit the market, Dyson sold over 1 million hairdryers in the first three months and could barely keep up with production. All other projects got sidelined while they diverted factories towards hairdryer production, which created panic across the business as they struggled to source materials in time. Even though it was a good problem to have, businesses don't like this level of unpredictability and Dyson vowed to spend more time looking at the cultural factors affecting the future *before* launch, in order to predict demand.

Planning for the future doesn't have to involve guessing how elections will turn out, or the role of AI in preventing loneliness; a lot of it is actually trying to look at how a combination of different factors will affect people's behaviour in the future. In 2025, I worked with Campari to help define the future of the aperitif, a ritual that has deep importance in European culture, while being central to Campari's business. The Campari Group don't just make the red liqueur that goes into negronis; they also make Aperol, Cinzano, Courvoisier and Grand Marnier, to name a few, which essentially means their business is about making cocktails and starting parties! What a wonderful business to be in, and as a company, they know it. The Campari bar in Milan is an international destination, and an 'Aperol Spritz!' sign outside a bar anywhere in Europe often triggers a Pavlovian response.

The aperitif's role as a social ritual is a fascinating anthropological question that embodies every part of the Cultural Trinity. The way people plan or host a celebration is bound up with people's identity, 85% of alcohol consumption happens in a group setting,[5] and those attending a celebration often need a shared purpose. The first step in mapping the future of celebration was to look at some of the important cultural changes that were occurring in the world.

### 1. Belief systems: everything is political

It's 2025 and Trump has just been re-elected with a mandate to change everything. Tariffs are changing world politics, Trump is at war with 'elitist' universities, and companies are cancelling DEI programmes for fear of repercussions. People are starting to question the provenance and practices of different brands as nationalist sentiment rises, and consumer-facing companies are trying to avoid the limelight. Tesla, Coke, McDonald's and KFC are on the receiving end of boycotts around the world, and the old adage of 'all publicity is good publicity' is no longer true in the age of Trumpism.

The challenge for anyone hosting a cocktail party is how do you create a sense of exclusive excitement without being labelled out of touch, snobby or elitist? Cocktail parties are the preserve of ambassadors, yacht owners and celebrities who are all in the firing line for populist attack. This cultural backdrop filters into the milieu and means people start to have an intrinsic desire to disassociate themselves from the elites. In reality, that's completely untrue – having a vodka tonic on a sunny day doesn't have any bearing on being elitist – but the association is there, and one to avoid when hosting an Aperol spritz event.

## 2. Community: bars aren't what they used to be

Urban centres post-Covid have been changing. European towns and cities have been moving towards the model of the 'fifteen-minute city', whereby services and businesses are within fifteen minutes of a person's home. This has been both a deliberate town-planning initiative as well as an organic business adaptation, and the effect is that the high street has come to people, rather than people going to the high street. As a result, some communities have become a lot tighter and more insular after Covid. While the concept of moving back to a village mentality might sound appealing, the reality of it is that a) wealthier communities thrive, while poorer communities do not have the same level of investment, and b) in becoming more insular, they turn into physical echo chambers of homogeneity. The future of the community is where your neighbours are 'people like us'.

The number of bars, pubs and restaurants that are closing in urban centres, particularly in less affluent areas, poses a challenge to serving a great drink like an Aperol spritz. The future – I suggested – is not that people will cease to celebrate, but that celebrations will move to new spaces, outside of bars, and we'll see a rise in pop-up bars in unused shops, street parties, school fundraisers and mini-festivals in parks or public spaces. It's human nature to party, and a street is as good as a bar, which is as good as a living room – as long as it has the right atmosphere, people and drinks.

## 3. Identity: AI will be making decisions for us

And thirdly, as discussed in Chapter 8, personal AI will change everything, including the aperitif. The way people plan parties, start parties and serve drinks at parties will all change when endless decision-making and creativity are done with the assistance of AI. Given your AI will learn where, when and how we like to party, it will inevitably affect how we find a party!

The interesting thing about these three near- to mid-term drivers of change is that they can all be imagined, but it was the first time we had put them together to imagine the future of celebration. Celebrations focused on food and alcohol tend to sit on a spectrum, where at one end people are seeking a special occasion, often based on new experiences and a sense of enlightenment, or they are seeking to lift the everyday, a sense of familiarity that gives people purpose, in a place that means something to them. It's a spectrum between aspirational novelty vs ritualised comfort; it's street food vs McDonald's; and in alcohol, it's a nightclub vs the local boozer. If celebration is about catering to a higher form of connection, the future celebration does it through two different types of community:

## Communities of possibility

In this world, the party doesn't wait for the weekend; it waits for your vibe to sync with others! AI will track your social rhythm; it will remind you and others of your flavour preferences and celebration styles, then triangulate these against a network of like-minded individuals to orchestrate gatherings with uncanny precision. You might find yourself at a curated rooftop soirée, surrounded by strangers who somehow feel like old friends, each sipping cocktails that match their mood metadata. These aren't elitist, invite-only affairs – they're algorithmically democratic, anchored not in class but in shared sensorial identity. In this space, you aren't just a person who likes negronis – you're someone whose celebration style leans spontaneous, creative, and your AI knows just who else shares that vibe.

Technology, rather than alienating, becomes the bridge to new forms of belonging, where identity is not static but constantly composed through finding the right celebration. When nobody knows how the event will go, it will be important to signify the start, and an aperitif will represent the moment of exploration into the unknown.

For the sceptics in the room – and there were some – I pointed out that some of these futures already exist:

— Particularly in the gaming world, where knowledge and experience of the game gives people kudos. Many online gamers are also starting to meet in the real world, having been friends online for years.

— AI is already matching people together. The dating world is the first step in this direction, with other services like Timeleft arranging dinner for you with like-minded strangers at a restaurant you are likely to enjoy, after you answer a few psychometric questions.

— The rise in immersive theatre, where the audience plays an active role in the performance, already shows there is a large appetite for celebration based purely on possibility rather than certainty (which is how most plays end).

## Communities of familiarity

As cities reorganise themselves around the principles of the fifteen-minute city and bars continue to shut in less affluent neighbourhoods, a new kind of celebration emerges: 'The NeighbourGood'. These are hyper-local gatherings formed not around status or spectacle but around proximity, participation and shared ritual. With public space reclaimed for joy, people take to the streets, courtyards and car parks with folding tables, Aperol carts and Bluetooth speakers. The emphasis isn't on exclusivity or trendiness but on co-creation and belonging – celebration as a civic act. Identity within these communities is rooted in contribution: who brings the best homemade lemonade, who DJed last Thursday or who fixed the garden fence.

In a world wary of elitism, these micro-festivals resist the optics of extravagance and instead offer the authenticity of shared labour and local joy. These celebrations have happened so many times before that people get excited because they know exactly what happens next. People reject the presence of technology because it inhibits the tempo of the moment, restricting the potential hedonism. They're not just parties, they're rehearsals for a more collective way of living, and starting with an aperitif is a reminder of their collective effervescence, a memory of previous joys.

The future based on familiarity created a lot more nodding heads in the room. While both scenarios were just as likely, this version tapped into our collective desire to inject humanity into the future. I didn't need to follow up with the signals for change because the audience did it for me, giving the following examples:

- Lockdown street parties continued long after Covid, with Halloween often becoming a neighbourhood gathering, and a revival in local history events.
- Businesses were moving out of the city centres towards the local high street as a result of people working from home.
- Many had been to new shows and clubs where everyone had to hand over their phone so they couldn't record the event, giving people a sense of freedom to be their best selves.

The problem for Campari is how does one Aperol spritz aperitif prompt an exploration into the unknown during immersive theatre while at the same time becoming the staple for a Friday night park gathering? This dualistic world can be difficult for products and brands to navigate, as every brand strives to have a clear and consistent positioning in the mind of the consumer.

But this obsession with a brand standing for one clear idea is outdated. As the world bifurcates into different experiences that are based on varied cultural experiences, so too can products and brands. Context is king in the mind of a consumer, and when Campari decide their aperitifs are there for anyone who wants to *start* a party, they start a ritual rather than an occasion.

# SO WHAT?
## Mapping the future in life, business and society

The only constant is change, though sometimes it's harder to see than we imagine. Our belief systems are typically slow to change but they do adapt to new scenarios, as we saw in the pandemic when people fought for social justice, and as we'll likely see in the future as we incorporate personal AI and synthetic companions into our lives. Imagining hoverboards and self-driving cars is fun, but using culture as the basis for future planning allows us to see more 'knowns' than we might expect, because we are extrapolating based on what we already know about ourselves and how we are likely to act. The future is murky, but mapping how our culture will develop is much clearer.

Borrowing from the futurists, there are five important rules for cultural change that apply to life, business and society equally.

### 1. You can only predict two to three years in advance

Mapping how change will happen in the short term is a much safer bet because our belief systems will likely be similar in that time. Predicting what we'll want to do in our career, how quickly a business can change its culture, or the way society treats gender fluidity are all easier to map if we are confident about the belief systems they're based on; our beliefs are the bedrock for cultural change.

### 2. Correct predictions sound crazy

This one is harder to do anything about but important to note. If it's not crazy enough as an idea, then it's probably wrong;

but if it's too crazy, nobody will believe you. Consider it the catch-22 of culture mapping.

### 3. Don't expect people to change

People are creatures of habit – whether it's the time we wake up, how businesses deal with their customers or whether society shifts to AI, you can expect the change to be slower than you'd imagine on paper. This is particularly important in business transformation plans, where bosses have spent months planning for a restructure or market announcement, only for staff to seemingly ignore them because they haven't been on the journey of change.

### 4. Look at the counterculture

Looking to the fringes is great fun. In life, countercultural movements arrive in fashion trends that you initially assumed weren't for you, only to realise that you've adopted that style six months later and wish you'd got on board earlier.

In business, the countercultural trends are the greatest source of innovation. If you're a market leader, your competitors will be demonstrating the countercultural innovations because they'll need to do something different to compete. If you're a small business up against Goliath, then taking the opposite strategy to the market leader will probably offer great dividends. Culture never stands still, and in business it's important to be vigilant about what's happening at the fringes.

In society, countercultural movements are moments of resistance. Each movement needs to be assessed on its merits and must never be discounted simply because it's different. Women getting the vote, wearing seat belts and not smoking indoors were all seen as countercultural movements that were challenging to the mainstream, but viewed with hindsight, they were obviously right.

## 5. The future is here, it's just not evenly distributed

This is an excuse to go somewhere interesting. Whatever you want to achieve in life, business or society, there's probably a place that's already trying it out in one form or another, and you'll learn a lot from going there.

# 10

## Life Lessons from a Business Anthropologist

Whenever an anthropologist conducts research, they learn as much about themselves as they do about the topic they're studying. This practice of 'reflexivity' is important in the academic world as it makes us assess how we might be bringing our own preconceptions, biases and judgements to a topic. In the early part of my career, I worked on a project with five other colleagues investigating sexual health practices in Essex. At the end, we all admitted that the work had inspired each of us to go for a check-up because talking about sexual health had made us reflect on our own behaviour. Most of us were in our late twenties and single, and we rarely thought about the consequences of our actions until we were forced to address them through researching what other people do. When studying obesity, I changed my nutrition; when studying home furnishing, I rearranged my home; when studying financial capability, I increased my pension contributions and opened a savings account. On the flip side, when I worked for a fizzy drinks company, I consumed many more cans of Coke; when working for a tobacco company, I began social smoking; and when working for an alcohol company, I started having a nightcap (or two) each evening. When you live and breathe a culture in order to understand it, you question your own behaviour too.

Anthropology is a fantastic analytical tool for business and government, but it also teaches us great skills for life. Anthropology helps you understand other people. I've spent years listening to other people and I've honed my skills of interpretation. I know when people talk about why they chose one brand over another, it is often really about where they see themselves in society. When people talk about their child's behaviour, it is often a conversation about their moral code. The skill of active, unconditional listening is incredibly important; when we listen closely, we hear more than words. Both anthropologists and psychologists approach a conversation similarly, but a psychologist will see forms of cognition, whereas an anthropologist will analyse how people sit within a culture. Both look beyond the words to draw different conclusions.

Beyond understanding yourself and others better, being reflexive – knowing where you sit in relation to a topic – helps you fit into new groups. There's a skill in getting people to tell their story honestly and openly, and it often comes through quickly picking up on the signals and gestures that are important to the group – its secret rules and peculiar rituals. A skilled anthropologist can become a cultural chameleon, accepted in numerous communities while remaining authentic to who they really are. In psychology, they call it 'mirroring', but I believe it's more than simply being a mirror to other people. I believe it's about embodying their behaviours to a point where an anthropologist actually thinks and acts like the group to gain deeper understanding.

We don't all have to *be* anthropologists, but any of the challenges that people face today – be that at work, at home, meeting new people and making new friends – could be improved with good anthropological training.

### The need for cultural intelligence

We are living through an era of *culture* wars, based on the rise of woke *culture*, that's often combined with cancel *culture*. Some of these behaviours are because of *cultural* insensitivity, but at times it's because of *cultural* appropriation. It takes a real *culture* vulture to point this out because it's easier to notice if you're on the *cultural* scene. You get the point – culture is being used to describe a lot of movements right now. At first, I thought the overuse of 'culture' was a gross simplification, a way to mobilise support for a cause through simple slogans. But over time, I've come to accept the increasing use of 'culture' in common vernacular is probably down to the fragmentation of mass culture into small cultural movements. The reason this zeitgeist has emerged is because governments, businesses and society have needed to navigate an ever-changing cultural landscape.

This is what cultural intelligence is. The ability to see how elements of our life are interconnected in a way that is bigger than the sum of its parts; it focuses on humanity as a series of interdependent actors bound together with a common goal. The pandemic gave people an opportunity to reassess their moral code and values, and it provided a much-needed reset on a lot of behaviours, like the amount of time people were willing to spend at work over being with their family. We created new routines, started new traditions and reaffirmed some important boundaries that meant that certain cultures changed. The medical shock the world went through was followed very closely by a culture shock that sharpened our cultural intelligence.

But we, as human beings, are not particularly good at *articulating* the presence of culture in our lives. We like to think our behaviour is a result of our fears, desires and motivations, and that we design the world around us according to our individual preferences: 'I have decided to spend more time at home rather than at work, so I will only go to the office three days a week.' Well, sadly not; you actually decided to go to the office three days a week because there is a new collective belief system that says this is acceptable, and it works to your advantage. The culture has shifted in a way that has allowed us to act on this preference.

Here I will lay out the techniques, analysis and cultural viewpoints that help anthropologists see culture. None of these methods require a PhD or a spreadsheet but rather seeing, listening and feeling. The practice of anthropology is a human skill that means we look beyond the brain for answers, and instead ask bigger questions about why we do what we do.

## Principles of participant observation (aka getting to know someone)

The fieldwork of anthropology (known as ethnography) is premised on 'participant observation'. Observation is crucial as we care as much about what people are doing as what they're saying. Anthropologists are not interested in being an impartial observer, someone without experience or feeling, instead they are expected to take part in the same activity as those they're observing. Polish anthropologist Bronislaw Malinowski developed participant observation out of pure necessity.[1] In 1914 Malinowski travelled to Papua New Guinea to observe and understand the Trobriand islanders, but his stay was extended from several weeks to several years due to the outbreak of the First World War. As a result, he learned that participating in the islanders' lives gave him the greatest insight.

One of the defining moments of my career came in an interview during my apprenticeship when I was asked to understand the causes of anti-social behaviour. When I went out to find the wayward youths of Tower Hamlets, we weren't sure whether sending a geeky anthropologist on to the streets of London was utterly inspired or likely to end in disaster. Participating in an authentic way was tricky (and potentially illegal), but hanging out in the shadows, with youths in hoodies, was the only way we were going to find the answers. Participation wasn't as hard as I feared – I was very upfront about who I was – and they thought it was amusing that someone like me would want to hang out with people like them.

Walking round the streets with them was both enlightening and petrifying. I was on edge; these kids had swagger, actively sought eye contact with strangers in the street and expected everyone else to move aside. If they weren't walking, they were on a busy corner surveying the street like aggressive meerkats, rather than talking among themselves. To me, it appeared as though they were looking for trouble.

The group jumped on to a wall, which led to another wall, which meant we could climb on top of someone's garage, which was one of their evening drinking spots. They were very proud to show me their spot. There was a mass of empty vodka and whisky bottles in the corner and a couple of wooden pallets to sit on, and importantly, no overlooking windows or paths from which to be seen. Suddenly, the mood relaxed. There was no swagger any more, no aggression and no surveying the environment for danger – they were safe here. I had found their teenage pub, where they were young, silly kids. They joked and laughed, teased each other about what their friend said in class, and talked about how they didn't want to disappoint their mums. On a different night we hung out in one of their older brother's cars, playing their favourite music and smoking cigarettes. These kids were only being antisocial because they had no place to be social, which I could only learn from taking part in their world.

Participant observation works just as well for public health interventions as it does for selling cans of Coke. Over a hundred years after Malinowski developed participant observation on the Trobriand Islands for the London School of Economics, the practice is alive and well in corporate boardrooms and government departments, with some well-documented techniques on how to achieve it. Whether you are looking to get involved in anthropological investigations or simply trying to understand your family, the following techniques and ways of looking at the world should help.

## Five techniques to help you understand people better in the field (and in life)

### 1. Walking a mile in someone's shoes

While culture is often thought about as a creation – a piece of art, a performance, some graffiti – an anthropologist thinks about culture as manifesting in people. The aim of the anthropological game is to understand people through hanging out together. Taking part in the culture will help you understand people's choices and decisions.

This technique is just as applicable at home as abroad. Many people live in the same area but never see their neighbours' lives. Maybe go to a motorbike meet-up or volunteer at a food bank and see if you feel comfortable there. International travel is an extreme version of this, but there are plenty of everyday opportunities to create new cultural experiences on our doorstep, and subsequently understand how different people live. There are also ways to walk a mile in someone's shoes without having to meet them, like doing our shopping somewhere new. You will start to understand other people's views if you buy what they buy and ask shop assistants about products you know little about. Walking a mile in someone else's shoes means you have more context behind why they're making the decisions they're making.

## 2. Building up our empathy muscle

Empathy does not have an on-off switch; it is something that can be practised, revised and improved by exercise. Done well, empathy is an incredible connector, but it is different to sympathy. Empathy is the ability to understand and share another person's feelings while sympathy is a feeling of concern for someone who is experiencing a difficulty. While both come from a place of kindness, empathy drives connection while sympathy drives disconnection (just think about the last time someone felt sorry for you!).

There are three different forms of empathy worth noting. Physical empathy is wincing when your partner stubs their toe, feeling tearful when your child is upset or getting goosebumps when watching a scary film. Compassionate empathy adds a layer to physical empathy, where you understand someone's need and you want to help them with it, like giving money or time to a charity or cooking your best friend their favourite meal. The act of kindness demonstrates that you are thinking of the person in need, even when you can't fix the problem for them. Finally, cognitive empathy is where most anthropologists want to get to, but it can often take time. Cognitive empathy is where you can feel how someone else is feeling, intellectualise their position and find a way to help them with their problem. Often, it involves a little bit of time between feeling their feelings and finding a solution, but with practice, that timeframe can be reduced. Cognitive empathy is more solution focused, like realising a coworker is stressed and taking some work off their plate, or that your child is sad to miss a birthday party, so you arrange another playdate. Many of the solutions are obvious, but it's empathy that compels you to act.

This might all sound very logical and straightforward, but none of this is easy. There are many factors that get in the way of us being more empathetic, like fear, fatigue, burnout, narcissism and distraction. When a partner is wagging a finger in your face, it's quite easy for your ego to get in the way of empathy. When you're tired at work, it's easier not to be empathetic with colleagues. In the technologically engrossing society that we live in, social media is designed to steal your attention away from truly understanding people in the real world. Empathy is much harder to practise in the online world, so getting people off their phones is a good start.

This skill is not unique to anthropologists; psychologists use empathy as part of the therapeutic process. Indeed, therapists often hope to get to a state of cognitive empathy because they can advise their client on the way forward based on their needs. The difference is anthropologists use empathy to create insight or change on a societal level rather than a personal one. If we take the early days of the pandemic, there were many question marks over whether people should wear a mask. A psychological insight would be that people felt scared when surrounded by other people, so they should be provided with masks to ensure they felt safe – which is true. An anthropological insight showed that mask wearing was a public display of fear – it was a marker of their identity – so the mask itself was a form of communication. Mask wearers were implicitly saying that the virus was serious enough to warrant taking new measures to protect the health of vulnerable people and the wider community (and those who didn't wear a mask often didn't want to express fear). In fact, many anthropologists argued for mask usage to be mandatory to remind everyone there is a disease in the air (an insight that many governments might have done well to observe). Both of these insights are derived from being empathetic, but anthropology creates a different insight to psychology.

In the commercial world, *business* anthropologists benefit from practising empathy because it drives commercial success.

For brands, being empathetic towards their customers shows they care. That might simply be an advert showcasing the additional barriers a disabled athlete has to break through (Nike), or a bank that gives you guidance on how to reduce spending when overdrawn (Monzo). Empathy creates customer loyalty, which increases frequency of purchase, which in turn means advertising budgets can be reduced, leading to greater commercial success. The same is true for new product design, where an empathetic approach shows an emotional awareness for what consumers are trying to achieve when using your product, so your design is more tailored to their needs. Cognitive empathy is used by business anthropologists because action without empathy is meaningless, and empathy without action is directionless.

In our everyday lives, empathy creates meaningful connections. Putting empathy at the heart of friendships will prevent heated arguments over politics or social issues, and practising empathy in our family means that people laugh at how kooky their parents are rather than letting it wind them up. Empathy strengthens our connections and minimises our differences, but it is a continual process gained through experience and exposure. We have to constantly fight our own biases to avoid making assumptions about people, things or situations. If we can be empathetic in our endeavours, we will embrace the strange and unfamiliar rather than shun anything that represents difference.

## 3. The power of observation

You learn an awful lot from people by simply watching what they do. We are notoriously bad at accurately reporting on our own behaviour, even though we don't know it – I probably run three times a week (well, I would like to), watch about four to five hours of TV a week (and then some at the weekend), and I don't drink more than fourteen units of alcohol a week (err, how many glasses is a unit, and who's actually counting?). These behaviours are hard to self-monitor because so much of life is conducted on autopilot, and when it comes to justifying our actions, we want to be better than we really are. Given we are so bad at reporting on our own behaviour, observation gets us closer to reality, which gives us more objective data to work with.

I once visited a diabetic man who told me on the phone that he ate 'fairly healthily', that he was 'always on the go' and took his dog for a 'long walk every day'. *This is a man who manages his diabetes well*, I thought. When I met him, I was dubious about his claims given he was rather overweight and didn't seem particularly mobile. When I observed him, I realised why. For lunch, he proudly microwaved sausages because that was healthier than frying them. True. He then got the mobility scooter out to take the dog out. True, it was a long walk, but he wasn't doing much walking. Observing context behind statements, whether that's related to health, finances or how people play with their kids, gives us so much more information than people tell us.

Much of the work that I've done with brands is about how people put their products on show (or not). The relationship Dyson's customers have to cleaning can be seen through whether they have their vacuum cleaner on display or hidden in a cupboard (indicating whether the home is cleaned by everyone in the home or by the 'cleaning fairies'). The relationship consumers have with Chanel differs enormously by country: in America it's communicated through a prominently worn handbag, in Spain through a fragrance people recognise from a kiss on the cheek, and in China through having the brand logo in a picture frame on the wall. Observing how products and brands are communicated visually adds an enormous amount of context to how the brand should behave and increase its business. In some countries, it's common to open windows regularly and have plants in the home because people want to be closer to nature and value the physical environment. This is true in countries with good air quality (like Germany) as well as terrible air quality (like China), where it's considered always better to have air flowing through the home. The Scandinavian aesthetic is seen as a calm, harmonious space to some and a complete waste of perfectly usable space to others. As humans, we are natural observers, and we can turn what we see into meaning.

Non-interventional observation can also offer helpful insight. Watching the flow of people through a train station, department store or supermarket offers insight into how spaces influence people's behaviour. A fragrance department can feel like a sensory overload, and you can literally see people rushing past the perfume stalls. Many aisles in a supermarket are wider than they need to be because even a small amount of human contact (known as the 'butt brush') makes customers stop browsing and move on.[2] McDonald's doesn't have any cushioning on their seats as uncomfortable people eat faster and leave space for more customers.

A golden rule for anthropologists in the field is to ask, 'Can you show me?' No matter how good, vivid and interesting someone is at describing what they do, you will almost certainly find out something new if you get them to show you as well. It's not that anthropologists don't trust people to tell the truth; it's just that they don't believe people can.

## 4. The art of a great question

While observation is a fantastic way to understand what people do, a great question can reveal why they did it. Great questions come in all shapes and sizes, and the proof of greatness is whether the answer tells the questioner or respondent something new. Sometimes great questions are philosophical –

'How is your relationship with your partner different now compared to when you met?' Others are designed to explain some of the things they do on autopilot – 'Why do you always stack the dishwasher after dinner while the kids go off and play?' A great question is perfectly timed and often reveals an inherent tension, like why people are still married, or why parents don't want their kids to learn housework. Great questions come from people who read a situation with all their senses and can feel something in the air.

When I'm exploring a topic, I try to be as naive as possible. If I'm studying personal care, I will know everything about the benefits, science and cost of every product – but I won't know what *the person in front of me thinks* about them, which is the part I am intentionally naive about. Being naive means you get to explore someone else's world without assumption, without prejudice, and you put it together one piece at a time from their point of view. Anthropological fieldwork often requires us to spend a whole day or more with an individual, listening to them talk about themselves. This level of indulgence often allows people to get deeper insight into their own life, allowing them to vocalise their thoughts without judgement.

There are two different lines of questioning available to anthropologists. Social questions focus on how people interact with other people, institutions, objects and brands. 'How did you meet your partner?' 'What do you think about your employer?' 'Why have you put this object/brand here?' Social questions relate to how people fit into a community and how they express their identity, and should reveal their underlying beliefs and values.

Personal questions are equally useful to uncover the root cause of a problem. A common line of personal questioning is the 'five whys' – an interview technique where you ask 'why' at least five times following the initial question. The science is utterly non-existent, but anecdotally, this works very well (and you can always ask it six or seven times, if required). I used this technique when interviewing adolescents who had received an Antisocial Behaviour Order (ASBO) from the police, which worked particularly well as they are a notoriously inarticulate bunch (note: 'Ian' comes from Tottenham, a working-class area of London where people have a gritty, fast-paced accent, with punctuation that makes more sense when heard than when written down).

>Me: So, can you tell me how you got your ASBO?
>
>Ian: Yeah, it was because I was out on my moped with my mates on the corners. They did warn me and that, the police, and they said I was doing it too often but I didn't think it was that bad, so I was a bit surprised when they slapped me with an ASBO.
>
>Me: Why?
>
>Ian: 'Cos I wasn't really doing nothing wrong. I wasn't trying to scare no one, I was just having a laugh with my mates and that, but they said it was antisocial to the people in the houses.
>
>Me: Why?
>
>Ian: I dunno why. I guess they think we're there to rob them or summink, but we ain't there for that, we're just out havin' fun, you know.
>
>Me: Why?
>
>Ian: 'Cos we haven't got anywhere else to go, have we? I can't be here with my mates 'cos my mum'll go nuts, and if I go to my room, then my brother's gonna be there. We can't go to Mark's because his place is tiny, and all my other mates ain't got anywhere we can go.
>
>Me: Why?

Ian: There ain't no place we can go. I'd live somewhere else if I could, but I haven't got the money for that. I can't afford a place which is why I'm still here. Mum doesn't exactly want me here either, but that's the way it is

Me: Why?

Ian: I can't get a steady job. I tried. The call centre had it in for me and my supervisor was a prick. He asked me to do the hard calls knowing I was gonna fail, so they got rid of me. I go down the job centre every week, but even in there they look at me and think 'he can't do that' 'cos I didn't really do school, so I just get the odd labouring day where I can. If I could go back and learn better I would, but that's all past now. And when you ain't got a job in London, what you gonna do?

The five whys successfully identified the root cause of why he has an ASBO, which is that he felt rejected by his mum because she wanted him to leave home, and rejected by society because he couldn't get a job. So he hung out on the corner and revved his moped repeatedly, which annoyed the local residents.

### 5. Listen to the silence

The final technique is to park your questions and listen to the silence. Silences are everywhere, and they generally fall into one of three categories: information that is a) omitted, b) neglected or c) unbearable to say. People omit information from a story regularly; we'd rather not say we got the job because we were in the right place at the right time; instead we'd rather say we spent a long time researching the employer. The truth is complex, yet we often tell simple stories that prioritise factors we want people to know about us. If there are holes in someone's story, ask them to retell it again later, and probe into the parts of the story that have shifted.

People also wilfully neglect elements of a story, partly because they are in denial. We might neglect to tell someone that we were out of work for six months because we don't want anyone to know that we were fired. Silences based on neglecting information are more carefully constructed and protect someone's identity, so the silence can be harder to find. You can test out a neglectful silence by asking them to confirm/deny your own theory as to why something happened, which allows you to probe for the holes in a naive manner.

Silence on topics that people just can't bear to talk about are often based on cultural avoidance. Whereas the first two types of silence are about identity protection, cultural avoidance is driven by a society's values around a particular topic (an anthropologist's dream). Many of these are often quite big and predictable topics, like not wanting to talk about sex, money or addiction. But there are a whole host of smaller silences that are indicative of cultural avoidance, like gender divisions in household chores, child poverty rates, housing inequality or maternity provision. Many of these topics are silenced in the media, in workplaces and around the dinner table, and the silence is hard to find.

Amusingly, the best people at finding silence based on cultural avoidance are people from another culture. If you approach the world with a different set of values, it becomes easier to spot the silences.

### Cultural viewpoints (and life skills)

Many of these techniques are intuitive because anthropological investigation is a very human skill. We bring out people's stories in a way that illuminates how culture affects their day-to-day lives, through understanding how identities are formed, the way they interact with their communities, and how they express their underlying belief systems.

Exploring these cultural factors is incredibly useful when trying to redesign a service or launch a new product, but it is also helpful in our daily lives. Culture is not owned by any one person or group, and it is not a fixed data point. Culture is ever shifting and is owned as much by anthropologists as artists, mechanics, midwives and street cleaners. Everyone has an identity, is part of a community and has an underlying belief system that guides them in life, which means these skills are everywhere.

### Identity – how culture shapes you

You don't meet a person so much as you encounter *an* identity. By observing someone, you will see they also have other identities in different places with different people. We are parents, children, workers, political ranters, players of games, hunters of products and makers of homes, all at once. Having empathy means we don't see someone simply as a football fan, or a mother, or (God forbid) an anthropologist because when we see people from several angles, we see they are many things. Empathy helps us understand the code switch and the links between these various identities because we're able to see the world from their point of view.

Often, these identity switches seem trivial, minor deviations, but they can come to define our lives and opinions. Two devoted fathers, hard-working salary men, who regularly attend church and love their families, football and dog walking might seem identical until you learn that one is a Republican and the other a Democrat. While American political identities are fairly easy to identify, some of our identities are more present at different moments in time – like being a banker during the day and a gamer at night. Serious gamers use a different language among fellow gamers, make different jokes and even adopt different personas to when they are offline (or at work!). Asking the right questions in various different moments will tell you a lot about who that person is, so you know what happens when they put their gaming identity away and switch into banker mode.

Our identity is affected by the culture we live in because every identity we have is recognisable to other people. It is a projection of who we are, and we act in a particular way because we (mostly) know how it will be received.

## Community – the stuff between us

Communities are where ideas are accepted or rejected, conversations become community knowledge, and our shared rituals and routines make up a 'collective effervescence' (to quote French sociologist Émile Durkheim). Friday night piss-ups in towns across the UK are classic moments of community effervescence, designed to generate conversations and rituals that become a bonding exercise (rounds, shots, kebabs, fights). American tailgating before football games is another moment of collective bonding, whereby turning up in the parking lot can create a fizz of excitement among strangers. If we want to understand communities better, walking a mile through the collective effervescence is the best way to do it.

Yet getting involved in other communities isn't as easy as it sounds as we live in a society that naturally restricts our view. Most communities have created echo chambers – places where people only tend to hear views similar to their own. This has two opposing consequences: our own communities feel ever stronger and more unified but we fail to see other communities that are completely different. This combination drives our tribalistic tendencies because all we see is a sea of sameness, and we cease to even notice our own tribalism. If we truly want to understand what it's like to be trans, working class, a Muslim woman, a Danish man or a gig economy worker, we need to walk a mile in their shoes.

Increasingly small communities are becoming fuelled by tribalistic tendencies, but this needn't be the only way forward. We need to forge bonds between communities rather than being scared of them. To do this, we need to put ourselves in the middle of a community we don't know – sit in a synagogue or mosque, shop in a different supermarket or hang out with some gym bunnies after spin class. If you have influence in the workplace, give staff time to help in a soup kitchen or put executives to work on the shop floor. These are mechanisms that reduce 'othering', improve mental health and morale, and develop lateral thinking when it comes to problem solving.

If observation and participation are great ways to understand another community, humility and empathy help us overcome barriers between communities. Realising that someone has voted Democrat ever since they emigrated from Mexico as a runaway teenager (empathy) might get you closer to liking a political enemy. Equally, realising that building a wall on the Mexican border isn't entirely aligned to your Republican values (humility) will close the rest of the gap. Neither of you need to change your political community, but it will help you overcome some of the ways a community influences you.

### Belief system – identifying our purpose

The cultural belief systems we are brought up in probably have the largest effect over why we do what we do, but they are also the hardest to identify in everyday life. We can't see what we can't see, which makes listening for the silences a crucially important tool. Start by noticing what people talk about and you'll learn their priorities, then figure out what they are not telling you.

Societies that naturally praise people (the US) are different from those that prefer people to be humble (Sweden), and the difference indicates whether the culture values competition or consensus. Similarly, whether people get uneasy with a lack of structure (Mexico) vs those that enjoy not knowing what tomorrow will bring (the UK) shows whether a culture inspires a need for certainty.[3] These traits can be mapped across national cultures which form the baseline of people's belief systems. When people from different countries meet, these baselines become ever more obvious. My Israeli friend often opens my fridge and helps himself to a beer. When I questioned him, he said, 'Asking you for a beer is rude. I know you're not going to say no, so asking is a formality among people that aren't friends. If you want me to ask, you're basically saying we're not friends!' This blew my formal British mind and made me realise that our cultural beliefs shape so much of our behaviour.

Belief systems are the baseline for how we approach authority, whether we respect hierarchies, the types of instinctive judgements we make, who we are likely to respect and what our 'house rules' are. It dictates our family structures and explains why so many children in Shanghai are brought up, in part, by their grandparents. Our belief systems are accessed through good questions, understanding the silences and a lot of analysis about what's important to people.

Culture is obvious, but it often hides from us. It influences the drinks we order, how people feed their dogs in Brazil, or how doctors treat drunk patients in A&E. It is the water fish live in but cannot even see, impacting our every action and decision. If we examine the interaction between people, the information that's shared and the desire for collective action, we start to see culture more clearly.

## Is culture dead?

No.

Social commentators, academics and journalists occasionally make grand pronouncements about the death of culture. Globalisation, consumerism, populism, technology, data and bureaucracy are all believed to be crushing cultural differences. This is not true. Culture will never die – but the *form* of culture is always changing. The very act of putting the thermometer in the water changes its temperature, and as soon as you get involved in culture, it changes. If we think culture is dying, then we should challenge ourselves to find the countercultural movements that sit on the fringes, as they often show us what's coming next.

Culture creates the rules that we collectively live by. Culture can only die when anarchy reigns, and that day is unlikely to come, not least because cultures have a vested interest in preserving themselves. So, until that day, we should all make it our mission to uncover some of the rules that make us.

## Acknowledgements

I've had the same yoga teacher for fifteen years and at the end of every session she says, 'Give thanks to the universe, the cosmos and to all our teachers,' at which point I always think about my children. Martha and Tilly have taught me more about culture, and who I am, than anyone else. They question everything, assume nothing, and have shown me the difference between culture and cognition.

No one person owns culture, we all do, and this book is no different. I've simply written the things that I've learned from being with other people. Beyond my kids, I need to thank my parents, Jenny and Derek, for showing me the world, and pushing me to explore all parts of it. My early adventures with them definitely set the blueprint for exploring cultures around the world. And to my grandmother, Annie, who always had another blinding story to tell every time I told her what I was writing about.

During my near two decades as a business anthropologist, I've had a team that's made me who I am today. Johanna Shapira is the boss that everyone should have at some point in life, but no one ever does. And if you're lucky enough to have a buddy like Vic Guyatt at the same time, you're truly made. The three of us had a golden era of laughter, tears, exploration and a dogged determination to show the world the importance of cultural insight. We were also blessed with a guardian angel of a CEO (a rare combination) in Ben Page, who could see we were changing the world of research, while also making him a loss for the first few years.

Once I'd established the ethnographic practice at Ipsos, the cultural stories really started to flow. We ran projects in thirty-five different countries in 2018 alone, with a team that decoded the rules of culture for breakfast, lunch and dinner. If I thought I'd earned my anthropological spurs, Lucy Neiland and Helle Thorsen pushed me to another level. Hannah Mills and Ellie Tait were never afraid to say that my 'clever phrases' sounded like bullshit, which taught me to say it like it is, and Heidi kept me real while making insight look easy. Sunny Sharma, Sophie Mathison, Alma Berliner, Angus Grant, Angus Smith, Gigi Zhang, Deana Kotiga, Anna Geatrell, Stephanie Gleeson and Murray Stanford have all given me stories for this book, because they are tireless in finding out why people do what they do. And not a single one of these people could have become the cultural gurus they are today without the support of Jo Ashun. Thank you, Jo.

With these people in my life, I had a book full of stories, but it was Helen Coyle who lit the fuse for me to write it. Effortlessly, she had all the right words, at the right time, that raised my motivation one level further at each moment. Never could anyone create that level of motivation as easily as she did. Emily Attree did the necessary on the early drafts until Charlotte Merritt, my insanely wise agent, came to my rescue. Everything she predicted came to pass, and she always knew when to step forward and when to step back. I could not have asked for better editors in Phil Connor at Headline and Emily Taber at Basic Books who have tagged in and out as if they job share (they don't). Towards the end, Anna Sanders got me over the line, and then the next line, when I was flagging. She reminded me of the vision when I was word blind, gave me perspective when I was lost, and had the kindness and unbelievable capacity to read everything I sent her.

And if you've got this far, I'd like to thank you, the reader. I believe our attention has been slightly misdirected when describing why we do the things we do, and I hope this book helps you to see the world from a cultural perspective, and to recognise that we are all cultural beings.

# References

## Introduction

1 Ipsos. (2024). https://www.ipsos.com/en-us/ipsos-again-named-worlds-no-1-most-innovative-insights-analytics-company-2024-grit-top-50-suppliers

## 1. Finding the Rules That Make Us

1 The quote is often attributed to Peter Drucker, management consultant and author, though the origin is unclear.
2 Culture Capitalist, Gamwell, A. & Surles, P. (2023, November 22). The enduring relevance of anthropology. *Substack*. https://culturecapitalist.substack.com/p/the-enduring-relevance-of-anthropology
3 'Nudging', a term derived from the iconic behavioural science book *Nudge* by R. H. Thaler and C. R. Sunstein (2008), refers to the idea of subtly steering people's behaviour without restricting their freedom of choice.
4 I've used the term 'favourable outcomes' to mean what the designers of the policy want to happen, not what may actually be for the common good. Even in government, where nudging is referred to as 'libertarian paternalism', there is much debate about whether governments are good at knowing what a favourable outcome is for citizens.
5 The Nobel Prize. (2002, October 9). *The Royal Swedish Academy of Sciences has decided that the Bank of Sweden Prize in Economic Sciences will be shared* [Press release]. https://www.nobelprize.org/prizes/economic-sciences/2002/press-release/
6 Stanford Prison Experiment. *Britannica*. https://www.britannica.com/event/Stanford-Prison-Experiment
7 Project Implicit. Harvard. https://implicit.harvard.edu/implicit/iatdetails.html
8 Gillian Tett has referred to the phrase several times in various podcasts and writings, but the original quote is 'The last thing a fish

would ever notice would be water' by the 20th-century American anthropologist Ralph Linton.

9 Kochhar, R. & Moslimani, M. (2023, December 4). *Wealth gaps across racial and ethnic groups*. Pew Research Center. https://www.pewresearch.org/2023/12/04/wealth-gaps-across-racial-and-ethnic-groups/

10 The Sentencing Project (2021). *The color of justice*. https://www.sentencingproject.org/reports/the-color-of-justice-racial-and-ethnic-disparity-in-state-prisons-the-sentencing-project/

11 Crockett, Z. (2016, September 13). 'Gang member' and 'thug' roles in film are disproportionately played by black actors. *Vox*. https://www.vox.com/2016/9/13/12889478/black-actors-typecasting

12 Wolf, E. R. (1964). *Anthropology*. Prentice-Hall.

## 2. How Culture Affects Life, Business and Society

1 Geertz, C. (1973). *The interpretation of cultures*. Basic Books.
2 Statista. (2025). *Number of consumers of tea including herbal/fruit/green tea in the United Kingdom in 2024*. https://www.statista.com/statistics/301982/tea-usage-by-user-type-in-the-uk/
3 Miner, H. (1956). Body ritual among the Nacirema. *American Anthropologist, 58*(3), 503–507. https://www.sfu.ca/~palys/Miner-1956-BodyRitualAmongTheNacirema.pdf
4 Wang, T. (2016, January 20). Why big data needs thick data. *Medium*. https://medium.com/ethnography-matters/why-big-data-needs-thick-data-b4b3e75e3d7
5 Change4Life. National Social Marketing Centre. https://www.thensmc.com/resources/showcase/change4life
6 Ipsos in the UK. (2018, June 8). *The power of culture – Matthew Walmsley, Public Health England*. YouTube. https://www.youtube.com/watch?v=PLhCqcBnEH8
7 HMRC. (2016). *Soft drinks industry levy*. https://www.gov.uk/government/publications/soft-drinks-industry-levy/soft-drinks-industry-levy
8 Public Health England. (2020, October 7). *Sugar reduction: progress report, 2015 to 2019*. Department of Health and Social Care. https://www.gov.uk/government/publications/sugar-reduction-report-on-progress-between-2015-and-2019

## 3. Culture Makes an ASS Out of U and ME

1 Freud, S. (2014 ed.). *Civilization and its discontents*. Penguin Classics.

2. Gelfand, M. (2018). *Rule makers, rule breakers: Tight and loose cultures and the secret signals that direct our lives.* Scribner.
3. Oreg, I. and Sverdlik, N. (2018, May 22). Translating dispositional resistance to change to the culture level. *European Journal of Personality, 32*: 327–352. https://bschool-en.huji.ac.il/sites/default/files/businesshe/files/oreg_sverdlik_2018.pdf; Ambrosino, B. (2014, December 29). What the world values, in one chart. Vox. https://www.vox.com/2014/12/29/7461009/culture-values-world-inglehart-welzel
4. The Sutton Trust. (2019, November 20). *Almost half of the public say today's youth will be worse off than their parents* [Press release]. https://www.suttontrust.com/news-opinion/all-news-opinion/almost-half-of-the-public-say-todays-youth-will-be-worse-off-than-their-parents/
5. World Bank Group. (2022, April 1). *Lifting 800 million people out of poverty – new report looks at lessons from China's experience* [Press release]. https://www.worldbank.org/en/news/press-release/2022/04/01/lifting-800-million-people-out-of-poverty-new-report-looks-at-lessons-from-china-s-experience
6. World Bank Group. (2024, October 23). *The World Bank in China.* https://www.worldbank.org/en/country/china/overview
7. Ipsos interviewed a representative sample of 22,285 adults aged sixteen to seventy-four from thirty-three markets. Data was weighted to match the profile of the population. Ipsos. (2020, January). *Global perceptions of social mobility.* https://www.ipsos.com/sites/default/files/ct/news/documents/2020-01/report-global-advisor-social-mobility-2020.pdf
8. Guy Shrubsole's 2019 book *Who Owns England?* suggests that over 50% of the country is owned by 1% of the population, which is largely made up of the aristocracy, gentry, corporations, bankers and the Crown.
9. Pew Research Center. (2023, April 13). *In a growing share of U.S. marriages, husbands and wives earn about the same.* https://www.pewresearch.org/social-trends/2023/04/13/in-a-growing-share-of-u-s-marriages-husbands-and-wives-earn-about-the-same/
10. Pew Research Center. (2017, June 22). *The demographic of gun ownership.* https://www.pewresearch.org/social-trends/2017/06/22/the-demographics-of-gun-ownership/
11. Yi, S. (2021). *Grandparents' co-parenting in urban China and its influence on parents and children.* Child Research Net. https://www.jstage.jst.go.jp/article/asiajapanbulletin/2/0/2_2.0_31/_pdf/-char/ja
12. World Economic Forum (2020). *The global social mobility report 2020.* https://www3.weforum.org/docs/Global_Social_Mobility_Report.pdf

## 4. Culture Starts at Home

1. Kondo, M. (2014). *The life-changing magic of tidying: A simple, effective way to banish clutter forever.* Vermilion.
2. Pelchen, L. & Allen, S. (2024, October 3). Home improvement, interrupted. *Forbes.* https://www.forbes.com/home-improvement/contractor/labor-materials-shortage-impacts-renovations/
3. Ipsos. (2011, June). *Children's wellbeing in UK, Sweden, and Spain: The role of inequality and materialism.* https://www.unicef.org.uk/wp-content/uploads/2011/09/IPSOS_UNICEF_ChildWellBeingreport.pdf
4. Pogosyan, M. (2017, February 21). Geert Hofstede: A conversation about culture. *Psychology Today.* https://www.psychologytoday.com/gb/blog/between-cultures/201702/geert-hofstede-a-conversation-about-culture
5. Żemojtel-Piotrowska, M. & Piotrowski, J. (2023). Hofstede's cultural dimensions theory. *Encyclopedia of Sexual Psychology and Behavior*, 1–4. https://www.researchgate.net/publication/371822907_Hofstede's_Cultural_Dimensions_Theory
6. Fox, K. (2004). *Watching the English: The hidden rules of English behaviour.* Hodder & Stoughton.

## 5. Finding the Rules That Change Us

1. Torches of freedom campaign. Omeka. https://omeka.uottawa.ca/jmccutcheon/exhibits/show/american-women-in-tobacco-adve/torches-of-freedom-campaign
2. Packard, V. (1984). *The hidden persuaders.* Pocket.
3. Thaler, R. H. & Sunstein, C. R. (2009). *Nudge: Improving decisions about health, wealth and happiness.* Penguin Books.
4. As terminology goes, I've always thought that the use of 'interventions', a word borrowed from the therapeutic side of psychology, feels rather sinister in a context describing social change.
5. Statistics Netherlands. (2024, August 28). *Over 4 million people withhold consent for organ donation.* https://www.cbs.nl/en-gb/news/2024/35/over-4-million-people-withhold-consent-for-organ-donation
6. Department for Work & Pensions. (2024). *Workplace pension participation and savings trends of eligible employees: 2009 to 2023.* https://www.gov.uk/government/statistics/workplace-pension-participation-and-savings-trends-2009-to-2023/workplace-pension-participation-and-savings-trends-of-eligible-employees-2009-to-2023

7 Wilkinson, A., Parker, M., Martineau, F. & Leach, M. (2017). Engaging 'communities': anthropological insights from the West African Ebola epidemic. *Philosophical Transactions of the Royal Society of London. Series B, Biological Sciences, 372*(1721). https://pmc.ncbi.nlm.nih.gov/articles/PMC5394643/
8 Art, V. (2024, November 18). Johnnie Walker's 'Keep Walking' campaign overview. *Oh Bev*. https://www.ohbev.com/blog/johnnie-walkers-striding-man-keep-walking-campaign
9 Cave, A. (2017, September 5). Deal that undid Bell Pottinger: inside story of the South Africa scandal. *Guardian*. https://www.theguardian.com/media/2017/sep/05/bell-pottinger-south-africa-pr-firm

## 6. How Tribalism Makes Us and Breaks Us

1 Kelly, J. (2020, November 30). How politics drive our personal relationships – and even where we live. *UVA Today*. https://news.virginia.edu/content/how-politics-drive-our-personal-relationships-and-even-where-we-live
2 Klein, E. (2020). *Why we're polarized*. Simon & Schuster.
3 Salvanto, A. (2022, September 5). Americans increasingly concerned about political violence – CBS News poll. CBS News. https://www.cbsnews.com/news/political-violence-opinion-poll-2022-09-05/
4 Pew Research Center. (2017, October 5). *The partisan divide on political values grows even wider*. https://www.pewresearch.org/politics/2017/10/05/7-global-warming-and-environmental-regulation-personal-environmentalism/
5 BBC News. (2016, June 24). EU referendum: England leads UK to exit. https://www.bbc.co.uk/news/uk-politics-eu-referendum-36606245
6 Ipsos. (2023, March 8). *Americans divided on whether 'woke' is a compliment or insult*. https://www.ipsos.com/en-us/americans-divided-whether-woke-compliment-or-insult
7 Lee, G. (2017, October 24). FactCheck Q&A: How many children are going to gender identity clinics in the UK?. Channel 4 News. https://www.channel4.com/news/factcheck/factcheck-qa-how-many-children-are-going-to-gender-identity-clinics-in-the-uk.
8 Department of Work and Pensions. (2016). *Performance of the Carer's Allowance Unit: Apr 2015 to Mar 2016*. https://www.gov.uk/government/publications/performance-of-the-carers-allowance-unit-apr-2015-to-mar-2016/performance-of-the-carers-allowance-unit-apr-2015-to-mar-2016

## 7. Social Silences Create Social Consequences

1. Canada Life. (2024, March 22). *Over half of UK adults do not have a will*. https://www.canadalife.co.uk/news/over-half-of-uk-adults-do-not-have-a-will/
2. NHS. (2022, August 16). *Loneliness in older people*. https://www.nhs.uk/mental-health/feelings-symptoms-behaviours/feelings-and-symptoms/loneliness-in-older-people/
3. Yi, S. (2021). *Grandparents' co-parenting in urban China and its influence on parents and children*. Child Research Net. https://www.jstage.jst.go.jp/article/asiajapanbulletin/2/0/2_2.0_31/_pdf/-char/ja
4. Gulino, E. (2024, February 20). When can you ask the person you're dating: 'How much money do you make?'. *Refinery29*. https://www.refinery29.com/en-us/how-to-talk-about-money-in-a-relationship
5. Naughton, J. (2018, December 30). The growth of internet porn tells us more about ourselves than technology. *Guardian*. https://www.theguardian.com/commentisfree/2018/dec/30/internet-porn-says-more-about-ourselves-than-technology
6. Statista. (2024). *Most popular pornographic websites worldwide as of November 2024*. https://www.statista.com/statistics/1445673/most-visited-porn-websites-worldwide-unique-visits/
7. Zattoni, F. et al. (2020, November 28). The impact of COVID-19 pandemic on pornography habits: a global analysis of Google Trends. *Springer Nature*, 33(8):824–831. https://pmc.ncbi.nlm.nih.gov/articles/PMC7699018/
8. FHE Health. (2024). *Revealing statistics re: pornography addiction*. https://fherehab.com/learning/pornography-addiction-stats?
9. Mann, S. (2023, January 10). *Teens are watching pornography, and it's time to talk about it*. Common Sense Media. https://www.commonsensemedia.org/kids-action/articles/teens-are-watching-pornography-and-its-time-to-talk-about-it
10. Abrams, Z. (2023, October 1). *Up to 19% of teens experience dating violence. Psychologists want to break the cycle*. American Psychological Association. https://www.apa.org/monitor/2023/10/disrupting-teen-dating-violence
11. FDA. (2025, January 22). *Results from the Annual National Youth Tobacco Survey (NYTS)*. https://www.fda.gov/tobacco-products/youth-and-tobacco/results-annual-national-youth-tobacco-survey-nyts
12. Rostad, W. L., Gittins-Stone, D., Huntington, C., Rizzo, C. J., Pearlman, D., Orchowski, L. (2019, October 1). *The association between exposure to violent pornography and teen dating violence in

grade 10 high school students. National Library of Medicine. https://pmc.ncbi.nlm.nih.gov/articles/PMC6751001/?

13  Macdowall, W. ,Gibson, L., & Tanton, C., et al. (2013). Lifetime prevalence, associated factors, and circumstances of non-volitional sex in women and men in Britain. *Lancet, 382*(9907), 1845–1855. https://pmc.ncbi.nlm.nih.gov/articles/PMC3898964/

14  Georgiev, G. (2019, November 20). $350 mln. in 6 months — the cost of the 2019 Gillette advertising fiasco?. *Medium.* https://georgi-georgiev.medium.com/350-mln-in-6-months-the-cost-of-the-2019-gillette-advertising-fiasco-86785f29a4bf

15  Pew Research Center. (2025, March 4). *Gender pay gap in U.S. has narrowed slightly over 2 decades.* https://www.pewresearch.org/short-reads/2025/03/04/gender-pay-gap-in-us-has-narrowed-slightly-over-2-decades/

16  Institute for Women's Policy Research. (2024, May). *IWPR #110* https://iwpr.org/wp-content/uploads/2024/05/IWPR-Retirement-Income-Gap-Quick-Figure-2024-1.pdf

17  Women's Bureau, U.S. Department of Labor. (2025, January). *Women and wealth.* https://www.dol.gov/sites/dolgov/files/WB/508_Older_Womens_Wealth_Review%20Issue%20Brief_01232025.pdf

18  Ipsos/King's College London. (2024, March 4). *Nearly half of Britons say women's equality has gone far enough.* https://www.kcl.ac.uk/news/nearly-half-of-britons-say-womens-equality-has-gone-far-enough

19  Ipsos. (2024, March 4). *Masculinity and women's equality: Study finds emerging gender divide in young people's attitudes.* https://www.ipsos.com/en-uk/masculinity-and-womens-equality-study-finds-emerging-gender-divide-young-peoples-attitudes

20  Ipsos. (2025, May 29). *Young men believe women prioritise attractiveness and financial status when dating, but young women say kindness and humour more important.* https://www.ipsos.com/en-uk/young-men-believe-women-prioritise-attractiveness-and-financial-status-when-dating-young-women-say

21  Chiliza, J., Brennan, A. T., Laing, R., Feeley III, F. G. (2025, December 31). *Evaluation of the impact of PEPFAR transition on retention in care in South Africa's Western Cape Province.* National Library of Medicine. https://pmc.ncbi.nlm.nih.gov/articles/PMC11704810/

22  MenStar Coalition. A community-based peer-support intervention to improve men's linkage to and early retention in HIV treatment. https://www.menstarcoalition.org/not-linked/coach-mpilo/

23 Tett, G. (2021). *Anthro-vision: How anthropology can explain business and life.* Random House Business.

## 8. How Technology Creates New Rules in Life

1 Lawrence, I. (2018, November 12). The F1 barcode that had everyone talking. *Smart Motoring.* https://smart-motoring.com/latest-news/the-barcode-that-had-everyone-talking/
2 Haidt, J. (2024). *The anxious generation: How the great rewiring of childhood is causing an epidemic of mental illness.* Penguin.
3 NHS England. (2022, December 15). *Health survey for England, 2021, part 1.* https://digital.nhs.uk/data-and-information/publications/statistical/health-survey-for-england/2021/part-3-drinking-alcohol
4 Buchholz, K. (2023, September 8). *Gen Z: The more sober generation.* Statista. https://www.statista.com/chart/30783/alcohol-consumption-by-generation/
5 Berry, K. (2024, November 24). 'I was scammed out of £75k by Martin Lewis deepfake advert'. BBC News. https://www.bbc.co.uk/news/articles/clyvj754d9lo
6 Ben-Zion, Z., Witte, K., & Jagadish, A. K. et al. (2025). Assessing and alleviating state anxiety in large language models. *npj: Digital Medicine, 8.* https://www.nature.com/articles/s41746-025-01512-6
7 Landymore, F. (2025, April 2). An AI model has officially passed the Turing Test. *Futurism.* https://futurism.com/ai-model-turing-test

## 9. The Future Is Here, It's Just Not Evenly Distributed

1 United Nations: Department of Economic and Social Affairs. *14.9 million excess deaths associated with the COVID-19 pandemic in 2020 and 2021.* https://www.un.org/en/desa/149-million-excess-deaths-associated-covid-19-pandemic-2020-and-2021
2 Brand, S. (2000). *The clock of the long now: Time and responsibility.* Basic Books.
3 Marr, B. (2023, September 5). Virtual influencer Noonoouri lands record deal: is she the future of music? *Forbes.* https://www.forbes.com/sites/bernardmarr/2023/09/05/virtual-influencer-noonoouri-lands-record-deal-is-she-the-future-of-music/
4 MINTEL. (2023). *China live streaming commerce market report 2023.* https://store.mintel.com/report/china-live-streaming-commerce-market-report?
5 Ritchie, H. & Roser, M. (2018, April). *Alcohol consumption.* Our World in Data. https://ourworldindata.org/alcohol-consumption

## 10. Life Lessons from a Business Anthropologist

1. Baker, V. J. (1987, January). Pitching a tent in the native village: Malinowski and participant observation. *Bijdragen Tot de Taal-, Land- En Volkenkunde, 143*(1), 14–24. https://www.researchgate.net/publication/41017766_Pitching_a_tent_in_the_native_village_Malinowski_and_participant_observation
2. Page, B. (2018, June 12). Shoppers' movements might come down to fears of caves and the 'butt brush'. *Ehrenberg-Bass News.* https://marketingscience.info/shoppers-movements-might-come-down-to-fears-of-caves-and-the-butt-brush/
3. Geert Hofstede's '6-D model of national culture' gives every country a score against Power Distance, Individualism, Masculinity, Uncertainty Avoidance, Long-term Orientation and Indulgence. These measures and the Country Comparison Tool published on their website are great for comparing national cultures. https://geerthofstede.com/culture-geert-hofstede-gert-jan-hofstede/6d-model-of-national-culture/

# Index

absorption, cultural, 5
Accident & Emergency (A&E) departments, 138–151
active listening, 254–255
*Adolescence* (TV show), 191
advertising
   AI use in, 214–217, 241–243
   Gillette, 188–189
   Marlboro, 206–207
   micro-targeting, 208
   Nike, 147–149
   social media, 207–210
   subliminal, 205–207
   virtual influencers, 241–243
ageing, talking about, 178
AI *see* artificial intelligence
Airbnb, 49, 129
alcohol use
   aperitif ritual, 244–250
   experimentation with, 210–212
   hospital admissions due to, 138–145
Anthropic, 225
anthropological fieldwork skills
   asking questions, 264–268
   empathy, 260–262, 269, 271
   listening to the silence, 267–268, 271
   observing others, 262–264
   participant observation, 257–259
   walking a mile in someone's shoes, 259–260, 270–271
anthropology
   business applications, 49–53
   codification of culture, 25–28
   Cultural Trinity and, 37
   life skills learned from, 254–255
   psychology vs., 9, 18–19
   as the study of culture, 5–6
   as the study of groups, 17–19, 25–26
*Anthro-Vision* (Tett), 198
*The Anxious Generation* (Haidt), 210
aperitif ritual, 244–250

Apple, 201
Arsenal, 153–156
artificial intelligence (AI)
   algorithms, 212–213
   in business, 226–227
   celebration planning and, 246–249
   companions, 243–244
   emotional responsiveness of, 216
   glasses, 228–229
   influencers, 242–244
   living with, 212–214, 222, 225–227
   personal, 214
   pushback against, 222–224
   social media and, 209–210, 212–213
   in society, 227
   therapy, 218–222
   Turing Test and, 225
attention economy, 209
Ayurveda, 51–52

*Back to the Future Part II* (film), 228
Barnhill, John Basil, 79
beauty routines, 85–86, 212
Bedouin, 41–44
behavioural economics, 121
behavioural science, 17–18, 22, 121–124, 135–144
behaviours
   belief systems and, 70–72
   brain and, 16–18
   changing, 8
   cultural influences on, 25, 36–37
   interventions for, 141–145
   nudge tactics and, 122–124, 138–142
   during pandemic lockdowns, 20–21, 230–233
   predictions of future, 233–234, 251
   reflexivity and, 254–256
   shared, 3
   *suzhi* (high-quality behaviors), 86–87, 88

*Being John Malkovich* (film), 216
belief systems
   AI therapy and, 221-222
   American national character and, 78-83
   aperitif ritual and, 245
   baselines in, 271-272
   behaviours and, 72-74
   brand purpose and, 147-149
   British national character and, 77
   Chinese national character and, 85-88
   community and, 126, 127-128, 129
   comparing, 72-73
   construction of, 33
   in the Cultural Trinity, 28-29, 32-33
   culture wars and, 171
   friction points in, 239-240
   house rules and, 105-108, 114, 272
   identifying, 271-272
   identity and, 72, 93-96, 125-126, 129-131
   interventions and, 145-146
   manosphere and, 191-192
   pace of change and, 70-72
   political identity and, 161
   pornography and, 186
   Pride movement and, 133
   public health campaigns and, 58-59, 62
   football culture and, 155-156
   stereotypes and, 95-96
   tea culture and, 46-49
   teeth brushing routines and, 52
   weaponisation of, 160
Bell Pottinger, 152
belonging, 4, 32
Bernays, Edward, 119, 120, 121
Betty Crocker, 119-120
biases
   in AI training, 213
   cognitive, 19, 22-24, 121
   creating change with, 121
   in-group vs. out-group, 81-82
   implicit, 23-24, 26-27
Biden, Joe, 233
Bill and Melinda Gates Foundation, 193-195, 197
Black Lives Matter movement, 128, 147-149, 232
Blair, Tony, 233
*Blink* (Gladwell), 22
Blockbuster, 201
Bourdieu, Pierre, 112
boycotts, 150, 246
Brahmins, 50

brain
   behaviours and, 16-18
   cognition and, 21-24
   cognitive biases, 19, 23-24
Brand, Stewart, 235-236
brand purpose, 129, 250
Brazil
   pace of change in, 72
   pet feeding habits in, 53-56
   support systems in, 73
Brexit, 15, 71, 128, 162-169, 171, 234
British National Party (BNP), 123, 166
Bush, George W., 193
business
   AI and, 226-227
   anthropology's applications to, 49-53, 261
   boycotts of, 150, 246
   as a community, 38
   cultural change in, 150
   Cultural Trinity's applications to, 63-64
   empathy in, 262
   multinationals, 94-95
   polarisation in, 173-174
   products for harmony in the home, 103-105, 114
   psychology's applications to, 15-18, 53-56
   social silences in, 200-202
   *see also* workplace

Cambridge Analytica, 15, 150
Cameron, David, 233
Campari, 245-250
cancel culture, 255
celebrations, 247-250
Chanel, 263
change
   belief systems and pace of, 70-72
   creating with psychology, 119-124
   cultural, 149-151, 251-253
   futurists on, 236-240
   mapping with the Cultural Trinity, 126-131
   as the only constant, 131-135, 251
   openness vs. resistance to, 70-72
   pace layers, 235-236
   polarisation and, 172, 173-174
   rules for, 251-253
   social, 146-149
Change4Life, 57, 61
character, 76

ChatGPT, 216, 218-219
Chauvin, Derek, 232
Chime, 180
China
   collectivism of, 73, 84-85
   Cultural Trinity and national character of, 88
   pace of change in, 71-72
   parenting and childcare in, 84-85, 272
   stereotypes, 83-88, 93
   tea culture in, 46-47, 48
   teeth brushing routines, 50-53
   traditional Chinese medicine (TCM), 51-53, 87
   virtual influencers, 240-242
   *xiào* (filial piety and elder respect), 180
class
   equity and, 74-78
   stereotypes, 95
   talking about money and, 179
   tea culture and, 45-46, 48
climate change, 128-131, 159, 235
Clinton, Hillary, 150
*The Clock of the Long Now* (Brand), 235
Coach Mpilo, 197
cognition
   AI undermining of, 223-224
   codified by psychology, 21-24
   culture and, 9-10, 19-21
   home as balance between culture and, 112-114
cognitive dissonance, 130
cognitive empathy, 260, 262
Coke, 150, 205-208, 246
collateralised debt obligations (CDOs), 199-200
collective effervescence, 270
collectivist cultures
   China, 73, 84-85
   home organisation and, 104-105
   privacy in, 107
colonialism, 43, 47, 135
commitment devices, 122-123
Common Sense Media, 184
community
   AI therapy and, 222
   aperitif ritual and, 244-250
   belief systems and, 126, 127-128, 129
   belonging and, 174
   brand purpose and, 148-149
   British national character and, 77
   broken by tribalism, 162-169

   Chinese national character and, 86-88
   components of, 32
   cultural change through, 130-134
   in the Cultural Trinity, 28, 30
   culture wars and, 171-173
   defined, 30
   familiarity within, 249-250
   football culture and, 155
   friction points in, 239
   identity and, 125-126, 127, 129-131
   interventions and, 143
   made by tribalism, 156-161
   manosphere and, 192
   norms expressed through the home, 100-101
   online, 186-192, 240
   participation in, 270-271
   political identity and, 160
   pornography and, 185
   Pride movement and, 132
   public health campaigns and, 58-59, 61
   tea culture and, 47-48
   technology and, 248-249
   teeth brushing routines and, 52
   workplace, 30, 142-143, 174-175
compassionate empathy, 260
corporate culture, 14, 198-199
countercultural movements, 237-240, 252-253
Covid-19, 20-21, 100-101, 135-136, 193, 230-233, 234, 246-247, 250
cultural avoidance, 268
cultural intelligence, 256-257
Cultural Trinity
   in action, 33-37
   AI therapy and, 221-222
   American national character and, 83
   aperitif ritual and, 245-247
   belief systems in, 31-33
   brand purpose and, 148-149
   British national character and, 78
   business applications, 62
   Chinese national character and, 88
   community in, 28, 30
   culture wars and, 171-172
   finding countercultural moments with, 237-240
   football culture and, 156
   framework, 28-32
   identity in, 28, 29-30
   manosphere and, 192
   mapping change with, 124-131

in pet feeding habits, 56
political identity and, 160-161
pornography and, 186
Pride movement and, 1324-135
in public health campaigns, 59, 62
in tea culture, 47-48
in teeth brushing routines, 52-53
*see also* belief systems; community; identity
culture
death of, 273
definitions of, 225
elements of, 3-4
questions about, 1-2
stories about, 1-2
uses of word, 13, 256
culture wars, 169-173, 255-256

dancing analogy, 40-41
data, thick vs. thin, 56-57
death, talking about, 178, 180
debt, 198-199
DEI practices, 171-172, 245
Democratic party, 157-162, 169-170, 173, 174-175
denial, 177, 268
desires, behaviours and, 17-18
Dichter, Ernest, 119-120
diversity, 169-170, 174-175, 188
divisiveness, 4
doomscrolling, 208
Dove, 49
dream analysis, 16
Durkheim, Émile, 270
Dyson, 244-245, 263

East India Company, 47
Ebola, 135-136
ego, 119-120
emotions, talking about, 16
empathy, 260-262, 269, 271
environmentalism, 237
equity, class and, 73-78
ethnography, 257

Facebook, 150
familiarity, 247-249
'fat words,' 25
fears, behaviours and, 17-18
feminism, 188-189
Ferrari, 206
fifteen-minute cities, 246-247, 249

Finkel, Eli, 159
five whys interview technique, 265-267
Floyd, George, 232-233
football culture, 153-156, 173
Fox, Kate, 113
France, stereotypes about, 89-90, 93
freedom, 80-81
Freud, Sigmund, 18, 66, 117, 119, 121, 155
funeral rituals, 136
futurists
on change, 234-236
craziness of correct predictions, 233-234
cultural change predictions, 236-240
on the distribution of the future, 240-244
rules for cultural change, 251-253
short-term predictions of, 229-233

Gamwell, Adam, 13
Geertz, Clifford, 45, 112
Gelfand, Michele, 68-69
gender essentialism, 190
General Data Protection Regulation (GDPR), 214
Gibson, William, 240
Gillette, 188-189
Gladwell, Malcolm, 22, 27
Google, 225, 227, 228
Google Gemini, 213
Google Glass, 228-229
Gorpcore, 240
Great Depression, 47
grounding, culture as, 3
group think, 173
Guthrie, Woody, 150

Haidt, Jonathan, 21-22, 210
hairdryers, 244-245
Harry Potter, 178
Harvard University, 23
hidden persuaders, 121
Hinduism, 90
hip hop, 237
HIV/AIDS, 193-198
Hofstede, Geert, 113
the home
belief systems and rules of, 105-108, 112, 272
community norms expressed through, 100-101
hosting, 102-103
identity expressed by, 97-99, 114
IKEA design for, 103-105

the home (*cont.*)
   organisation of, 104–105
   pandemic renovations, 101
   as a place of cultural apprenticeship, 112–114
   society and, 114–115
hospital emergency departments, 137–146
hosting, 102–103
humility, 271

id, 119
identity
   AI therapy and, 221
   aperitif ritual and, 245
   belief systems and, 70–71, 93–95, 125–126, 129–131
   brand purpose and, 147-8
   British national character and, 76
   Chinese national character and, 85–88
   community and, 125–126, 127
   components of, 31
   in the Cultural Trinity, 28–33
   culture wars and, 171–173
   expressed by the home, 97–105
   football culture and, 154–155
   friction points in, 238
   group role and, 26
   influences of on culture, 38–39
   interventions and, 143–144
   manosphere and, 191–192
   mega-, 157–162, 164
   online, 212
   political, 158–162, 269–270
   politics, 149–151
   pornography and, 185–187
   Pride movement and, 131–134
   public health campaigns and, 57–59, 62
   shaped by culture, 269–270
   social media and, 29–30
   stereotypes and, 67
   tea culture and, 47–48
   teeth brushing routines and, 50–51
ideology, 32–33
IKEA, 103–105, 112
Implicit Association Test (IAT), 23–24, 27
India
   Ayurveda, 51, 52
   British colonialism, 43–44, 47
   pace of change in, 72
   Rajasthani Bedouin, 41–44
   restraint of, 73
   stereotypes, 90–91, 93

   tea culture in, 46–49
   teeth brushing routines, 41, 40–51, 52
individualistic cultures
   home organization and, 104–105
   hyper-individualism, 9
   privacy in, 107–108
   United Kingdom, 76, 76–78
   United States, 72, 78–81
Industrial Revolution, 223
influencers, 240–242
influences, cultural, 25, 68–70
Instagram, 208, 209, 212, 242
instincts
   brain and, 16–17, 19
   of children and babies, 20
   cultural, 4
   following, 22
Institute for Motivational Research in America, 120

Japan
   multinational businesses, 95
   stereotypes, 91–92, 93
   as a tight culture, 68–69
   views on Americans, 82
Johnnie Walker, 150
Jung, Carl, 16, 18

Kaepernick, Colin, 147–148
Kahneman, Daniel, 21
KFC, 150, 246
King, Martin Luther, Jr., 169
Klein, Ezra, 157–158, 164
Kondo, Marie, 101

Lewis, Martin, 215
LGBTQ+ communities, 125, 131–135
liberty, 79–81
*The Life-Changing Magic of Tidying Up* (Kondo), 101
Lineker, Gary, 170
listening skills, 255, 267–268
loneliness, 178, 244
loose cultures, 68–69
loss aversion, 122–123
Luddites, 223–224, 226, 227

Ma, Jack, 84
Malinowski, Bronislaw, 257, 258
*Man and His Symbols* (Jung), 16
manosphere, 129, 189–192, 201, 244
Marlboro, 206
mask wearing, 136–137, 261

McDonald's, 150, 246, 247, 264
meaning
   cultural, 3
   systems of, 25
Meta, 229
#MeToo movement, 188
Mexico
   indulgence of, 73
   pet feeding habits, 55
   views on Americans, 82
Miner, Horace, 49
mirroring, 255
money, talking about, 179
Monzo, 262
morality, 33, 115, 169
Moro reflex, 20
Musk, Elon, 234

nanny state, 57, 115
narcissism of small differences, 66
national culture, 38
neoliberalism, 237
Netflix, 191, 201
Nike, 129, 147–149, 262
Nokia, 201
non-interventional observation, 264
norms
   belief systems and, 31
   cultural, 3
   social, 32
*Nudge* (Thaler & Sunstein), 121–123
nudge theory, 121–124, 141–142

Obama, Barack, 78, 233
objects
   identity expressed through, 97–98
   treatment of, 98–99
observing others, 262–264
OCEAN profiling, 146, 147, 150
OpenAI, 216, 225
othering, 171, 173, 271

Packard, Vance, 121
pandemic lockdowns, 20–21, 101–103, 230–233, 234
parenting and childcare
   in China, 84–85
   communities, 125
   in Russia, 65, 93
   in Spain, 108–111
   in Sweden, 108–112
   in the United Kingdom, 75–76, 105–112

participant observation, 257–259
Patagonia, 128
Pedigree, 53–56, 64
perception, of others, 31, 67
personality tests, 146
pet feeding habits, 53–56
Philip Morris, 120
physical empathy, 260
polarisation, 157–162, 169–172
police brutality, 232–233
political parties, 156–162
politics, 14–15, 149–151
populism, 129, 161, 235
Pornhub, 183–184
pornography, 181–187, 201
possibility, 248–249
predicting the future, 229–234, 251–253
President's Emergency Plan for AIDS Relief (PEPFAR), 193–198
Pride London, 131–133
Pride movements, 131–134
privacy, 56, 106–108
programmatic imprint of culture, 112
psychology
   anthropology vs., 9–10, 18–19
   business applications, 15, 17–18, 53–57
   codification of cognition, 21–24
   creating change with, 119–124
   empathy in, 261
   political applications, 15
   self-improvement and, 14–15
   as the study of individuals, 18–19
public health campaigns, 57–62, 135–137, 193–198
Public Health England (PHE), 57–62, 63, 237
purpose
   brand, 128, 249–250
   identifying, 271–272
   shared, 3

question asking, 264–267
queueing, 65–66

race, stereotypes about, 95
racial profiling, 232–233
racism
   implicit biases and, 23–24, 25–26
   systemic, 23–27, 25
Rajasthan, India, 41–42
reciprocity, 102
reflexivity, 254–256
Replika, 242, 243–244

Republican party, 156-162, 170, 171, 174-175
respect, 45, 48
rituals
   aperitif, 244-250
   belief systems and, 31
   funeral, 135-136
   social, 44-45
   tea, 44-49
   teeth brushing, 41-42, 50-51
Ronson, Jon, 170
Royal London A&E department, 137-146
Russia, parenting and childcare in, 66, 93-94

Samsung, 201
Saudi Arabia, house rules in, 106
Scandinavia, multinational businesses in, 95
secrets, 176-178, 182
self-expression, 31
Sensodyne, 50-53, 63, 64
sex, talking about, 181-182
'SFW' catchphrase, 38
Shapira, Johanna, 33-34
silences, listening to, 267-268, 271-272
   *see also* social silences
*Slumdog Millionaire* (film), 90
smoking, 119, 122-124
social isolation, 178
social justice, 158-159
social media
   addiction, 210
   algorithms, 187, 209, 210-214, 226
   communities, 187, 189
   doomscrolling, 207
   friction points in, 238
   hacking your feed, 226
   identity and, 30-31
   influencers, 240-242
   subliminal influence of, 205-210
social silences
   aging, 178
   consequences of, 183-187, 200-202
   culturally defined, 179-180
   death, 178
   debt, 198-200
   money, 179
   overcoming, 200-202
   pornography, 183-187
   as public health issues, 193-198
   secrets, 177-179
   sex, 181-182
   unhealthy workplaces and, 198-200

society
   AI and, 226
   cultural change in, 128-131, 152
   culture wars, 169-172
   the home and, 112-114
   morality and, 112-114
   social change and, 146-149
Soft Drinks Industry Levy (UK), 61
South Africa, HIV rates in, 193-198
SpaceX, 234
Spain, parenting and childcare in, 108-111
Stanford Prison Experiment, 23, 26
Starbucks, 150
stereotypes
   American, 78-83, 93
   belief systems and, 94-96
   British, 74-78, 93
   Chinese, 83-88, 93
   French, 89-90, 93
   Indian, 90-91, 93
   Japanese, 91-92, 93
   national, 65-68
   reasons for looking beyond, 94-96
Stonewall riots, 131, 133
stylistic codes, 32
subliminal advertising, 205-207
suffragettes, 119, 120
Sugar Tax (UK), 60-61
Sunstein, Cass, 121
support, 32
Sweden
   IKEA and Swedish aesthetic, 103-105
   parenting and childcare in, 109-111
   support systems in, 73
   as a tight culture, 68-69
sympathy, 260

taboos, 177, 179, 187, 197-197
talking therapy, 176
Tate, Andrew, 190-191
tea culture
   in China, 44-45, 46
   Cultural Trinity, 47-48
   in India, 46, 47-48
   in the United Kingdom, 44-48
technology, uses of, 6-9
   *see also* artificial intelligence
Tech Sabbath, 226
teeth brushing routines
   in China, 51-52
   Cultural Trinity and, 52-53
   in India, 41, 50-51, 52
Tesla, 234, 246

Tett, Gillian, 25, 198-199
Thaler, Richard, 121
therapy, 14, 17, 176-177, 218, 221
thick data, 55-56
thin data, 56
*Thinking, Fast and Slow* (Kahneman), 21
Thylmann, Fabian, 183-184, 187
tight cultures, 68-70
TikTok, 209, 212, 242
toileting practices, 41-43, 103
Tottenham, 153-155, 173
Tower Hamlets, 33-36, 257-258
toxic masculinity, 187-193
traditional Chinese medicine (TCM), 51-53, 87
tribalism
   Brexit, 162-171
   culture wars, 169-173
   polarisation and, 172-174
   political, 156-169
   sporting, 153-156
   tendencies towards, 270-271
Trobriand Islanders, 257, 258
Trump, Donald, 15, 78-80, 149, 161, 171, 233, 245-246
Turing, Alan, 225
Turing Test, 225

uncertainty, 76, 93
UNICEF child wellbeing study, 108-112
unification, 47, 49
United Kingdom
   Brexit, 15, 71, 130, 162-169, 234
   class system, 45-46, 48, 74-78, 95, 179
   Cultural Trinity and national character of, 78
   culture wars, 170
   football culture, 153-156
   Gen Z alcohol consumption, 211
   individualism of, 77, 79-80
   LGBTQ+ community in, 131-134
   pace of change in, 70-71
   parenting and childcare in, 65, 105-109
   political polarization, 162-169
   politics, 233
   public health campaigns, 57-62
   Royal London A&E department, 137-146
   stereotypes, 74-78, 93
   talking about sex in, 181-182
   tea culture in, 44-48
   Tower Hamlets, 33-36, 257-258
   toxic masculinity in, 190
United States
   Cultural Trinity and national character of, 81-82
   cultural values, 78-81
   culture wars, 169-172
   Gen Z alcohol consumption, 211
   house rules in, 106
   individualism of, 73, 77-80
   as a loose culture, 69, 79
   masculine characteristics of, 79
   multinational businesses, 95
   pace of change in, 70
   political parties, 157-162
   politics, 233-234
   presidential elections, 149, 161
   stereotypes, 78-83, 93

values, 30, 31, 66-67, 72-73, 271
   *see also* belief systems
vibe shifts, 5, 13, 151
Vicary, James, 205-206, 208
virtual influencers, 240-242
voice notes, 6-9
Voldemort, 178
Vote Leave campaign, 162-169, 171

*wabi-sabi*, 92
walk a mile in someone's shoes, 259
walking a mile in someone's shoes, 270
Wang, Tricia, 56
*Warhammer* (game), 125
*Watching the English* (Fox), 113
webs of meaning, 44-49
West Africa, Ebola epidemic in, 135-136
WhatsApp, 6-8, 73, 184, 230
white collar quarantine, 231
Winnicott, Donald, 18
Winter, Alex, 223
woke culture, 169-173, 255
Wolf, Eric, 37
workplace
   community in, 30, 142, 174-175
   corporate culture, 14, 198-200
   identity, 127
   social silences in, 198-200
   *see also* business
World Economic Forum, 90
World Values Survey, 70-72
Writers Guild of America (WGA), 223

Xi Jinping, 83

Zimbardo, Philip, 23
Zoom, 230

# RAISING READERS
## Books Build Bright Futures

Dear Reader,

We'd love your attention for one more page to tell you about the crisis in children's reading, and what we can all do.

Studies have shown that reading for fun is the **single biggest predictor of a child's future success** – more than family circumstance, parents' educational background or income. It improves academic results, mental health, wealth, communication skills and ambition.

The number of children reading for fun is in rapid decline. Young people have a lot of competition for their time, and a worryingly high number do not have a single book at home.

Our business works extensively with schools, libraries and literacy charities, but here are some ways we can all raise more readers:

- Reading to children for just 10 minutes a day makes a difference
- Don't give up if your children aren't regular readers – there will be books for them!
- Visit bookshops and libraries to get recommendations
- Encourage them to listen to audiobooks
- Support school libraries
- Give books as gifts

Thank you for reading.
www.JoinRaisingReaders.com